The Last Frontier

D0815808

Also by Howard Fast

The Last Frontier

Howard Fast

It is a matter of historical experience that nothing that is wrong in principle can be right in practice. People are apt to delude themselves on that point, but the ultimate result will always prove the truth of the maxim. A violation of equal rights can never serve to maintain institutions which are founded upon equal rights.

—Carl Schurz

NORTH CASTLE BOOKS

*An imprint of M.E. Sharpe,*INC.

Armonk, New York
London, England

Copyright © 1941 by Howard Fast

All rights reserved. No part of this book may be reproduced in any form
without written permission from the publisher, M. E. Sharpe, Inc.,
80 Business Park Drive, Armonk, New York 10504.

Originally published in 1941 by Duell, Sloan & Pearce

For My Father
WHO TAUGHT ME TO LOVE
NOT ONLY THE AMERICA THAT IS PAST,
BUT THE AMERICA THAT WILL BE

Library of Congress Cataloging-in-Publication Data

Fast, Howard, 1914–
The last frontier / Howard Fast ; with a new introduction by the author.
p.   cm.
ISBN 1-56324-593-0 (alk. paper)
1. Cheyenne Indians—History—19th century—Fiction.
I. Title.
PS3511.A784L37   1997
813′.52—dc21
96-48628
CIP
Printed in the United States of America

The paper used in this publication meets the minimum requirements of
American National Standard for Information Sciences—
Permanence of Paper for Printed Library Materials,
ANSI Z 39.48-1984.

BM (p)   10   9   8   7   6   5   4   3   2

North Castle Books
An imprint of M. E. Sharpe, Inc.

CONTENTS

INTRODUCTION

It SEEMS an eternity ago, and I suppose it is, a small eternity, when my wife and I went out west to seek out the facts about the Cheyennes' flight north from their reservation in Oklahoma to their old hunting grounds in the Black Hills. I had read a paragraph or two about this incredible trek in Struthers Burt's book on the Powder River Country. That was in 1939. We had been married two years—both of us kids in our early twenties.

We had never been to the West before. I suppose you could say we had never been anywhere much before. I was making a bare living as a writer—very bare in those depression days. We owned a 1931 Ford that we had bought for forty dollars, but it did not seem capable of a long trip, so we traded it in for twenty dollars and bought a 1933 Pontiac for seventy-five dollars. It was a great car, and we drove it some five thousand miles through the West. We covered the territory the Cheyennes did, the story I tell in this book. We spoke with some old Cheyennes who had taken part in the flight. At the University of Oklahoma, in Norman, where we lived for a while, we spoke to young Cheyenne and Arapaho students who had heard the story from their parents and their grandparents; and we spent the best part of a day with Stanley Vestal, who was then the greatest authority on the Plains Indians in the country. We made a few hopeless efforts to learn some of the Cheyenne language but then gave it up in despair, and whenever we spoke to the old Indians, we used a translator.

We were two city kids in a strange country, seeing the reality of people we had encountered only in books and films, and very soon we came to understand that everything we had read and seen on film was part of a gigantic lie. We were in contact with a noble and beautiful people—and perhaps we were overwhelmed by the difference between the fact and the fiction.

This was years before books began to be written and films made that attempted to tell the truth of our battles with the Plains Indians; so in a way, we were breaking a trail.

When I came home and when we put together the notes my wife had made and the sum of our experience, I wrote the book called *The Last Frontier*, and it was published by Duell, Sloan and Pearce in 1941.

I was totally unprepared for the torrent of praise it received. Pearl Harbor was still in the future, but against the suffering of the people in occupied Europe, it took on the form of a sort of parable. The book became a best-seller—my first—and it has been translated into fifty-one foreign languages. It has sold, through its various editions, over a million copies; and now, in my eighty-second year, it has been brought back into print.

At the time of its first publication, Carl Van Doran, the historian, said of it: "I do not know of any other episode of Western history that has been so truly and subtly perpetuated as this one. A great story lost has been found again, and as here told promises to live for generations."

FOREWORD

Sixty-two years ago, Oklahoma was called Indian Territory. A hot, sun-baked, dusty stretch of dry earth, dry rivers, yellow grass, and blackjack pine, it was intended to be what its name indicated—Indian Territory.

For two hundred years, like a sprawling young giant, America had flung itself across a continent, ocean to ocean, peak to peak. In 1878, the job was done, the mountains climbed, the valleys filled. The frontier had gone, and already it was a wistful refrain in songs and stories.

The railroads spanned the plains, north to south, east to west. You could send a telegram from 'Frisco to New York in two minutes, or you could cross over the plains by train in two days.

The Texans had driven their cattle north to the lush valleys of Wyoming, and already the Swedes and Norwegians were swarming onto the prairies to get the feel of the rich brown earth winding back from their plow blades.

It was a good time, with a nation coming of age, with

Tom Edison inventing the electric light to spill away the darkness once and forever, with prosperity coming back, with the wounds of that bitter, best-forgotten war healing themselves, with Rutherford Birchard Hayes concluding his inaugural address with these words:

"A union depending not upon the constraint of force, but upon the loving devotion of a free people; 'and that all things may be so ordered and settled upon the best and surest foundations, that peace and happiness, truth and justice, religion and piety, may be established among us for generations.' "

The best of all possible times. And not so long ago but that many people alive today will remember.

In this swirl of a country completing itself, Oklahoma had remained as an island in a continent. After all other frontiers were gone, a circular frontier still bound Indian Territory.

This land of many states and territories, which God had given to Americans and which Americans had given to the world, had once been inhabited by another people. They were darker-skinned, and the first white men to reach this hemisphere had called them Indians, being somewhat confused as to geography. Indians they became and Indians they remained.

They lived a simple life; they hunted and they fished, and sometimes they raised crops and sometimes they killed one another, sometimes with as little reason as white men have for killing one another. There were not many of them. They took no census, but we can estimate that at no time in the past three hundred years were there many more than three hundred thousand of them. In tribes, in clans, in scattered villages, they were in most of the land, from the Atlantic to the Pacific.

However, they had one unforgivable fault; they considered that the land on which they had always lived was their own. They believed that it was enough their own for them to fight and die for it. And the eloquent persuasion of the white men, who taught them many refinements in the art of killing, and also the gentle art of scalping, could not change their simple beliefs.

So they fought back, as savages will; and they fought for what they fondly believed to be their homeland. They lost because they were "savages," and because even in the beginning they were woefully outnumbered. They lost because their way of life was in the stone age.

In the end, they signed treaties, so that some of their land might remain with them. But the treaties were broken, and land companies sold their acres for anything from twenty cents to twenty dollars.

The colonies became a nation, and the nation rushed westward with such a mighty surge as the world had never seen before. What we called the "frontier" was like the edge of a surf when the tide comes in. It went on until it reached the Pacific Ocean, and then America had come of age.

But always on the edge of this surf, on this frontier, were Indians, men fighting for their homes and their way of life. At first, the surf swept over them ruthlessly; but then America developed what might be called a conscience—or perhaps only a weariness of these dark-skinned people who persisted in fighting the inevitable.

They had to go somewhere, and the solution was discovered in Oklahoma, in that dreary and least-attractive part of all the plains country. So Congress set it aside for them, called it Indian Territory, and proceeded with a plan to settle there what tribes of Indians still roamed as free men.

So our story begins there. Our story of an incident—a very small incident—in the history of a great nation.

The Last Frontier

PART ONE   July 1878

THE INCIDENT AT DARLINGTON

I⊤ WAS a hot day, midsummer in Oklahoma. The metallic, cloudless sky appeared ready to loose its bolt of molten sun. The heat came from everywhere, from the sky and the sun, from the Texas desert, blown by the south wind, from the ground itself. The ground had given up its moisture, and now it was dissolving in little puffs of fine red dust. The red dust spread up and out and over everything. It coated the stunted, blackjack pine and it coated the yellow grass. It fell on the unpainted houses and gave their warped boards an affinity with the earth from which they had recently come.

Everything shimmered to distortion in the heat. A rabbit, bounding across the clearing, was like a brown rag blown by the hot wind.

Agent John Miles paused in his morning walk of inspection over the agency grounds. He had been six years in Indian Territory, yet he could not grow used to Oklahoma summers. Each one was hotter, or else he forgot how bad the last one had been.

He passed a careful finger around the inside of his starched collar. It was now eleven o'clock, and by noon, usually, the last bit of starch had lost its grip, leaving the collar a wilted wreck. Aunt Lucy, his wife, had often pointed out to him how foolish it was to wear a starched white collar all summer long. A neckerchief, which also served as a handkerchief, was more comfortable and more practical, nor did it mean a loss of dignity.

As to the last, he wasn't quite sure. Dignity and authority were composed of a host of little things; give up one of them and you're on the road to give up all of them. And the further you are from civilization, the more those little things matter.

He could not conceive of any place further from civilization than Darlington, the agency for the Cheyenne and Arapahoe Indians.

He took out his handkerchief and wiped his face. Then, after glancing about quickly to see whether he was observed or not, he bent down and wiped the red dust from his black shoes. He folded the handkerchief carefully, so that the dirty part would be hidden if he took it out of his pocket again. Then he sighed and continued his walk toward the agency schoolhouse.

The schoolhouse had been one of his first achievements after he had been appointed Indian Agent. He was very proud of it, just as he was proud of his other improvements at Darlington; yet he knew that his pride could be humbled, quickly and mercilessly. He was a Quaker, a more or less devout one, so he hid his pride carefully.

4

When it was humbled, along with despair came something that was almost satisfaction.

Now he realized that the schoolhouse needed painting again. In other climate, the cold of winter wore paint, but here the merciless heat fairly boiled it from the boards. He shook his head, knowing it was hopeless to ask for increased paint rations when even the food supply was being cut down.

He crossed a pocket of sifted dust in which he sank to his ankles. There was no use wiping his shoes again. He walked on, coughing in the swirling red cloud that had sifted up and over him.

An Arapahoe, barefoot and wrapped in a dirty yellow blanket, barred his path and loosed a stream of soft Indian words. The dust from the Indian's shuffling feet rose between them.

Miles knew the man, whose name was Robert Bleating-Hawk. The man could speak some English. Six years had not made Cheyenne or Arapahoe much more intelligible to Miles; and often he thought that sixty years would not.

"Speak English, man," he said impatiently.

"My wife—she say dat chicken no lay egg, dat damn chicken."

"Well, see Mr. Seger about that."

"Johnny, he no give damn about egg," the Indian said stolidly.

"I'll talk to him," Miles said, forcing himself to be patient.

"You see, we eat dat damn chicken."

"Then you'll get no more chickens from us," Miles said, and walked on.

5

He was glad to get into the shade of the schoolhouse veranda. It was a little less hot there, and the house was some protection from the dust. By now, a tight, knotty pain was gathering at the point where his brows met. That meant that he would have a headache in the afternoon, and Lucy would scold him for exposing himself to the sun. She wanted him to carry an umbrella and make himself the laughingstock of every Indian on the place. Still her scolding would give him an excuse to take a cold bath before dinner.

He stood on the veranda, listening to the hum of voices from inside the schoolhouse, and thinking comfortably of the cold bath that would come later in the day. From where he stood, he could see the fall of land to the dry bed of the Canadian River, dust and withered yellow grass, on which somehow thickets of blackjack pine managed to find an existence. Beyond, the yellow and red Oklahoma landscape dashed headlong to the metal sky. The Indian village of cone-shaped lodges sucked futilely at the dry riverbed. Aside from the shuffling shape of Robert Bleating-Hawk, not a thing was alive in all that braised surface. Most of the Indians had already left on their summer buffalo hunt, from which they would return bitter and empty-handed. The rest would not move from the shelter of their lodges until the sun had set.

The schoolbell rang and the doors opened, and the Indian boys and girls came tumbling out, shrieking and laughing. They were already scattering onto the grass when Mrs. Hudgins, the matron, came out and saw Miles standing on the porch. She was a large, powerful woman, with heavy thighs and a bosom like a pouting pigeon; she had loose cheeks, tiny blue eyes, and gray hair. Sweat poured from her face and neck, staining the collar of her dress.

When she saw Miles, she clapped her hands together and cried: "Boys and girls, boys and girls—I want you to say a proper good morning to Agent Miles."

A few paused, but the rest ran on.

"That's quite all right," Miles said.

"I'm so sorry. In the summer everything's so difficult. It's so hot. You can't concentrate in the heat."

Miles nodded sympathetically.

"I'm not complaining," Mrs. Hudgins said.

The two other teachers came out onto the porch now. Joshua Trueblood and his wife, Matilda, were also Quakers. They had followed the *call* to Indian Territory, and the territory was beating them into jelly-like submission. Joshua Trueblood was a small man with a limp, straw-colored mustache. His life was hell and his fear of the Indians was exceeded only by his wife's. As a teacher, he was futile and plodding. His wife was a mouse-like woman, a sort of shadow to him. For all that, a strange sort of moral conviction had kept them at the agency.

"It seems a shame," Joshua said, "that they should have school in the summer."

"I know," Miles nodded. "We'll let them off in a few days more. I didn't want them along on the hunt. It's bad enough for their fathers and mothers to go wandering through this wasteland, looking for buffalo where no buffalo exist, without dragging their children with them."

Matilda clicked her tongue, and Mrs. Hudgins said: "Things are so difficult in the heat."

Miles stirred himself. His head ached now, and it re-

7

quired an effort to leave the shade of the porch. "I'll be going along," he said. "I'll see you at lunch—"

He forced himself to walk down the slope toward the Indian village. He passed the fields where the Indians, under the supervision of the agency farmers, had put in a crop of corn and potatoes and cabbage. The fields were a spread of dust, like refuse from a swept floor. No force on earth could bring the Indians out to work under that sun.

He passed through a flock of chickens. They drove the dust into his face and eyes, and he coughed. Pain in his head was like hammer blows. He turned and watched the chickens rooting in the fields.

On his way back to his house, he passed several of the newly constructed shacks which were to replace the tepees the Indians lived in now. They had not been painted, and already the green pine boards were curling and warping with the heat, drawing the nails that held them to the beams. Miles shook his head, set his face stolidly, and plodded home.

There were five of them at lunch, Agent John Miles and his wife, Lucy, Joshua and Matilda Trueblood, and John Seger, man of all work about the agency. Seger, a dark-haired, dark-skinned, dark-eyed rock of a man, had been at the agency almost as long as Miles. Coming originally as a handyman, he had by now turned his hand to everything from teaching school when the situation became too much for the Truebloods, to hunting down whiskey smugglers.

The Indians called him Johnny Smoker, from the refrain of a little nursery rhyme he taught the children at the school. He, of all that group at the table, was the only one who loved his work. He understood the Indians, and they understood him.

Now he came into the dining room hot and sweating and angry, hardly able to contain himself until after Agent Miles had said a long and leisurely grace. Then Mr. Bunk, the cook, entered, following Aida, their Arapahoe serving girl. She was carrying a bowl of hot pea soup, and Bunk was edging after her, watching fearfully that she didn't drop it.

"I do believe that hot soup is cooling in weather like this," Mrs. Miles said.

"Maybe it is, Aunt Lucy," Bunk nodded, standing back from the table and not taking his eyes from the Indian girl until she had set the soup in its place. "Maybe it is, but my God almighty and lovely Jesus, that kitchen is so hot. My God almighty, I had to come out or else just go crazy. Sure as God almighty, it's no wonder so many cooks go crazy."

"It looks like rain tomorrow or the next day." Mrs. Miles smiled sweetly. "And you shouldn't take the Lord's name in vain, Bunk."

"Sorry as the devil, Aunt Lucy," Bunk said, and then he wiped his hands on his apron and returned to the kitchen, pushing the Indian girl in front of him.

Mrs. Miles began to dish out the soup, and Seger, who could contain himself no longer, growled:

"I ran two buffalo hunters off the place today."

9

"Buffalo hunters?" Miles asked uneasily. "There's no buffalo here—no buffalo anywhere near the agency."

"I call them buffalo hunters," Seger said, nodding at Mrs. Miles and Matilda Trueblood. "Lord knows what I'd like to call them. Scum and riffraff. Dirty-shirts—you know the kind, in buckskin. Maybe they hunted hides once, but they don't no more. There's more low characters and rustlers and two-bit gunmen right here in the territory than in all the rest of the states together."

Miles shook his head. "What do you suppose they wanted here?"

Seger nodded at the women, and then said in a whisper: "Squaws."

"That's no good."

"Lord, don't I know it. And in this weather. I go to bed and dream about something setting them off. And when the tribes come back from the hunt without seeing hide or hair of a buffalo, it'll only be worse."

"We'll finish eating," Miles said slowly, choosing his words carefully and trying to hear them through the throbbing pain in his head, "and then you can ride over to Fort Reno and have Colonel Mizner send a detail back here. We'll all feel better then."

"I hope so," Seger said, without enthusiasm.

They had almost finished their meal when Miles, who sat facing the window, saw the Indians riding toward his house. At first it seemed to him that his eyes were deceiving him, that this was a mirage, a heat-manufactured dream of some sort. There were about twenty of the Indians, half naked and painted; their ponies were lean as skeletons, a leanness which the riders matched. They rode in billows of sun-soaked dust, red clouds on which their horses' bellies appeared to float.

"God bless me," Miles whispered. Then the others followed his eyes.

"God bless me," Miles said again, and Seger murmured: "It never rains but it pours."

Seger led the way out to the porch, sighing with relief when he saw that the Indians, who were now filing around to the front of the house, were without weapons. They were Cheyennes, and Seger recognized the two old chiefs who led them—Dull Knife and Little Wolf.

Dull Knife's band of Northern Cheyennes were the last Indians to come into the Cheyenne and Arapahoe Agency. Their original home was in the Black Hills of Wyoming; from time beyond memory they had lived there, making seasonal trips onto the plains of Montana and North Dakota to hunt buffalo, but always returning to their home in the hills. Of all the Cheyenne bands, they were the last to be touched by civilization. In their hills and in the lush fertility of the Powder River valley, they had all that they wanted, and the white men were a long time coming.

In 1865, the Harney-Sanborn Treaty was signed. It guaranteed to the Indians of the northern plains, the Sioux, Cheyennes, and Arapahoes, the land which they occupied, the whole basin of the Powder River. This land extended westward from the Little Missouri River to the Black Hills and the foothills of the Rocky Mountains. It seemed at the time that the Indians would be able to live in this great stretch of land for generations to come. It was well-stocked with game and beyond the railroad's reach. And the cattle country was fifteen hundred miles to the south.

Then the Union Pacific finished building. In the Powder River country the grass grew as high as a horse's rump. In all the world, there was no such cattle country. The Texans drove their herds north fifteen hundred miles, opening the Chisholm trail, and the government built forts to protect them from the Indians. The Indians struck back, and Congress sent diplomats to break the Harney-Sanborn Treaty. It was the old story all over again, cattle, railroads, land-companies—and the Indians had to go.

Dull Knife and his people fought on longer than most of the tribes. It wasn't until the spring of 1877 that they surrendered to General Mackenzie and his troops. They were told that they would have to leave their homeland and go south, where a great territory had been set aside for the Indian tribes. They were also told that once there, the government would care for them, and they would live in peace and prosperity. A branch of their tribe, the Southern Cheyennes, had been living in Oklahoma for generations; that was added to other arguments, and the final argument was a regiment of U. S. cavalry. The final argument persuaded them, and by now they had been on the reservation for something more than a year.

The year hadn't dealt gently with them. Coming from the dry plains and hills of the north into the malaria-ridden lowlands of Indian Territory, they came down like flies with fever and disease. A hunting, meat-eating people, from a land thick with game, they were in a place as bare of game as it was of beauty. Even before they arrived,

Miles was always short of rations. And since his supplies were not increased, he was not disposed to waste what he had on godless savages who sulked in their skin tepees. For a year they had been dying, and starving, and now the thin men on their thin ponies seemed like the very ghosts of the dead.

They rode around to the front of the agency and halted there. They leaned forward over their ponies and gazed, almost without interest, at the five people who stood on the veranda. And the red dust eddied and settled, like the smoke of evil puffballs.

"Take Matilda inside," Miles said to his wife. The two women went inside, and Joshua Trueblood shifted from foot to foot, nervously. The chiefs, Little Wolf and Dull Knife, rode up to the porch and dismounted.

Both the Cheyenne chiefs were old men, but Dull Knife was the older, the weaker and less sure of himself. He stood with his feet in the dust, staring down at his toes, poking through the holes in the ancient, beaded moccasins he wore. Little Wolf stepped up onto the porch; there was nothing of humility in his manner.

Little Wolf was short for a Cheyenne, who were the tallest of all the plains people. He stood at Seger's height, a stooped, thick-shouldered man, with a leathery face and long, stringy hair. His face was handsome, a big jaw, a wide mouth even for an Indian, a broad, curved nose, and small, wise and compassionate eyes, set close together and lost in a maze of wrinkles. He had the clean look of a man who has lived all his life out of doors, seasoned with wind and rain and hot sun. There was something about him that stilled their fears, perhaps the calm way he

13

stepped up onto the porch, offering his hand in turn to
Miles, Seger, and Trueblood. His grip was strong and
tight.

He spoke in smooth, soft Cheyenne that was almost a
whisper. No one of the three men knew enough of the
language to follow all his murmured words.

"Sabbe English?" Seger asked.

"Leetle beet."

"Try to find out why they're here, John," Miles said
nervously.

Seger managed the Cheyenne haltingly. The chief
cocked his head to one side, concentrating upon the words.
Seger stumbled along, and the chief waited patiently until
he had finished.

"Same old thing," Seger told Miles. "As far as I can
make out—not enough food, no buffalo, sickness, heat,
same damn thing as always. Maybe I got him wrong. The
old man's burned up, all right. You'd better send for
Guerrier to make talk with them."

Edmond Guerrier was a halfbreed who lived at the
agency, doing odd jobs, interpreting, and acting as a useful contact between the agent and the Indians, many of
whom were Guerrier's relatives. Now Miles sent Trueblood after him, while Seger invited the two chiefs into
the agency office to have a smoke. Before entering the
house, Dull Knife shook hands with the white men. He
had none of Little Wolf's assurance, and in spite of his
age and dignity seemed almost like a frightened child.

In the office, Seger stuffed his pipe and lit up, but the
chiefs would neither sit down nor smoke. In spite of the
heat, they held their blankets close about them and

14

pressed back against one of the walls of the little room. The minutes during which they waited for Guerrier ticked by slowly, and Miles, glancing out of the window, saw the other Cheyennes sitting stolidly on their skinny mounts. There was no use trying to make conversation in what broken Cheyenne Seger knew or in the few words of English Little Wolf could speak.

In a little while, Mrs. Miles came into the office with a plate of sugar cookies. She had been nervous for her husband, but when she saw how quiet everything in the room was, she smiled cheerfully and offered the cookies to the two chiefs. When they refused, she seemed surprised and hurt.

"I've never known one of them to refuse my cookies before," she said plaintively.

"These Northern Cheyennes are kind of wild, uncivilized," Seger explained.

"They look hungry enough," Mrs. Miles said.

"Now look here, Lucy," her husband protested, "this may be serious. We have to talk with these men and we've already sent for Edmond to interpret. Now you'd better go back into the house and wait for me there."

"If you wish. Shall I leave the cookies here?"

Miles nodded absently, and she set the plate down on the desk and went out. He took out his watch, a large silver turnip, and stared at it impatiently.

"Where is he?" he demanded of Seger.

Seger shrugged and went on smoking. It was hot and close in the room, and the two old chiefs smelled of horses and rawhide and burnt wood.

Seger rose, went to the window, and wrenched it up.

Miles began to nibble at one of the cookies. His head still ached and he had not taken the cold bath he planned.

"They're here," Seger said.

Trueblood was panting as he led Guerrier into the room. "I ran down to the village," he gasped. "I thought—"

Seger grinned maliciously, and Miles said: "Would you mind taking notes, Joshua?"

Trueblood nodded and began to busy himself with pad and pencil, trying desperately to regain his composure. Guerrier wiped the sweat from the inside of his hatband and then from his face, nodded at the two chiefs, and then addressed them in nimble Cheyenne. He left out all ceremony and attempted to be businesslike, as white men were.

"Ask them what they want here?" Miles said. "If it's food they want, tell them to go back to their camp and I'll have some extra rations sent down."

"It's not food," Guerrier said. "They want to go home."

"Then let them go home. I'm certainly not keeping them here. Tell them they can go as soon as they please."

"They don't mean to their camp," Guerrier explained. "They mean home to Wyoming."

"Now that's impossible," Miles cried, slapping his hand down on his desk. "That's out of the question. Tell them it's impossible. As a matter of fact, they know it's impossible. Tell them no one can leave Indian Territory without permission from Washington. And make it clear to them that the Great White Father is not giving such per-

16

mission. This is to be the home of the Indians for all time to come, and it will be just the sort of a home they make it. If they're lazy and worthless and lie in their lodges all day, then they will be repaid in coin of like kind. Make that clear to them. They have to stay here."

Guerrier translated and Joshua Trueblood scribbled in his notebook. Seger puffed his pipe stolidly. When the halfbreed had finished speaking, the two chiefs glanced at each other. An expression of hopeless, dazed uncertainty had come over the features of Dull Knife. He shook his old head wearily and made as to go. But Little Wolf laid an affectionate yet restraining hand on the old man's arm.

Little Wolf began to speak, and the halfbreed translated directly, in the first person. He was less at ease translating from Cheyenne into English, and he chose his words carefully, eyeing Trueblood who was scribbling in the notebook.

"For how long must we stay here?" Little Wolf said evenly, never raising his voice. "Until all of us are dead? You mock my people for staying in their lodges, yet what would you have them do? Work? Hunting is our work; we always lived that way and we never starved. For as long as men can remember, we lived in a country of our own, a land of meadows and mountains and tall pine forests. There was no sickness and few of us died. Since we've been here, we have all been sick and many of us have died. We've starved and we've watched our children's bones poke out the skin. Is it so terrible that a man should want to go back to his own home? If you can't give us permission to go, let some of us go to Washington and tell them how we suffer. Or send to Washington and get permission for us to leave this place before we are all dead."

Some of the old chief's simple eloquence had been transmitted to Guerrier. He finished speaking with his hands spread out, and for a moment there was intense, hot silence in the little office. Then the spell was broken and Guerrier began to study the inside of his hat, turning it slowly between his fingers. Trueblood was reading what he had written. Agent Miles looked at Seger, who continued to puff stolidly on his pipe.

Miles envied Seger's detachment. He could sit by and watch. For himself, how could a man make savages understand the policy of a nation? For them it was a simple matter of right and wrong, of having their wishes satisfied. They couldn't see that already that northland of theirs was being stripped of its game and planted with farms and ranches. Nor would it be any use for him to attempt to explain the dream he had once had of bringing civilization to the Darlington Agency. It was out of the question for him to bother the Indian Office with this; he had to handle it by himself or with the aid of Colonel Mizner and his garrison at Fort Reno. He tried to temporize.

"I can't send to Washington now," he said carefully. "Perhaps later, but not now. Suppose you try one more year at the agency. If things don't go better, I promise you that I will endeavor to place the matter before the proper officials at Washington."

Little Wolf shook his head. "If we're all dead in another year, what good would it do? We have to leave now. If we do as you say, perhaps there will be none left to travel north."

"I gave you my answer," Miles said stubbornly. His

head was pounding like a drum. He began to see the two chiefs as shimmering grotesques behind a mask of heat. He was trying not to hate them, to reason with himself and see some of the justice behind their complaints.

But it was all mixed up—with the cold bath they were keeping him from and which was the only thing that would relieve his headache, with the heat and the dust, with the unpainted green pine boards pulling the nails out of the newly built shacks, with the short rations, with the loneliness of Darlington, with the struggle within himself against the cause he believed himself called to serve.

"Tell them I can't promise them anything else!" he snapped at Guerrier.

The two chiefs heard the answer silently. They nodded and mechanically shook hands with everyone in the room. The handshake was alien to them, but precise and formal, as if they were bent on carrying out to perfection the one ceremony of the white men they knew. Little Wolf's face was set in an expressionless mask, but Dull Knife's reddened eyes were almost senile in their sorrow and despair.

Miles sighed with relief as they left the room, but Seger followed them out to the porch and watched them climb onto their skinny ponies. The other braves were still waiting in the same position as before, sitting limply and leaning forward over the bone pommels of their rawhide saddles. Then the whole band filed away as they had come, their horses' hoofs making almost no sound in the deep red dust, the strangling clouds of pulverized clay rising beneath them until again they seemed to be floating on horrid red clouds.

Seger was puffing his pipe reflectively when Miles poked

his head through the door and said: "John, I'm going to take a cold bath. Will you keep an eye on things?"

Seger nodded.

"Think we've seen the end of that?" Miles asked anxiously.

Seger shook his head. "Only the beginning," he murmured.

PART TWO   August 1878

T H R E E   M E N   W H O   R A N   A W A Y

THE AFFAIR of the three men
was brought to Agent Miles' attention by an Arapahoe
called Jimmy Bear, who had gone north from the agency
to look for game. That was some weeks later, and it had
not rained and the heat had not abated. The Arapahoe
was Oklahoma stuff, but he had never seen such weather
as this. He had never seen the earth turn to dust and
choke up a man's throat and nose and eyes. He was out
hunting for two days, and in all that time he had seen
nothing alive, although the earth rippled and undulated
with the heat.

In the bitterness of noontime, he crouched in the yellow grass and hid from the sun in the shade of his horse's
belly. When he touched his finger to a dry, white buffalo
skull, it was hot enough to make him wince.

Then he got on the horse, and the saddle cut his legs
like a hot knife.

"By God, I die soon in this damn wedder," he moaned aloud. He was a Christian, and he spoke so much English that the other Indians referred to him as "the one who has lost his own tongue."

So maybe it was the heat that made him almost crazy when he saw the three Cheyennes galloping north. His first thought was that they would kill their horses, and his next thought was that they had a good reason for riding north that way, sure as God to kill their horses sooner or later. He spurred after them, and then saw them wheel their horses and stare at him so desperately that he was afraid they might shoot him before he could say a word. They were wild men, not Christians—Northern Cheyennes from Dull Knife's village.

"Where are you going?" he yelled at them, this time in their own tongue.

"North!" came the reply."To the place we came from." And then they wheeled their horses again and rode off like madmen.

It made him almost crazy, all the way back to the reservation, thinking of the cool winds and the green trees in the place they were bound for.

Agent Miles questioned the Arapahoe carefully, thinking meanwhile, "Why did he have to tell me this? Do I care if three or ten of them go off or to the devil?" But he knew that in another hour it would be all over the agency. Such things had a way of getting around. In this heat, there was needed only a spark to start a raging fire.

"You're sure they were three men of Dull Knife's band?" Miles asked.

Jimmy Bear nodded. He held up his hand and counted off on the fingers, "One, two, tree."

"Riding north, you're sure?" Agent Miles persisted.

"By God, I know dat—dey ride like crazy."

"What were their names?"

The Arapahoe shrugged. "Dem Nordern Cheyenne—"

Miles half doubted him. He wished that Seger were there in his office. Not that Seger would have helped him to come to a decision, but Seger would have puffed his pipe and looked the Indian down. The agent had a feeling that an Indian would tell the truth to Seger sooner than to him.

"If you don't know their names, how do you know they were Northern Cheyennes?"

The Arapahoe motioned eloquently. He wrinkled his eyes and looked at Miles as if the agent were a fool.

Then Aunt Lucy came in with a plate of her sugar cookies and a pitcher of cold lemonade. She set them down on the desk, and the Indian pressed his hands together and looked at Miles anxiously. Miles nodded, and the Indian began stuffing his mouth with sugar cookies.

"Are they good, Jimmy Bear?" Aunt Lucy smiled.

He nodded, but didn't stop eating. He ignored the lemonade, but swallowed the cookies rapidly until the plate was empty.

"Now wouldn't you like some of that nice, cold lemonade?" Aunt Luck asked.

Shaking his head, he rose and edged toward the door.

Miles said, "That's all—you can go." And when the Arapahoe had left, continued:

"Lucy, why do you persist in feeding them?"

"Well, they do expect it."

"They shouldn't expect it. They shouldn't expect to
stuff themselves with sweets every time they come near this
place. I try to be perfectly fair and just in apportioning
their rations."

"I'm sorry, John," she apologized.

"Yes, yes," he nodded absently, playing with a pencil
and making little circles on the paper in front of him.
"Do you know where Seger is?"

"At the barns, I think."

Miles took his hat and left the house. He walked toward
the barns slowly. A slight fainting spell the day before
had been a lesson to him; if he came down with ague, the
agency would drift like a ship without a rudder. He saw
Seger sitting in front of the barn, comfortable in the
shade, splicing a broken harness strap, and he envied the
man's rock-like brown strength. Seger glanced up as Miles
approached, nodded, but continued with his work.

While Miles told Jimmy Bear's story, Seger continued
to work, intent upon the leather. And when Miles had
finished, Seger said softly, "Three don't make much difference."

"If three can leave with impunity, then a whole tribe
can."

"They haven't yet," Seger said.

"It will be all over the agency by sundown," Miles
said.

"It's your business. You can say you gave them permission to leave."

"They'll all be asking for permission," Miles said hopelessly. "Every Indian on the reservation will want to go back where he came from."

"I would have beat that Arapahoe's head off—taught him a good lesson and make him keep his mouth shut."

"It's too late for that," Miles said, "even if I were to condone such methods. You'd better hitch up the buckboard."

"Going to the fort?"

Miles didn't answer. He envied the indolent way Seger could crouch in the dust. That was the difference between a working man and a leader.

As a leader, driving the buckboard to Fort Reno, Miles felt tired and insecure and puzzled. He had put on his black coat and a black bowler hat, and again as always, he felt that the soldiers in their graceful cavalry uniforms would laugh at him. He hated the thought of Fort Reno and its garrison being located so close to Darlington, a perpetual reminder that he and the others at the agency were in no way able to deal properly with the Indians. Yet at the same time he was thankful, thankful a hundred times, thankful at night when he awoke from troubled sleep and realized that the army of the United States of America was almost within call.

Yet he couldn't reconcile peace at the bayonet's point with his devotion to that prince of peace whom he had once pledged himself to serve. If you came with your arms wide open in love, then the bayonet should be left behind. Give in love and serve in love, and with love you will be received. Even by the lowliest savage. Yet what was the use? He didn't truly believe, not even the way Lucy believed, making a simple service out of her plate of sugar cookies. He remembered coming on Seger once when the handyman was beating a Cheyenne boy unmercifully. He had caught Seger's upraised hand, crying:

"John, if we come to them with our fists clenched and hate in our hearts, will they give us their love?"

Seger's face didn't change, although his eyes seemed almost contemptuous. "Agent Miles," he said, "this little bastard tried to knife me, so you'd better go away and let me finish with him. He'll love me all right when he knows who's his boss."

The memory of that disturbed him, but nevertheless stiffened his resolve to be firm this time. Love and heat don't go well together. Let the Indians obey the law, and then he would show them how gentle he could be with their welfare. Anyway, his head was aching again and his collar and shirt were wet with sweat. Also, the cloud of dust thrown up by the horses' hoofs was settling all over his black clothes.

He drove into the fort, through the log gates and past a sentry who saluted stiffly. Miles was never able to return a salute; things military always oppressed him. He pulled in the horses and sat on the buckboard for a while, trying to catch his breath and ease the pounding of his heart. Then he climbed to the ground and wiped his face and his hat carefully with his handkerchief.

Fort Reno, a rectangle of log and mud walls, log and

26

mud barracks, was in almost no way different from the other U. S. Army posts which spotted the plains from the Canadian border in the north to the Rio Grande in the south. A regiment drilled and sweated and curried their horses, while their officers whiled away days and nights of unending boredom with whist and penny poker and malaria. There were few women, and almost no social life, not even a trade store to bring the diversion of dirty buffalo hunters and unscrupulous whiskey peddlers. The Indian wars were over and done with, and here in Indian Territory there were not enough cattlemen to plague the commanding officer with their complaints about rustlers. Rustlers were at least a diversion; they might be hunted down and brought back to the fort to entertain the West Pointers with their tales of lynching bees, herds run off, brands changed, hairbreadth escapes. . . .

But here there was nothing except monthly leave and a trip to St. Louis. And the months were long and hot. So the men cursed and drilled and the young officers wrote letters home and listened bitterly to veterans' tales of the glorious old times, of Sitting Bull and Custer and Crooks and Sheridan, when there were Indians to be killed and brave men to do the killing.

Colonel Mizner greeted Miles pleasantly enough. Sometimes there was more friction between the military and the agency people, and sometimes there was less; for the past month things had been going smoothly. Quakers, both as people and as a sect, were something out of the colonel's ken, but he prided himself upon a certain broad-

27

mindedness, the result of having seen many things in many places. Also, he was the sort of a person more at ease being asked than asking. The uniform was his God, and when someone begged service of the uniform, they begged it of his God. The more so when it was someone like Miles, a person whom he considered not quite competent for his task—a task far more suited to the military than to a pack of Quakers.

So he greeted Miles pleasantly and condescendingly, asking about his health and the health of Mrs. Miles. He was almost pleased to note the marked anxiety in the agent's face.

Mizner was a tall man, narrow-faced, who prided himself on his small waist and his tight mouth. He had a habit of running his hand across the front of his uniform, as to assure himself that he had not put on weight in the past few hours. He liked to think that he, with his erect trimness, was a pleasing contrast to many of the easy-going plains officers, so many of them brevetted products of the war who had never seen the all gray walls of West Point. Now he stood straight and easy, as if the mercury were at sixty instead of one hundred and five in the shade.

"This heat," Miles said, in uncomfortable apology for his dusty appearance and dripping brow. "It seems cooler here at the post."

"The way you take it," Mizner smiled. "One gets used to the plains—heat, cold, it's the same story. Are your red men cutting up?"

Miles shook his head wearily, and Mizner invited him to share the shade of the veranda. They settled themselves

28

on the porch of the officers' mess, and Mizner called for drinks.

"Just a lemonade," Miles said. He was staring moodily at the parade, where in the shade of a stunted pine two young lieutenants crowded close to a laughing girl. She didn't seem to mind the heat, and he grudged her the shrill laughter which was so clear in the dry air. He had never seen her before, and his second thought was that it would be nice if someone like that, a total stranger, should come up to the agency and have dinner with him and Lucy and the Truebloods. A Roman Catholic priest, bound south and east for his parish with two loaded mules and a donkey, had taken shelter at the post for the night. Now he stood by the well, a shapeless black club of a man, staring at the laughing girl with lonely eyes. Miles felt a sudden kinship for him, a sudden knowledge of all the other's woes and troubles.

The lemonade made him feel better. He sipped it slowly and told Mizner the gist of his troubles.

"So you think Little Wolf wants to go bad," Mizner nodded, after the agent had concluded.

"Not that perhaps, but the situation must be kept in hand."

"Naturally. I agree with you," Mizner said easily. "He's bad medicine, that Dog Soldier. I fought him up north. You can't reason with an Indian, and you can't change them once they're bad and wild. The only good ones are the dead ones. But really, there's nothing to be disturbed over. The post is here and I have a smart troop, and even if an outbreak should become general, I could hold the post a month if I had to. Two months," he amended. He said to himself, "By God, I only wish they'd try."

"No, no, it's not a general outbreak I fear," Miles said hastily. "Nothing like that at all. Things are well in hand at the agency. As a matter of fact, there's been a noticeable improvement every week for months. It's just that these northern Indians are unused to reservation discipline. They must be punished for the three who ran away. They must understand that they are here on the reservation once and for all."

"I'll send a detail up to their camp," Mizner smiled. "We'll read law to them and have the chiefs up to your office for a dressing down. Meanwhile, you can decide on the punishment. And I warn you, Agent Miles, make it stiff. I know these damned Dog Soldiers."

"I'd be careful," Miles said uncertainly.

"I'm never careful." The colonel was fatherly now. "Give it to them and we'll back you up. The army's still good medicine in these parts. . . ."

The detail consisted of Sergeant Jonas Kelly, Private Robert Fritz, and Steve Jesky, a sort of unofficial scout who hung around the post and traded his few abilities for a place to sleep, food to eat, and drinks whenever he could steal them. He lied as easily and graciously as any famous plains scout whose biography had appeared half a dozen times in half a dozen eastern newspapers; and he would spill his lies for hours on end to any stranger who would buy him a bottle of forty-cents-a-pint raw whiskey.

He wore dirty, ancient, stinking buckskins, a withered

30

Indian scalp, and long hair, the trademark and union card of supposedly accomplished scouts and Indian killers. He had an oversized, tumorous wart on his nose, and a tobacco stain which ran from his mouth across his beard and halfway down his shirt. But among his few accomplishments was a sort of knowledge of the Cheyenne language.

His knowledge was brief and elementary, but he considered it more than sufficient to make him an expert interpreter. To him, the rich, beautiful, abundant, flowing tongue of these Indians was savage gibberish, and he translated accordingly. As a matter of fact, his own English vocabulary was so limited that he could not have interpreted correctly, even if he had known all that the Indians said. And there were few to contradict him; the army knew as little of the language of the people they held down as armies of occupation do the world over.

Now he rode in advance of the two enlisted men, who held their distance with reason. The weather was hot enough to bring out hidden smells and to increase ordinary smells. Both Sergeant Kelly and Private Fritz were weather-beaten, dry-faced men whose years on the plains were many. Their skin was healthy and brown, their eyes light and small, and soldiering was a trade they had been in for enough years no longer to ask whys or wherefores. They were competent and steady, not eager for trouble and not men to avoid it if it came. Their job was to protect the scout, and they would do just that; and the fact that they were going into a more or less hostile camp of Indians did not bother them greatly. They were convinced of the purpose of the U. S. Army, and if ordered to do so, they would have ridden into hell in just the same matter-of-fact fashion.

Their talk was between themselves, excluding the scout, who was used to being excluded by fancy-dress army boys. Sergeant Kelly had recently been confessed by the wandering priest; he told Fritz:

"I want no heathen women, mind you, whose souls are blacker than their hearts."

"You never rode agin the Apaches then," Fritz prodded him. "They uncover the bosom like you and me pull off a pair of gloves."

"Ye're a liar."

"Am I? By God, red women or black women—it's better than no women. You ever had a squaw, Sergeant?"

"Nor did you. And I'll mind you to keep your eyes off them."

"I'll keep my hands off them," Fritz said. "But Christ, I been so long at that damned fort my eyes'll have to do the work for me."

"A Dog Soldier'll soon as not cut your throat for looking at his women."

Fritz spat. "They're all the same red bastards. I seen pretty squaws, but they get old like a dry apple."

"I been with one," Kelly said, after a long moment.

"Yeah? Where?"

"It's best forgotten," Kelly said. "But don't go to thinking they're all the same. They're bad medicine, the Dog Soldiers. They're not like the Comanches or Pawnees or Sioux or Kiowas. They're proud, silent people, like the Irish."

"I never saw a silent Irishman," Fritz said.

32

"A deep silence of the soul. You wouldn't understand."

They rode on until the scout held up his hand. Through the stunted trees ahead of them, they saw the high, matchwork tops of skin tepees.

"That's it," Jesky said.

"Let me go ahead," Kelly ordered. "They have a proper respect for a uniform."

"I seen them shoot a hole into their proper respect," Jesky snickered.

The little detail crowded through the pines. A dog barked. They saw children racing for the camp. The troopers loosened the flaps of their holsters.

"Keep your gun down!" Kelly told the scout.

The Cheyenne village was planted in an open circle on the dry river-bank, in the shape of a letter C. The horses were herded outside the circle, in a stick-and-brush corral. As the two troopers and the scout approached, the men came running out of their tepees, some of them with arms in their hands. They wore little, leggings on some, only breechclouts on others. They were most of them lean and tired-looking, tall, broad-shouldered men with hard faces. Nor were there many. All told, the village couldn't have held more than three hundred souls.

The two troopers and the scout rode in with their hands high. Once they were within the camp circle, the Indians closed around them. But in their lined faces there was less of hate than of bitter curiosity. After the first flush of surprise, the children were back, poking their heads out of the tepees and crawling between the legs of the men. Their darting black eyes, tangled hair, and naked copper skin reminded Kelly of imps from some half-re-

membered childhood story-land. But the women held
back; they either stood at the edge of the circle or sheltered themselves in their lodges.

"Chief," Kelly said. "Make talk with chief—headman."
And turning to the scout, "Ask for the chief. Make sabbe
with them, keep them talking."

Jesky gabbled Cheyenne. Three or four elderly men
pushed their way up to Kelly's horse.

"Ask for Little Wolf," Kelly said.

A heavy-shouldered Indian nodded.

"And I'm glad to meet you," Kelly said, dismounting
and offering the Cheyenne his hand. They shook hands,
and then both troopers and the scout shook hands with the
other chiefs.

"Tell them there's trouble," Kelly said. "We're not ones
to be after trouble, but there's trouble all the same. Men
running away. Tell them it's Colonel's orders for them to
come into the agency, the whole lot of them, and make
talk with Agent Miles. Tell them Big White Father wants
to make talk with them."

Jesky put it into his broken Cheyenne. Two of the
chiefs frowned, but Little Wolf smiled slightly. Old Dull
Knife spoke slowly and haltingly, and Jesky struggled with
his Cheyenne once more.

The scout spat and turned to Kelly. "These God
damned Dog Soldiers are laughing at me. They're not
going into the agency. The colonel should have sent a
troop and given them a little lead. That's what they
sabbe."

"Tell it to them again," the sergeant said.

"I don't think they sabbe his talk," Fritz put in.

"They sabbe," Jesky snapped. "You ain't seen a nigger wouldn't play dead if he had to."

"Keep talking," Kelly ordered.

The chiefs spoke slowly and painstakingly. Jesky said: "They're going to break camp and move up the river a ways. The agent can go to the devil and be damned."

Kelly nodded. "Mother of God," he said under his breath, "but I am glad the father came by and heard my sins. We'll go back to the post now."

Colonel Mizner was glad that Miles had gone back to Darlington. Miles would hem and haw and splutter, and in the end he would try his milk of human kindness on the Indians. As Mizner said to Captain Charles Murray of Company B:

"By that time, a long line of burning ranches and scalped bodies would testify to the wise policy of the Indian Office. And just so long as they keep the agencies in the hands of doddering Quakers, they'll have this sort of thing."

"But there's been no hostile act yet," Murray ventured.

"My dear Captain, in time, when you've had as much dealings with the Indians as I have, you'll learn that it's too late to mend an Indian's handwork. But you can prevent it."

"Then you intend to wire Washington for permission to round them up?"

"I already have blanket permission to keep order on this reservation. That's my duty, and if I let a band of homicidal Dog Soldiers run wild, then I'm neglecting my

35

duty. If I put them in jail, lock, stock and barrel, then I'm doing my duty. That's all."

Captain Murray nodded. He didn't like Mizner, but Mizner was his superior officer, so he simply nodded and hoped that he would not be sent out with a detail and given the job of jailing a whole village of Cheyenne Indians. Rights and wrongs did not trouble him greatly, but he was the sort of officer who nurses an almost womanish concern for the lives of his men. He had been taught, and thoroughly believed, that the duty of a good officer was not to kill off his men, but to conserve their lives. And he had fought Dog Soldiers before; in his opinion, the whole regiment was not enough to jail the village.

"Take your company and bring them in," Mizner added.

"Sir?"

"I said, bring them in. Don't use force unless necessary, but if you have to—"

"My company, sir?"

"I think that will be enough. I think it a shame to the service if we couldn't arrest a few filthy savages with a company of cavalry."

"They're Cheyennes, sir, Dog Soldiers," Murray said uncertainly.

"I know that, Captain. If you're afraid—"

"I'm not afraid, sir," Murray said coldly. "Do you want me to bring in the whole village, or just the braves?"

"Just the braves. There shouldn't be more than fifty of them from what Miles says. Never mind the old men."

"And if they show fight?" Murray asked evenly. "Do you

want me to go into the village? They have their women and children there."

Mizner shrugged. "Take a howitzer with you and drop a few shells on them. That should start them out."

"A shell doesn't know a man from a woman."

"You have your orders, Captain," Mizner said.

And then Murray rose and saluted and left.

Even with the howitzer, Company B made little noise as they dipped down to the river-bed where the village had been. But as Murray expected, the village had moved. The troops milled in the dust for a while, looking at bits of rubbish, and then, as darkness was coming on, Murray gave the order to dismount and make camp.

Early in the morning, they were up and following the easily discernible trail the Cheyenne travois had left in the sand. These primitive sledges, made of crossed lodge-poles lashed to ponies, could only move slowly, and Murray was sure that they would soon overtake the Indians. As a matter of fact, they had gone no more than seven or eight miles when, on topping a rise, they saw the Indian village beneath them.

The lodges were pitched in a narrow, peaceful valley, a well-wooded spot, somewhat sheltered from the sun, and watered by a little stream which ran through the center. The still-green, peaceful aspect of the valley made it seem like a haven of cool delight to the hard-riding, sweating troopers. They closed up on the hilltop and sat their horses, remarking that the Cheyennes had picked the one bearable spot in a land that was remarkably like hell.

37

"And from here," Murray thought, "to the jail at Fort Reno."

He shrugged his shoulders, gave the order to dismount, and told the gunners to train the howitzer on the village. The horses were led back toward the river-bed, where they would be well protected, and the men were spread out along the edge of the ridge. Two wagons, brought along to take the Indians back to the fort, were kept close at hand with the horses harnessed. It was in Murray's mind not to give them too much time to think about things, but to hustle the braves into the wagons and back to the fort.

But the time the men were in place and preparations completed, the Indians were well aware of the presence of the troops. Some had mounted their ponies and were riding back and forth, watching the soldiers; but others went on with normal pursuits, currying horses, sitting and chatting, gossiping. The whole village, men, women and children, seemed willfully ignoring the fact that a company of U. S. cavalry had taken up positions around their village and trained a piece of artillery upon them.

Lieutenant Freeland, who had come to Fort Reno only three months before, fresh out of West Point, filled full with all the Indian wars of a hundred years past, and now satiated with boredom, asked eagerly:

"Do you think we'll see some action, sir?"

"I hope not," Murray answered morosely. "I'm going down there, Lieutenant, and I want you to hold on here without making a move until I come back."

"But, sir—"

"Don't worry, I'll come back.

"Sergeant," he called to Kelly. "Come along. And bring that scout with you."

Murray lit his pipe, and then he led the others down to the village as if they were three invited and welcome guests. The captain wasn't exactly afraid, not yet; there would be time enough for that later, and he was used to the sensation of fear. He knew he wasn't a brave man, but he could make his body do as he wished it to, and that was enough for him. Indians were a lasting puzzle to him, though he understood them better than many of his fellow officers. He could not understand a people who resisted overwhelming odds, who fought and fought even when defeat was assured, and who had finally fought themselves close to extinction. He could never believe that they held ideas of freedom and liberty similar to that of most white men; he put it down to primitive stubbornness and race suicide.

Now he was seeing a fragment of that race suicide completed, in fact helping to complete it himself.

They walked on, and soon they were in the village. The Cheyennes crowded around them curiously, but made no attempt to halt them or molest them. And when Jesky asked for Little Wolf, they were led to a tiny fire where three aged men sat, Little Wolf, Dull Knife, and Tangle Hair, who was a chief of the Dog Soldiers, a warrior society, whose name was the familiar plains term for all Cheyennes. These Dog Soldiers combined in themselves the duties of policemen and soldiers, directing the affairs of both the camp and the battlefield.

The three chiefs rose, shook hands, and then motioned for the soldiers to join them at the fire.

Murray admired the three old men, who could sit with dignity and calm, while preparations were being made to blow their village off the face of the earth. There was something about Indians, their faces, especially the lined, leathery, earth-colored faces of the old men, which gave him the feeling that here was strength enough to bear all the blows the white men could deal, and then more and more.

They smoked, and then Murray said, Jecky translating:

"I have to do this because the law says so. You know what the law is. The law is the word of the people in Washington, who rule the whole nation. They said that all Indians must stay here in the territory, on their reservations. Now three have run away from your village, and the rest of you have left the agency. That's not good; that's breaking the law. So I must take the men of the village into the post, where they will be kept until the three men come back and until we are sure they won't break the law again."

Jesky struggled with the words. Often, he halted to make Murray repeat something he had said, and then to find the Cheyenne equivalent in his own mind. When he had finished, he cocked his head for the reply, rubbing his beard and chewing his cud of tobacco owlishly.

"Them Dog Soldiers want trouble," he told Murray finally.

"How do you make that out?"

"They don't sabbe. They figure they didn't do nothing for you to take them to jail, only come away from the heat to where it's cool and better to live. They say they can't

40

make out to live in this country anyway, and if they have to die, they want to die here where it calls to mind the Black Hills or wherever the devil they came from. They say they didn't run away, and that even a child can walk eight miles, which is all they are from the agency."

. Murray shook his head, and then for a long moment puffed furiously on his pipe. "Tell them I must carry out my orders and they will have to come to the fort with me," he said.

"They say that when you lock a man up to die, there should be a reason, but for this there's no reason. They figure to stay here and keep the peace."

"Tell them that if they don't come in peace, I'll have to use force."

Over the granite features of Little Wolf, there passed the faint trace of a smile. As if he had known all this a long time ago.

"They say that you must do whatever you have to, and they must do whatever they have to."

There followed the same solemn ceremony of hand-shaking, and then the soldiers and the scout walked back to the ridge.

"Now I'm thankful that we brought the howitzer," Kelly said.

And Murray snapped: "You'll keep your remarks to yourself until they're called for, Sergeant!"

When Miles heard that Colonel Mizner had sent a troop of cavalry to bring Dull Knife's men into Fort Reno and jail, he was torn by two conflicting emotions, the first being relief that the matter had been taken out of his hands and would now be settled by competent military authorities, and the second shame, for he knew Mizner's action was neither just nor necessary.

The Cheyennes had not left the reservation, nor was it certain that they were making any preparations to leave. Therefore, they were still under his authority as Indian Agent. And as agent, how could he allow Mizner to arrest fifty or sixty men, not only for a crime which they had not committed, but for a crime which as far as he knew might not have taken place at all? He had no more than the word of Jimmy Bear as proof that three men of Dull Knife's village had run away. And that day was so hot that a saner man than Jimmy Bear might have doubted the testimony of his senses. If indeed he had seen the men at all. If he had not been lying to satisfy some fancied grudge. Or if the three men had actually been going back to the north and not merely hunting.

The more he thought of it, the more his head ached, the more his conscience troubled him, the more his doubts overwhelmed him. He was a sincere man; as Indian Agent, he was trying to follow his own creed and to benefit the small portion of the human race he controlled. The fact that the obstacles were almost insurmountable, that the rations were short, that he lacked competent and sufficient help, that the government preferred to quarter a regiment of cavalry upon the reservation rather than a regiment of schoolteachers or carpenters or plumbers or engineers, made no difference. His work was not changed, except that it was made more difficult.

He came to Lucy Miles with his problems, his aching

head, and wet, uncomfortable shirt. He drank her cold lemonade and tried to take some pleasure in her delicious sugar cookies.

"But, John," she said, "isn't it true that once those Indians are in jail at Fort Reno, everything will be settled and then you'll be able to decide who is guilty and who isn't guilty?"

"Everything won't be settled," he said miserably. "You don't arrest fifty or sixty men because some of them might be guilty. As a matter of fact, I don't know whether any of them are guilty of anything, except moving their village up to Cotter Creek, where I should have put them in the first place. At least there's water there and some green things and not all this hellish red dust."

"But the three men who ran away," Lucy reminded him gently.

"Damn the three men! I'm sorry, Lucy, but I'm not sure three men ran away. I'm not sure of anything."

"But everyone at the agency knows that three of that band ran away. It will just make things worse if men can run away whenever they take it into their heads to do so."

"Yes—"

"So you could tell Little Wolf or Dull Knife that the three men must come back and that would solve everything."

"How could they bring the men back? No, you don't understand, Lucy, it's not that, not three men, but this whole rotten reservation policy—putting a people into a prison." He hesitated, then shook his head. "No, they have to be punished for the three men. But not this way.

43

Mizner sent a gun up there. I wouldn't put it past him to drop a few shells into the village. And what can I do now?"

"Send someone over there. You're still agent at Darlington."

"That's true. Seger could go, make them wait until I've had a chance to talk with the chiefs. It would be better than Mizner's way."

He put on his hat and went out to find Seger.

He felt better already; he was doing something, at least, and regardless of what happened, he would have that small satisfaction. Also, Seger would not be bullied down by a few army officers. Certainly, he as agent was competent enough to dictate and enforce the law at his own agency.

While Seger saddled a horse, Miles spoke long and earnestly, not so much to Seger as to rid himself of all puzzling uncertainties. He begged Seger to hurry; that was the main thing. In all probability, Little Wolf would not surrender. Who had ever heard of Dog Soldiers giving in meekly unless they thought that theirs was the least just and reasonable part of the argument? So he begged Seger to hurry and avert, if not a new Indian war, at least a massacre. Seger listened stolidly to Miles' importunate pleading and instructions, to all of which he simply nodded.

"I'll do the best I can," he said.

It was dusk when Seger rode onto the ridge where Company B was encamped, and things were so quiet that at first he imagined that it was all over and that Miles would have to make his own peace with his own conscience.

Then, in the half darkness, he made out the still forms of troopers, sitting silently over their guns all the length of the ridge; and beyond them, in the fold of the valley, fires from the Indian village twinkled like night insects.

He sighed with relief and asked the sentry who challenged him: "Who's in command here?"

"Captain Murray."

"Let me see him. I'm Seger from the agency."

All afternoon and until now, Murray had put off the attack. At first, he had busied himself with preparations, and after they were completed, with a study of the tactics of the situation. Yet he knew that there were no tactics involved, nothing to do but drop a few shells and then advance into the village and take his prisoners. As the afternoon progressed and the net result of all his procrastinations was nothing at all, his mood grew blacker and blacker. Even Sergeant Kelly was afraid to address him, and once he flew into an almost insane fury at the scout, who was draped lazily against a tree, spitting tobacco juice all over the place.

The truth was that he had now come to realize the impossibility of taking even half of the men prisoner. The Cheyennes would fight and he would lose a dozen men and he would bury the mangled bodies of women and children. And in the end the net result would be a futile, foolish Indian war that might rage like a fire across half the plains country before it was finally settled, leaving in its wake dead and wounded men and broken lives. That the responsibility for this should have been summarily placed in his hands made him hate Colonel Mizner as much as he had ever hated any man. He saw himself

45

caught in a position where he could neither go ahead nor retreat, and he knew only too well the power a colonel of a plains regiment had where the making or breaking of his subordinate officers was concerned.

So from hour to hour, he put off the eventual outcome, and when at last he saw Seger, he felt that heaven itself had raised a hand to aid him. He welcomed Seger eagerly.

"Evening, Captain," Seger said. "I see you started the barbecue, but you ain't eating yet."

"It's no picnic to take fifty Dog Soldiers into jail."

"You're talking sense there. I reckon you know your colonel kind of overstepped himself this time."

"Did he?"

"I think so. So does Agent Miles. Maybe the Indian Office would think so too, and maybe there'd be all hell to pay if that pretty howitzer of yours began to drop shells into their village. Maybe Washington would sit up and take notice and even break a godalmighty like Colonel Mizner."

"Maybe," the captain said noncommittally, yet he could hardly keep from grinning with relief.

"Those Indians are still on reservation. That means under the supervision of Agent Miles, not of the military. And Miles warns you solemnly that he'll hold every officer of the regiment to account if anything breaks loose. You have no right to arrest those men, and the colonel knows it. Do you want me to put that in writing?"

"It's quite all right," Murray said.

"Are you going to camp here all night?"

"I have to—at least until I communicate with Colonel Mizner and receive further orders. But your precious savages won't be disturbed. I'll keep an eye on them, and that's all."

"I'll take your hand on that, Captain," Seger nodded. "I'm going down there now and try to get the chiefs to come into camp and make talk with Agent Miles. So don't start shooting if something comes out of the dark."

"Kind of risky," the captain warned him. "They know what we're up to."

"Do they? I'll leave the army to make the worst of anything. I'll take a chance. I don't think they'll shoot me."

"Want Jesky to go along and make talk?"

"Him? No, I sabbe a little Cheyenne, enough I guess. I don't want any part of the army with me."

"All right—go ahead. It's your own skin."

Murray stood there and watched Seger ride off into the night. A few paces, and he was lost in the murky darkness, and then there was only the sound of his horse's hoofs until even that faded away. For a long time, Murray remained where Seger had left him, staring at the twinkling fires of the Indian village, at the vaguely glowing tepees, like jack o' lanterns, full of the fire inside of them and giving off light from the openings at the top and from places where the buffalo skins were worn thin.

He heard the scout drawl from somewhere in the darkness: "That damnfool Seger'll get his head blown off. Serve him right. By God, I got no respect for a man that don't know niggers."

It was about an hour later that Seger came back. He leaned over in his saddle and told the anxious Murray:

"The chiefs'll be coming in in the morning. Let them through."

47

"Sure. Have any trouble?"

"Only with my Cheyenne. By God, how them little kids talk that language is more than I understand."

Colonel Mizner and Lieutenant Stevenson rode up to the agency early the next morning. Mizner was furious with Miles for countermanding his orders; but saner reasoning had shown what his gesture might have cost, and look at it as he might, he saw that Miles had pulled his chestnuts out of the fire. But now that Miles was going to handle the matter himself, Mizner wished to follow the proceedings, so that he might put his own end of the record in order.

Miles' little office was already crowded when the two officers arrived. Seger was there, and the agent, and Trueblood, and Edmond Guerrier to do the interpreting. Mizner entered with scarcely a greeting, nodding at the agency people and taking his place in a chair by the window. The lieutenant stood by his side. Seger sat on the edge of the desk, stuffing his pipe; Miles was behind the desk, and Trueblood in a corner with his pad and pencil. Guerrier stood unobtrusively against one wall, his head bent, his fingers rolling his broad-brimmed straw hat around and around.

For the half hour before the Indians came, little was said, and hardly anyone moved, except once when Seger rose to open the window wider. There were a few remarks about the weather and a lot of wiping of brows, but that was all. Miles bent over his desk, working on a report, but he seemed nervous and ill at ease.

Finally, Seger nodded at the window and said: "There they come."

Everyone turned to see. Three Indians were riding toward the veranda, two of them old men and in the lead, the one behind a huge middle-aged man, muscled like a gladiator with a deeply scarred face. They rode slowly and thoughtfully, leaning forward in their saddles, and behind them ran a crowd of agency children. At the house, they dismounted, and the children gathered in a circle around them, digging bare toes into the dust.

"The scarface is Crow," Seger said. "He's bad medicine, so maybe they expect trouble. They say he killed six Pawnees with his bare hands once at the old Twin Forks fight. The other two are Little Wolf and Wild Hog."

Seger lit his pipe and went out to bring the chiefs in. There was hot, cloying silence in the room until he returned. Miles stopped writing.

When the Cheyennes entered, they shook hands with everyone in the room and then took their places against one of the walls and waited for the agent to speak. But the silence continued. Then Little Wolf said something, and Guerrier translated:

"He wants to know why you have sent for them."

Mizner smiled suddenly. Miles said: "He knows why I sent for them."

"He says he doesn't know. He says they were living peacefully and doing nothing to harm any man. Even when the white soldiers camped over their village and trained a cannon on them, they continued to live peacefully. Isn't that what the white men want?"

Now the agent turned to Little Wolf and said: "Three

49

of your men have run away. An Arapahoe saw them traveling north, and he knew who they were. You know it's
against the law for any Indian to leave the reservation
without permission from me. Now you must give me ten
of your young men to hold here as prisoners, and meanwhile the soldiers will go out and search for the three who
escaped. When those three men are brought back, I will
give your ten men their liberty."

As Guerrier finished translating, Little Wolf murmured
something to Wild Hog. The other nodded. Little Wolf
shook his head slowly. "That's no good," he told the
agent. "I cannot do what you ask. How can you find three
men in a country big enough to hide a thousand men? If
one of your helpers at the agency ran away, would I come
and ask you to give me ten of your men? Is that the law
of the white men, that innocent people should suffer for
those who are guilty? The ten men have done nothing,
but you would put them in jail and keep them there
until they died. How many Cheyennes have you sent to
prison in Florida? Have any of them ever returned? No, I
cannot give up ten men for three men you will never see
again."

Mizner was still smiling. Guerrier shuffled nervously as
he translated. Miles said angrily:

"You will give up those men or receive no more rations
from me! I'll give you nothing to eat until I get them!
You'll starve until they are handed over! I want those
men, and I want them at once!"

Little Wolf shook his head. "I cannot give up those
men. It is no use to threaten to starve us; we are starving already. But I cannot give up those men. I am a

friend to the white people; I have been for a long time. I saw that it was better to work with the white men than to die fighting them. For myself, I do not care; I am an old man, but I saw that only a little of the tribe was left. It is a terrible thing when a whole nation dies, but if we have to die, it is better to die fighting than by what you call the white man's law.

⌐ "Maybe you think I do not know, but I have been to Washington and I have spoken to the president and I shook hands with him. He said there should be peace between us; I have tried to keep that peace."

Miles shook his head stubbornly. He was hardly listening to Guerrier's halting words. He was watching Mizner's smile, and feeling the colonel's contempt for a man who couldn't enforce law he pretended to administer.

"You must give up the ten men," Miles said. "I want them brought here, and I want them brought here today."

Little Wolf smiled curiously. "We have been friends, Agent Miles," he said. "But I cannot do what you ask. I must do what I think is right. I do not want trouble and I do not want bloodshed at this agency, but I cannot do what you ask."

"Then you'll starve!"

The two other Cheyennes looked at Little Wolf. The scarred man's face was contorted with anger, but Little Wolf gripped his arm so tightly that the fingers left marks in the skin. Then Little Wolf went from person to person, shaking hands with each.

"I'll expect the ten men today," Miles said.

"I am going back to camp," Little Wolf smiled. "We will do what we have to do, both you and I, Agent Miles.

Here at the agency you fed some of my people, so it would be a shame if I wet the grounds with blood. But this is what I must do and what I am going to do. I am going to take my people and go back north, to our own home in the Black Hills. We want to go peacefully, and so long as no one tries to stop us, we will go peacefully. But if you must send your soldiers after us, wait until we are a little way from the agency. Then if you want to fight, I will fight you, and we can shed our blood at that place."

Miles stared at him without speaking. Mizner said:

"By God, Miles, you're a fool if you don't jail the three of them now while they're here!"

"Let them go, Seger," Miles said dully.

"Miles, you don't mean to let them ride out of here?"

"They came at my request," Miles said. "I told them they would be free to come and go. That's the least I can do." Then he sat there with his aching head in his hands, while the others trooped out into the lesser heat of the veranda, to watch the three Cheyennes ride away, their skinny ponies swaying through the clouds of dust.

As Mizner was leaving, he said to Miles, smiling a little, "I'll keep Company B where they are. You might need them yet."

And Miles, crushed, made no reply. A while later, he sent off the following telegram to William Nicholson, Superintendent of Indian Affairs at Lawrence, Kansas: "LITTLE WOLF, NORTHERN CHEYENNE CHIEF, THREATENS TO LEAVE RESERVATION FOR NORTH WITH ENTIRE BAND, NUMBERING THREE HUNDRED. PLEASE ADVISE PROMPTLY."

He was nervous and upset while he waited a reply. Lucy, seeing his condition, invited the Quaker pastor, Elkanah Beard, and his wife to dinner. The good pastor did his best to ease Miles' mind. Beard was a stout little man with watery blue eyes, and he kept repeating that the way of love was the right way, and that all concerned should have faith that matters would right themselves.

"You see, brother Miles," he said, "one can only follow one's own right conscience."

"A savage," Lucy said gently, "cannot comprehend Christian law, even though he is baptized. We must have patience and love, as I always tell John, and in the end things will work out right."

"Assuredly," Pastor Beard nodded.

It was almost night before the reply came. Nicholson wired: "NO INDIANS MUST LEAVE RESERVATION. ABSOLUTELY IMPERATIVE TO WHOLE INDIAN RESETTLEMENT PLAN THAT NORTHERN CHEYENNES REMAIN AT AGENCY. INFORM COLONEL MIZNER."

Miles sat in his office for a long while, reading and re-reading the telegram before he sent for Seger. Then, tonelessly, he asked him to take the telegram to Colonel Mizner at Fort Reno.

Agent Miles had little peace that night; for long hours he sat in his office, watching the flies and mosquitoes buzz about the lamp, asking himself over and over whether he had done the right and the best thing. But Colonel Mizner was a man of action; within minutes after he had read the telegram, Company A was saddling, and a half hour later Captain Wint was leading them to join Murray's force.

Murray accepted Mizner's orders philosophically. He advised Captain Wint to spread out his men so that they might cover the whole of the eastern ridge.

"It wouldn't be wise to spread out further than that. I'll put out pickets, although it's hardly necessary. You can see their tepees down there and their fires."

"The colonel said something about going in there tonight."

"That would be insane. The place is full of women and kids. If the colonel wants a blood bath, he can draw it himself. This is a police action, not a massacre. We'll wait for morning."

PART THREE   September 1878

THE CHASE BEGINS

Captain Murray spent a
sleepless night. He had discovered in the past that it was
impossible for him to sleep when he expected any sort
of action the following morning. Regardless of how he
had exhausted himself the day before, the mere fact that
morning might bring to an end his existence on earth
was enough to point his mind to sharp and aggravating
focus. How he envied men like Wint or Freeland or
Stevenson, young men so immersed in the business of living that death was beyond their power of conception.
They were brave men, and he knew that he wasn't; the
mere sound of the word coward was enough to evoke all
his past life. Yet sometimes he wondered whether his own
fear wasn't universal, whether all other men didn't hide
it as well as he did. He had been in the army twelve years
and he was considered a brave man and a sound officer.

After the first few crawling hours, each of which left

his mind wider awake than before, Murray gave up his attempt to sleep, rose, pulled on his boots and stuffed his pipe with tobacco. He struck a match, stoked his pipe to hot flame, and then lay back on his cot, his knees jackknifed, his spurs caught on his blanket. The pipe didn't taste good; it never did in the dark, when he couldn't see the smoke.

Someone came to the tent, lifted the flap, and stood there.

"Yes?" Murray demanded.

It was Sergeant Kelly. "I saw you strike the match," he said. "I was thinking you might—"

"I'm quite all right," Murray said brusquely.

"Yes, sir."

"Wait a minute," Murray said. "Sorry. Makes one short tempered, not to be able to sleep."

"I have that trouble myself, sir," Kelly said stolidly. "I was taking a look over the place."

"Quiet?"

"Like a home of the dead," Kelly nodded. "The fires are burning down in the lodges, but what their need of fires on a hot night like this is, I don't know."

"Light, I suppose."

"Sir?"

"Nothing," Murray sighed.

"Light, did you say? Maybe to light their black souls to hell."

"Sergeant," Murray said curiously, "there'll be a fight tomorrow. You'll enjoy it, I suppose?"

"Sir?"

"I said you'll enjoy killing tomorrow, won't you?"

"I never looked at it that way, sir," Kelly said uneasily.

"How do you look at it?"

"It's good pay and there are worse things a man can do."

"Get some sleep, Sergeant," Murray sighed, and when the man had gone, unhooked his spurs from the blanket and walked out of the tent. As the sergeant had said, a glimmer of light still pricked out the shape of the tepees. The sky was black and starless, and a heavy pressure in the air gave promise of rain that night or on the morrow. Murray walked along the edge of the ridge, past the sentries, until he stood next to the howitzer. The gunners lay under the ammunition cart, snoring heavily. Murray laid his hand against the wet, cold barrel of the gun, and then let the moisture slide across his face.

He paced back and forth until he had smoked out two pipefuls. Now and then, a low roll of thunder broke the night, following hard on white flashes of light. The first two times caught Murray unprepared, but the third time he was staring directly at the Indian village; he had the instant impression of a man in the center of the village, alone and mounted.

He asked one of the sentries, but the trooper had seen nothing, and then, expecting rain, Murray walked back to his tent. He sat on the edge of his bed, one leg perched on the other, playing with the spur; but the rain didn't come. He sat like that until a gray, wet hint of dawn crept into the tent.

Then he went over to Wint's quarters and woke the other captain. "Morning," he said harshly. "Come out of it."

Wint sat up, rubbing his eyes. "What is it? What in hell, Murray, it's still dark out."

"It's morning. Get up. I want to have a look around, and you'd better be up while I'm gone."

"It's quiet," Wint said sleepily, fumbling for his boots.

"Too damn quiet. I'm going down there."

"That's a crazy thing to do. Why don't you wait?"

Murray shrugged and walked away. He had had no intentions of going into the village alone; it was fear that made him fling the challenge to the half-awake Wint. Now he wanted a drink, badly. He went to his tent, found a half-full pint in his bags, and finished most of it. He stuffed mints into his mouth, took the bottle with him, and as soon as he had passed the sentry, flung the bottle into the brush. He went on, soaking his breeches as he passed through the wet underbrush. The little gully was full of mist, and soon he could see the tall tepees poking out of the fluffed, cottony lather. Almost every other tepee was stripped of its skins, skeleton structures of skinny poles.

He wasn't surprised to find the village empty. Rather was he amazed at his own stupidity. He should have seen through their simple trick, to leave fires in half the lodges, strip the skins from the rest, muffle the horses' hoofs and go quietly from the place. How long ago was that? Now there would be hell to pay. Suppose Wint smelled the whiskey and reported?

Murray lit his pipe. Tobacco helped to take away the taste of his drink, and he hoped it would take away the smell. He walked through the village, and the mist loosened and broke in waving, feathery tendrils. He poked over the still warm fires and stared curiously at the scattered rubbish. There was something pathetically human about any place where men had been recently and were no more. In their presence the Cheyennes had never been as alive and real to him as they were now. He found himself picking up one thing and then another, a split bow that was not worth taking along, a little buckskin doll, beaded cleverly and daintily, a worn out pair of moccasins, a fire stick.

His mind traced the alternative course of events, the howitzer dropping shells on the village, the cavalrymen storming down over the lip of the gully, the crazy, raging anger that came over men who were being shot at—otherwise simple, decent men—and made them kill anything and everything, horses, children, women. He had heard stories of the brutal Sand Creek massacre of Cheyennes, and he was almost childishly relieved that he would not be involved in another action of the same kind.

As he walked back to where the two troops were encamped, he found himself humming lightly. He was tired now; he would like to lie down and sleep for a while.

Wint met him as he came over the lip. The clouds had broken up, and rays of sunshine spotted down into the gully. Captain Wint was fingering his small, black mustache and staring at the skeleton tepees.

"Cleared out," Murray said.

"All of them?"

"Every last one. How they did it without the horses making a whimper, I don't know. They're devils with horses."

"We should have gone in last night," Wint said worriedly.

"And then take hell for shooting up the women and kids?" Murray demanded.

"You can't choose with Indians," Wint said.

"If you don't mind making out the report, I'll nap just a bit," Murray said. "I didn't sleep well last night."

Colonel Mizner had just finished breakfast and was walking across the compound towards the stables. No word had come from Troops A and B out at Cotter Creek, and since by this time they should have come in with their prisoners, he was beginning to feel somewhat anxious. He had in mind to ride over to Darlington and see whether Agent Miles had received any further news either from the superintendent or from Washington; but he thought he would wait until some word came in from Murray and Wint. At the stables, he inspected the horses and told them to have his black mare, Jenny, saddled in about an hour. He was returning to his quarters when he saw Trooper Angelus drive a hard-worked horse through the gates. Mizner continued on to his quarters, showing less concern than he felt, although he knew that if there had been a fight during the night, Murray would have reported.

He sat down on his porch and lighted a cigar, watching calmly while Angelus ran across the compound. The men were on their way to morning parade, but they knew something was up and they gathered into little knots, watching the colonel and the dust-covered Angelus.

"Report from Captain Wint, sir," Angelus panted.

Mizner took the dispatch, but before he read it called to Captain Treebody:

"I'll have no loitering on the compound, Captain!"

He read it quickly, and when he had finished told Trooper Angelus:

"Get something to eat and report back here. Just a moment—do you know whether Captain Murray made any attempt to bring in those Indians last night?"

"I don't think so, sir."

Mizner went to his office, and there he read the dispatch again. His first impulse, the result of his mounting anger, was to order Troops A and B back to the post and have Murray put under arrest for gross negligence in the face of the enemy. But after a little consideration, he decided that the whole case could not stand up under a court martial. Too many sore points would be brought to light, one being whether his duty had been to arrest the Cheyennes or simply to detain them from leaving the reservation, and the second being a consideration of what might have occurred had Murray decided to shell the village. Massacres had a way of getting into the eastern papers, and pressure on Washington had put an end to the career of many an aspiring officer.

However, as things stood now, the matter had been simplified extremely. The Cheyennes had left the reservation and his duty was to bring them back. And if that were done easily and unostentatiously, thereby averting another Indian war, it might be General Mizner instead of Colonel Mizner. However, it was just as well to proceed cautiously; if he consulted Miles and things went wrong later, it would be just as well to have the civil Indian authorities take the consequences.

So when Trooper Angelus reappeared, Mizner was already mounted. They rode together to Darlington.

Agent Miles listened nervously to Colonel Mizner's account of what had happened the night before at Cotter Creek. When Mizner had finished, Miles shook his head and murmured:

"But that shouldn't have happened. They were not to leave the reservation."

"Many things shouldn't have happened," the colonel said.

"Still—I don't see how—you had two companies there."

"It was your policy to wait, Mr. Miles. My officers could not take the responsibility of shelling that village in the dark. If you had let us arrest those Dog Soldiers before, all this would have been averted. As matters stand now, the only thing to do is to go after them and bring them back."

"Yes, they must be brought back," Miles said uncertainly.

"Have you considered what might happen if this gets into the papers?"

"I did what I could," Miles said wearily. "What else could I do?"

"Will you countersign the order for their arrest?"

Miles stared at the colonel, then looked down at his desk, where his hands played nervously with a sheet of paper.

"They won't surrender," Miles said.

"They won't. Still, if they're not brought back, what about the other tribes at your agency?"

"I'll countersign," Miles sighed.

"Good!" The colonel became brisk and businesslike. "I'll dispatch two troops on their trail immediately, and we should see the end of this business within a week. Meanwhile, I'll wire the War Office at Washington and have your orders confirmed. Now how many people are there in Dull Knife's band?"

"About three hundred," Miles said listlessly. "Eighty-five or ninety men—the rest are women and children. Some are sick, a good many I guess. They can't go very fast."

"Then the two troops will be enough," Mizner said decisively. "We can save time that way by starting from the creek where my men are encamped. I'll leave it to you to notify the Indian Office, and I'll send you a report as soon as those Indians are safely in jail."

Agent Miles nodded, and Mizner strode erectly from the room. After he had gone, Miles sat at his desk, staring dully ahead of him. When Lucy entered, about an hour later, to remind him that his lunch was on the table, he was still sitting like that.

"What is it?" she asked.

"Nothing, nothing, Lucy. I did all I could."

Mizner's orders to Murray were brief and to the point. He told him to go after the Cheyennes and arrest them. The wagons would follow the troops to bring the Indians back to the post. The howitzer would have to be returned to Fort Reno, since it would impede the progress of the troops; but Mizner anticipated no great difficulty, even without the gun. The main thing was to locate the Indians. And the soldiers had with them, aside from Steve Jesky, an Arapahoe scout called Ghost Man.

"If they resist?" Murray asked.

"Bring back all who are alive. I'll see that you get full credit for the action, Captain. It may mean a promotion."

Murray nodded slightly, and the colonel said to himself, "This is a sullen brute, but he'll do it."

Wint, rated below Murray, was a good man to follow, but not to lead. Murray would drive on and come back with some of the Indians, those who were left. And Murray wouldn't lose too many men; if he had a fault, it was being overcareful in his command.

Mizner rode back to Fort Reno, well-satisfied with the way he had handled the situation, and A and B troops drove north. The trail of three hundred people on horseback, a village, a tribe and a nation, many people of many ages and many hopes, young and old and beautiful and ugly, with all their worldly possessions, large things and small things, gross and delicate, intimate or public—such a trail was not hard to follow. And how could they hide? Riding hard, the thunder of their horses' hoofs would wake the prairie for miles around. They would be heard and seen and pointed out. Doors would be closed against them, windows barred, stock driven out of their path. The plains they rode north on were not the plains their fathers and grandfathers remembered; the plains were bridled with fences and saddled with farms. Roads and houses and telegraph wires, and there was more than that, for three railroads, east to west, made three iron belts on the belly of the land.

⌐The troops drove north. Jesky and the Arapahoe picked up the trail, through the dust, brush trampled flat, a broad drag in the bottoms of dry river-beds. The dry earth was mangled, and the Arapahoe held up fluttering hands to show that the Cheyennes were running hard. The troops drummed under the bitter sun and they ate up the miles through the dry gullies of the Chautauqua Hills. Dust, foul and red, turning to mud on their skin and in their mouths, closed out the world. They sweated and panted and rode without talk, and the sun set like a pinched coal in a haze of scarlet. That night they made camp on Red Fork.

Murray was black and silent, and the men feared him. He was filthy, his body nasty with dirt and sweat, but the river was dry and there was no place to bathe; he took his bad temper out on the men, lashing them with his tongue and trying to find places where it would hurt most. They kept away from him as much as they could.

"What's eating you?" Wint asked him.

"That's my own damned business, Captain."

"All right. But if it's too much heat, try to be a little decent about it. We're all hot."

"Sorry," Murray said. He looked at Wint queerly.

"Think we'll be up with them tomorrow?" Wint asked. "Maybe."

"I've known Dog Soldiers to ride a hundred and twenty miles a day," Wint said. "They run their ponies on a string and change every ten miles. There's no cavalry in the world can ride them down."

65

"These have no string. Their ponies are skinny enough to die walking. And the women and kids are with them."

"Still, they'll move," Wint said.

"They'll move all right. Maybe we'll come up with them tomorrow. Maybe the next day. Make it an early reveille, four-thirty."

"That won't give the men much sleep."

"If the squaws can stand it, they can," Murray said.

They were up and on in the half light of dawn, the men cursing softly, the officers looking at Murray with curious eyes. The trail might have been hard to follow in that light, had the Cheyennes made any attempt to hide it. But their passage north was the line of a crow flying, the hungering of a people to be back on their own sod, in their own hills and valleys. North they went and north, and again the Arapahoe flapped his hands to show how Indians could ride, women and children and old men, when the land of their fathers called to them. He was with the white men, but he was proud of his own kind—and prouder when they passed the bodies of dead ponies, torn by coyotes and black with flies.

"Run to death," the troopers told each other. They knew that an Indian who runs his pony to death will run himself to death.

They rested in the heat of the morning, walking their horses and currying the sweat. They were in good grass country now, high and yellow in fat clumps, with dry dung all over to tell a memory of the great buffalo herds that had once rolled across the plains.

"And not so long ago," Kelly said. "Ten years ago, they were like black maggots on the land."

Already, Murray was telling the bugler to sound. He was beginning to feel the pain of long hours in the saddle, and he saw how the men stretched themselves to ease their cramps. How did women and children stand it? They could be Indians, savages without too much sensitivity, without any real knowledge of good or bad or right or wrong or pain or comfort; but still their flesh was flesh. He had once tasted the bitter comfort of a Cheyenne rawhide saddle.

"Better the sooner it's over," he muttered to himself, thinking that men kill a dog when they can no longer watch its suffering.

They drove on. North was the direction the Indians held to, and the sun was a hot knife on the troopers' backs. But the dust was thinner here, and the ripple of grasslands was like a yellow sea in front of them. They crossed the Salt Fork and reined in at a squatter's cabin.

"Indians?" Murray croaked.

The man was skinny and long, a horse face and shabby overalls. He rubbed his neck slowly, while his wife and two children crouched in the door behind him. He was something lawless and afraid, from the edge of a wave that had cast him into Indian Territory, and he feared and hated the soldiers as much as he feared and hated the Indians.

"They come by," he said sullenly.

"When?"

"Morning."

67

"How many? Speak up!" Murray snapped. "You're not dumb, are you? Speak up!"

"Maybe I'm dumb, mister," the squatter drawled. "You got no call to know my business."

"How many, mister?" Murray said again.

"Like as many as you—bastards, God damn you!" he yelled after them as they pounded off.

They were close to the Kansas border before they stopped again. They climbed down from their saddles, cramped in the legs, many of them tumbling over and rolling prone on the grass. There was a creek-bed near by, a succession of mudholes, and the men led their horses down to drink. Afterwards, the troopers lay on the ground and munched their rations and swigged from their canteens. Murray and Wint put their heads together over a map.

"They'll want water to camp by," Wint said. "Salt Fork is dry. They'll go on to the Medicine Lodge River."

"If there's water there. If not, they'll go on."

"They can't go on."

"Don't you think I know that?" Murray growled. "Their horses were half dead before they left Darlington."

Wint shrugged.

"I'll post a man to Dodge City," Murray said. "They should know already if the colonel telegraphed, but it won't hurt for them to have a company or two out north of here. They can shove a train along the Sante Fé and make a bear trap of it."

"The colonel might think—"

68

"I don't give a damn what he thinks," Murray said. "I want to finish this."

"All right," Wint nodded, "all right."

The trooper left for Dodge City, and the rest of them drove north again on the Cheyennes' trail. Once in Kansas, the ranch houses became more frequent, but when a ranch barred the path, the broad trail of the Indian village looped away. Then they came into broken country, and all they saw alive were two far-off figures riding range.

Once Lieutenant Freeland spurred up alongside of Murray and said: "The horses can't stand much more of this, sir."

"Can't they?"

And Freeland said no more; but Murray could see well enough that the horses were driving to death, sweating, lathered, all a-tremble even as they ran.

It was late afternoon when the scout, Jesky, pulled up his horse and pointed to a trail of smoke across the sky. Murray held up his hand for the troops to halt. The smoke was in many thin streams, running together and then apart.

"Trail's end," Wint said softly, and Murray noticed that he had slipped open the flap of his revolver holster. The men had bunched up; they were leaning forward over their saddles, breathing hoarsely. There was brown and gray dust all over their blue uniforms and their faces wore a three-day coat of beard. They watched the smoke.

Murray led them down to the river slowly, but there

was brush on the river bank, and about a hundred yards away he halted. Wint pointed upstream; about a mile off the ground humped almost to a butte, and it appeared that the Cheyennes were camped there.

"I don't like that brush," Murray said.

Lieutenants Freeland, Gatlow, and Auslander had pushed their horses close to the two captains. They were so excited that they had to bite their lips to keep from spilling words all over the place. It would be their first action, and already they were picturing what it would mean back east to tell tales of real Indian fights. Gatlow, a pink-cheeked, sandy-haired boy of twenty-two, was the son of an old plains man; he saw himself standing up to his father, swapping stories man to man. Auslander tried to keep what he considered calm dignity, but Freeland was grinning like a baby.

"Fall back and deploy your men," Murray told them gently. He seemed very tired; he kept rubbing his eyes and yawning.

"Kelly!" he called. "Oh, Kelly!"

When Kelly came up, the captain nodded at him wearily. He pointed toward the river. "Take the scout and two or three men, Sergeant, and beat out that brush.'·

"Yes, sir," Kelly said.

Murray and Wint sat close together, watching the five men, spread wide apart, go through the brush to the river. The sun was sinking low now and the shadows of the mounted men slipped sidewise, flat and long and slippery with the motion of the grass. A cool wind blew from the north, and the ribbons of smoke ran from each other.

Sergeant Kelly came back out of the brush, waving his arms.

"All clear!" he called.

Murray led his troops down to the river. The brush was full of birds; they threshed up and whirled over the heads of the dusty riders. There was about a foot of brown water standing on the sandy bottom, and as the troopers rode through they had to pinch their bridles to keep the horses from drinking. On the further bank, they formed in marching order, four by four, their flag spilled out, men mixed with shadow, a long snake in the grass and stunted trees.

They rode upstream slowly, resting their horses, and soon they were able to distinguish the shapes of men and ponies on top of the hill.

"They've seen us," Wint said, and Murray motioned for the bugler to blow. The trumpet notes were silver clear, like thin arrows sent into the late, rosy sunlight. The horses took life, and the whole pace of the column quickened.

Then Murray held up his hand for the column to stop.

An Indian had detached himself from the group at the top of the hill and was swooping smoothly down to where the troops had formed themselves for the attack. He rode erect, his arms above his head, his hair streaming behind him, his little pony running with wild and effortless grace. The sun dipped lower, and suddenly the hillside behind him was deep in shadow, a ball of fire resting on the lip of the butte. He came out of the shadow, and the pony stopped running. Still with his hands above his head, he walked his horse to within twenty paces of Captain Murray.

"Little Wolf," Wint said.

The old chief let his hands drop slowly; his earth-colored face was seamed in a smile that was half pity and half regret. Naked to the waist, unarmed, he sat on his horse in the quiet judgment of ages. He was something that was gone, that was dead and would never live again; and he knew it. As if all the two hundred years of bitter, bloody warfare between his kind and the white people had culminated here in the two opposing factors, Captain Murray in his dusty blue uniform and the old, half-naked Cheyenne chief.

Yet the only sensation Murray knew was sullen anger—an anger which included himself, Little Wolf, his men and all the forces that had driven him in two days of furious pursuit.

"Ask him what he wants," Murray said to Steve Jesky.

Little Wolf spoke slowly, nodding his head as the words fell from his wide mouth. It was difficult to believe that the man was a savage, speaking in a savage tongue. The words sounded reasonable, and the intonation was that of a wise grandfather speaking to hot-headed youth. All of the troopers were leaning forward in their saddles, trying to catch his words, even though they understood not a word he said.

"He don't want to fight," Jesky said.

"That's all right," Murray nodded. "Tell him to bring his people down here and we'll place them under arrest. They'll be well treated and wagons of food and clothes will come up tomorrow."

72

"He won't do that," Jesky said. "They ain't going back. They're going up north, and if he has to, he'll lead them cross the Canady border."

"It's no use," Murray said wearily. "Tell him we're going to attack and we're going to bring in his tribe if we have to kill every man he has. Tell him there'll be troops coming down from Dodge City tomorrow and more troops along the Sante Fé railroad. There's no way in the world for him to reach Canada or even Wyoming."

Little Wolf smiled again and held out his hand to Murray. But Murray didn't take it. Jesky drawled:

"He says he figures to do what he has to do, and you'll do what you have to do. But sometimes it's better for people to be dead than slaves."

Murray snapped: "Tell him to get to hell out of here before I have him shot!"

By now the whole side of the hill was in deep shadow, nor was there any sign of people on top. Half of the sun was glazed onto it, like orange icing on a Halloween cake. Little Wolf swung his pony and trotted into the shadow. Then he reined back once more, as if he wanted to speak with Murray again. Murray's reaction was the outpouring of all the rage and disappointment inside of him. He ripped out his revolver and flung a shot at the Cheyenne chief.

Little Wolf didn't move. Murray stared at his smoking revolver and said to Freeland without looking up: "Have the advance sounded."

Little Wolf swung his pony and raced away. The trumpet notes etched through the stillness, sharing with

73

the drum of the pony's hoofs the effect of wind and percussion playing to some lonely amphitheater. And from the men, tensing to the sudden unleashing of their horses, there came an almost audible sigh.

And then Wint flung his arm at the hilltop, where suddenly, against the flushed sky and ruddy sun edge, there appeared a long line of mounted men. There were more than eighty, all the men of the tribe, very old men and very young men and braves in the full manhood of good life.

The two companies of cavalry surged forward, and the fierce drumming of almost a thousand hoofs drowned out the sound of the trumpet. Their sabers flashed, and then the bits of light flickered out as they raced onto the shadowed upswing of the hill. And yet the silhouetted figures against the sky remained still.

Then the Cheyennes poured over the edge, their cry of defiance completing the unholy orchestra. Not on the troops, but almost on the troops in a wild charge that would have spitted them on stiff saber-arms; and then suddenly breaking into two parts, spinning around the troops and away from them, breaking out like bits of a shattered kaleidoscope, dancing on their wiry, tiny ponies, dark feathers in the breeze, somehow around the troops and past the troops and through the troops.

The bugles called back the blue uniforms, and Companies A and B pulled in their tired horses and reformed. They swung around on the dusky hillside and saw the Indians scattered beneath them, racing for the river-bed. And all they had to show for the charge was a

74

Cheyenne who lay on his back, twilight mercifully hiding his saber-split skull.

Murray, who had fired his revolver twice and still held it in his clenched, wet palm, waved at Captain Wint and yelled for him to take his company and pinch the Cheyennes in the river. The lines of blue fanned apart and then spilled down to the river, the men shouting hoarsely and stiffening their saber-arms once more. Troopers Harding and Defray trailed behind, the one nursing a bullet hole in his shoulder, and the other an arm broken by the blow of a war club.

When the troops reached the flat, the Cheyennes had already crossed the river. The flailing hoofs of Companies A and B beat the brush down, but the sandy river bottom slowed their progress. The tired horses, broken by the long day's run, could not be urged beyond a feeble trot, and many of them slipped trying to clamber up the further bank. Meanwhile, the Cheyennes, who had given their wiry ponies a few hours' rest before the attack, flung a few shots at the troops, raced upstream, and crossed the river again, leaving the muddied, crestfallen, wearied cavalrymen on the further bank.

It was almost night now. The pale pink sky still lay as a backdrop to the hill. The troopers dismounted, stood by their panting horses, and watched the Cheyennes file back to where they had left the women and children.

Wint was smiling foolishly. He murmured to Murray: "I once saw a vixen lead off from her cub's nest—"

"We should have gone into their camp," Murray said. "They would have come along once we had the women and kids. I'll know better next time."

75

"Their ponies were half dead before they left Darlington, still they ran us out of it."

"We'll do no more running," Murray said.

After the horses had been watered, Murray recrossed the river and camped his men about half a mile downstream from the hill. There were six casualties, none very serious, and all of them able to sit in the saddle. Private Tempor, a middle-aged man who had served as a hospital orderly all through the Civil War, dressed the wounds as best he could. Tempor, a big bearded man, was as gentle as a woman, nor did he complain about the lack of anything better than firelight.

While the men were eating, Murray and Wint rode toward the hill. The Cheyenne fires were hidden by the lip, but a rosy glow fanned out from the top, giving it the fantastic appearance of a small, smoldering volcano.

"They don't seem bothered," Wint said.

Vaguely, Murray could understand the strange fatalism of a people who would make up their minds to do something and then proceed to do it, regardless of what stood in their way. As if they had died already and had lost fear in the knowledge that men can die only once. But he was unable to put that feeling into words, and he didn't answer Wint.

"They can't have much food," Wint remarked. "Seems that Miles has been near starving them."

"Not so much the food as water. They can eat their horses."

"Oh, Indians don't, you know," Wint said.

"Don't they? Dog Soldiers will. They'll break every taboo they own before they surrender."

"Nasty job," Wint said. "Shall we go in there tonight?"

"I'd like to. They don't seem to have much more than small arms, a few pistols, maybe a carbine or two. When they were brought into the territory they had only a few hundred rounds of shells. They can't shoot much with that."

"Maybe they won't shoot," Wint said. "That old man's no fool."

Murray said: "I shouldn't have taken that shot at him. I lost my temper."

"I wasn't thinking of that."

"You can think whatever you damn please," Murray said.

"All right. But I wasn't thinking about that. I can see how you would lose your temper with people like that."

"You never lose your temper," Murray said.

"Oh, sometimes I do. You need sleep. If I slept as little as you—"

"Shut up!" Murray cried.

They rode on in silence, Wint's lips pressed into a fine thread. Finally, Murray said:

"I'm sorry, Wint."

"All right. Forget it."

They rode back to camp. Wint dismounted and walked away without speaking to Murray, who dropped to the ground near a fire and began to fill his pipe. Lieutenant Freeland came over and stood near him.

"Sir?"

"What is it?" Murray said.

77

"What are your orders for tonight?"

"We'll sleep," Murray said. "That's all. Put a guard on the horses and send out two-hour pickets all around that hill. Tell them to shoot anything that tries for the water. That's all."

The lieutenant nodded, but still stood there.

"That's all," Murray said. "Get some sleep yourself."

The captain lay back and stared at the sky. He hadn't eaten; he had no appetite. He lay there and stared at the black background to the white bits of light. Right now, he wanted two things very badly, a drink and a woman. Any kind of a drink and any kind of a woman—even one of those squaws from up there on the hill. He had never married, and there was no Mrs. Captain Murray to think of coming back to, like there was a Mrs. Captain Wint— if Wint thought of that.

After a while, Murray fell asleep. It was the first real sleep in three nights.

He was awakened by a spray of cold rain on his face, and he looked up at a low, leaden sky. During the night, someone had covered him with a blanket, and now he threw it off and rose stiffly. His feet were swollen and tight in his boots, and the first few steps were fine torture. He looked at his watch and saw that it lacked a few minutes of five. The troopers lay around the dead fires, rolled in their blankets, and faintly he heard the clop-clop of the pickets' horses.

He stumbled around, searching for Wint. Some of the men had been awakened by the rain, and they got to their feet awkwardly, saluting him. He found Wint and shook him awake.

"Get up," he said. "I want to go in there before it gets light."

Wint climbed to his feet and began to run his hands through his hair. He had a heavy beard, and his face looked haggard and worn.

"Where?" he said thickly.

Murray nodded at the hill. He hoped Wint would pull with him now; he was afraid; he would be less afraid if he had Wint to fall back on.

Wint kept untangling his hair. "You have infantry coming down from Dodge City," he told Murray. "We can hold them until then."

"I like to finish a job," Murray said.

"You didn't feel that way yesterday."

"I feel that way today," Murray said.

The rain was increasing. Wint pulled on his wet hat and said: "Your orders."

Murray shrugged. "Get the men up," he said. "We'll go in on foot. It's easier that way."

"I don't like to see cavalry dismounted."

"I don't like to see them killed."

Murray walked away. He found Kelly trying to kick a fire to life. "How was it up there, Sergeant?" he asked, nodding at the hill.

"Quiet."

"We're going up on foot. Start waking the men and draw the pickets in."

"Yes, sir."

"And no murder," Murray added. "Spread that around. That place is full of squaws and kids."

79

"I think they dug trenches, sir."

"I'll ask for your thoughts when I want them, Sergeant," Murray said.

The two companies of cavalry, dismounted and spread out in a thin skirmish line, began to advance slowly through the rain. They made a half moon around the base of the hill, and even when they began to climb, there was no sign or sound from the Indian camp. The gray dawn changed to dulled daylight, and when they were halfway up the hill Murray began to believe that they would walk into the camp without the Indians firing a shot.

Then he realized that they had dug trenches. He saw an Indian stand up, and afterwards he believed that it was Little Wolf. The blast of fire from the Cheyenne trenches tore the ranks of Companies A and B to pieces. They must have had little ammunition, because they only fired once, but the troopers gave back down the hill, leaving blobs of twisted blue in the wet grass behind them. They fired as they retreated, and Murray cursed and tried to make something of his lines. But behind them, on the hilltop there were no Indians to be seen beside the one man, who appeared to be sitting on the edge of a trench and calmly smoking a pipe.

The men lay in the wet grass at the base of the hill, while Murray stamped among them and tried to realize his losses. Wint, unhurt, never took his eyes off Murray, except once to look up at the hillside, where the twisted blue shapes were still visible in the grass.

"Freeland's up there," Wint said to Murray.

Murray shook his head and stamped on. Kelly was missing, and along with him five privates. At least thirty men were wounded. Steve Jesky, the scout, had been shot through the head; his buckskin-clad figure was almost invisible in the long grass. The Arapahoe, Ghost Man, his chest ripped open, was trying to crawl down the hillside. Lieutenant Gatlow ran back and helped him the rest of the way down. He lay in the rain droning a strange death song which no one understood, and after a while he died.

Murray stood next to Wint and whispered: "Christ, don't blame me for Freeland."

"We're all in it," Wint said, gently.

"They wanted to go home," Murray said. "God damn it, that was all they wanted."

"I know. What are you going to do now?"

"Go up there again," Murray said tiredly.

The wounded men were helped back to camp, and then the troopers who were left spread out into their thin skirmish line. They crawled this time, pulling themselves through the wet grass on their bellies, but for all that they could get no further than halfway up the hill. They lay there, firing whenever an Indian's head showed; but the Cheyennes held their own fire so long as the troops made no effort to advance.

The morning wore on, and toward midday the drizzle stopped and a hot, sulphur-colored sun broke through the clouds. The grass steamed, and the river, which had risen almost a foot, flowed like a sluggish red snake. Murray passed the order for the men to fall back.

They finished the last of their iron rations and then

lay around, drying out in the sun. Murray sprawled out with his head against a saddle and a handkerchief over his eyes; he was comfortable that way, and for a little while he was able to close out all thought, to be aware only of the heat of the sun and the brush of the cool wind across the prairie. The birds flew up out of the river brush, chattering and sending their shadows dancing over the earth, and a coyote made a long, quick ripple in the grass.

Wint sat down next to him and asked: "Are we going up there again, Captain?"

For a long while Murray didn't answer. Then he sat up, folded the handkerchief, and stared at Wint curiously.

"I don't know," he said.

"They'll bring up the howitzer with the wagons," Wint suggested.

Murray shrugged. "I thought this way was better," he said.

"It doesn't matter," Wint said. "Up there, they're as good as dead."

"I guess they wanted it that way."

"That's why it doesn't matter."

"I keep thinking about Freeland," Murray said. "We'll wait for the howitzer. There'll be troops coming down from Dodge City."

Neither the wagons nor the howitzer came. Murray waited until six o'clock, and then he sent Sergeant Geety and Private Hennesy back to see whether the supply train had lost the trail somewhere between Medicine

Lodge River and Darlington. He enclosed a report for Colonel Mizner, which he instructed the sergeant to send on with Hennesy once they had made contact with the wagons. Geety was to return with the supply train. As an afterthought, he told Geety:

"If the troops are gone, put the wounded in the wagons and carry them to Coldwater. There's a doctor there, I believe."

"If the troops are gone?" Geety questioned.

"You had better leave now, Sergeant," Murray said.

He watched the two men ford the deepening river, and then he turned back to his troops. The afternoon's rest had put them and the horses in better shape, and had picked up their spirits after the morning's defeat. But they had been on iron rations for three days, and dead and wounded had reduced their strength. Pickets were out, circling the hill, but as yet the Cheyennes had neither showed themselves above their trenches and rifle pits, nor made any move to escape.

Murray recalled stories of the old days of the Oregon Trail and the first wagon trains to cross over the plains. In those days, the situation had been curiously reversed, yet he doubted whether any wagon train of emigrants had ever faced a situation half so desperate and hopeless as that which confronted Little Wolf and his people. Hemmed in already by troops that outnumbered them two to one, their path to the north finally blocked by the detail sent out from Dodge City, surrounded over all by a network of army posts and forts, there was not a chance in a million that any of them could break through. Whatever meager food supplies they might have had were

83

almost certainly exhausted; sooner or later they would shoot out the last of their ammunition; and the constant flight would break both the ponies and the people who rode them. He had heard how Cheyenne boys and girls were set on ponies' backs at the age of four; he had seen, the night before, a feat of horsemanship beyond anything he had ever conceived possible; yet he knew that nothing human could stand the motion of a running horse hour after hour, day after day. They would break, even if they escaped; and he didn't believe they could escape.

He told Wint: "Let the men rest easy. The troops from Dodge will be here in the morning, and probably the howitzer."

"They might make a break tonight."

"They might," Murray admitted. "I'll keep the pickets riding all night."

"I'd like to get the wounded to a doctor. It's hell in this heat."

"The wagons will be here in the morning," Murray said.

"I hope so."

Murray slept again that night. It was curious how calm he had become since he realized the absolute certainty of the Cheyennes' fate; as if that thought had launched itself like a ship on a flowing river where the destinies of all men floated.

He was never at ease putting emotional conceptions into words or even thoughts; but he seemed to see his own fate as linked terribly close to the fate of the little village of savages. Just as they were an abstract in freedom, he was an abstract in bondage. But he no longer

84

struggled, nor did he care to struggle. He was a uniformed servant with a gun, and he would go on to destroy the one thing that personalized all his vague dreamings and longings. He didn't know how he was wrong, just as he didn't know clearly how they were right, naked savages with no sense of law or order or decency. But he did know that in finally destroying them, he would kill the last whimpering of his conscience. He would be able to say, as the deceased Sergeant Kelly had said:

"It's good pay, and there are worse things a man can do."

So he slept well, more than half the night, until he was rocked out of his sleep by a crackle of shots from the pickets. He came awake in all the confusion of men running for their saddles and horses, to hear the majestic orchestration of a thousand hoofbeats.

"Bugler!" he shouted. "Bugler!"

But there was no need for *Boots and Saddles*. Already the men were mounting, and already the young lieutenants were grimly ordering their troops. The pickets swept in and rolled down to report.

"Had their fires burning, and they were singing, sir— them damn heathen songs. It came like a bolt out of the blue."

"Tempor!" Murray shouted. "Take another man and stay with the wounded! Geety will pick you up tomorrow! Captain Wint, lead off!"

They drove into the dark after the vanishing hoofbeats of the Cheyenne village. The Indians had fled with the hill between them and the troops, and as Wint led the way around, on the narrow strip of ground fronting the river, the noise was already muffled and faint in the distance.

Suddenly, Wint gave the order to halt. Murray rode past the tight group of snorting and milling horses; when he came up to the head of the column, he saw that Wint had already dismounted and was bending over something on the ground.

"What is it?" Murray demanded.

Wint straightened with an Indian child in his arms. The boy couldn't have been more than five years old, and he was quite dead, shot through the neck. He had a round, wise Chinese face, and his black eyes were wide open.

Gordon, one of the pickets, pushed through and said miserably: "It must have been me, sir. I took a few shots at them. I couldn't see anything in the dark, just the lot of them. I took a few shots without thinking."

"That was the right thing to do," Wint said evenly.

"He's dead," Murray remarked.

"I was thinking we should bury him."

"Our men are dead back there—and they're not buried."

"I was thinking we should bury him," Wint said.

Murray stared at him, then nodded slowly. A few of the men dismounted, and without speaking began to scoop out a grave with their knives. They didn't go very deep, only about two feet. Someone threw a blanket into the circle. Wint wrapped up the Indian child and laid him in the shallow grave.

"It don't matter a hell of a lot," someone said. "The coyotes know."

"They know if you put him ten feet deep," someone else said.

They pushed back the dirt and pressed it down with their boots. A voice out of the darkness drawled: "Maybe you ought to speak a prayer, Captain."

Murray cried: "Shut your God damn mouth or I'll close it for good!"

"It wouldn't matter," Wint said, smiling a little with his thin lips. "He wasn't baptized. He's not a Christian, so it wouldn't matter."

They mounted again. The hoofbeats had vanished in the night, and as there was no use driving the horses, they rode northward slowly.

PART FOUR   September 1878

A WASHINGTON INTERLUDE

Meanwhile, Colonel Mizner
had wired a complete report to the War Office at Washington. And Agent Miles had reported his side of the matter to the Indian Office. William Nicholson, who was superintendent of Indian Affairs at Lawrence, Kansas, sent a more or less detailed report to the Department of the Interior. He also sent a warning to Agent Miles to make no statements for reporters.

Mizner's report, with many connotations and a few footnotes, reached its ultimate destination in the basement of William Tecumseh Sherman's house. The general in chief of the armies of the United States loved his family. In fact, he loved them so much that his name had become a sort of byword throughout the nation for an indulgent and gentle father. It made magnificent press

89

every time a reporter went through the Sherman household, down into the littered basement room that was the
general's study and office. As often as not, he might find
a child or two pestering the commander-in-chief at work.
The reporter would say to himself:

"My God, is this the man who cut a path of glory (and
destruction) through Georgia?"

It was magnificent; it was as good as the sign at the top
of the cellar stairs, a sign which read simply: General
Sherman's Office. It all proved that you knew nothing
about any man, regardless of his fame, until you saw him
at home with his family around him. Big men who were
simple human beings, not like the stuffed shirts who had
to have their huge offices paneled in solid mahogany.

And it was there in the basement, on a warm, cheerful
early fall morning, that General Sherman read Colonel
Mizner's report. The report had come through as a matter
of routine, with a stack of other communications concerning troop movements in the plains country. There
were disturbances among the Apaches and two Comanche
raids in the south. A drunken Nez Percé had killed a
white man, and a cavalry company was out hunting him
down. Sherman shook his head wearily; a cavalry company to hunt down a drunken Indian. A Major James T.
Fredricks wrote an impassioned denunciation of a gang
of whiskey peddlers who were running the stuff into the
Panhandle by the thousands of gallons. "How," he demanded, "is the army to preserve any form of law and
order when this scum can sell their sugared alcohol freely
and openly?" The whole thing was a maze of intricacies.
In the administration of the plains country, there were

concerned the army, the Indian Office, the Department of the Interior, the Society of Friends, the Justice Department working in the form of United States Marshals, civil law, state police such as the Texas Rangers, state militia . . . it went on endlessly. He wrote a violent note, tore it up, wrote one more judicious, referring Fredricks' complaint to the Indian Office.

Sioux had crossed the border from Canada. "Someday," Sherman said to himself, "we will take this whole matter of Canada and put it to rights." He and many other army men thought it should have been done immediately after the war between the States, when the Federal Government had in uniform hundreds of thousands of hardened fighting men. A march to the north, two quick blows at Montreal and Quebec; and the result would have been a nation that stretched from the North Pole to the Rio Grande. Well, it could still be done and it would be done; and for a while the general was lost in dreams of new campaigns—in the mingled warmth and coolness of the cellar, hardly minding the flies that buzzed around his head and beard and walked stiff-legged over his papers.

A strike in Chicago; two troops to preserve order. He read that over twice. The general hated strikes; they were a vague menace that made him hot with a helpless sort of rage. You couldn't fight them as you should; you couldn't even define to yourself what ominous seeds of the future they carried. Only, you knew they were a menace; you knew they were men mocking at the uniform you wore.

And starting to read this next, he hesitated, glancing down at the bottom of the paper to see whose name was signed. He couldn't recall a Colonel Mizner. He asked himself, "What regiment would that be—in the Territory?" Not the Fourth, the Fourth was further north, not the Eleventh. Perhaps the Fourth after all. It was a pride of his that he carried almost every colonel in his mind. He located Mizner in the obscurity of Indian Territory. Twisting the hairs of his beard, he stared into the drizzle of sunshine that touched the edges of his desk and tried to make a picture of Oklahoma. Wet country? Perhaps it had been raining in his memory, but it would be dry now. They had dry summers out there, dry and long. Red dust; he remembered a complaint: the red dust got into the blue uniforms, and you could hardly wash it out. The British, in their campaigning in hot, dry countries, wore drab, and perhaps that was more practical. More nearly the color of dust and took washing better. Somewhere he had read about white being good in hot countries; hadn't Benjamin Franklin written something of the sort? But put a soldier in white and he'll do nothing but pick at his clothes . . . nonsense, of course. Blue was a good color, look what the blue had been through. He read:

". . . to advise you of the fact that three hundred Northern Cheyennes have recently left this reservation. The action was taken contrary to the orders of Hon. Jn. Miles, Indian Agent at Darlington, who has been much disturbed by the insolence of these savages. As my instructions were to enforce the authority of the agent, I dispatched two cavalry companies to bring these Indians back. Their progress is north, and as I understand they intend to return to their former villages in the Powder River Country. About ninety of their number are armed and in condition to resist, and unless halted they will undoubtedly do harm to farms and citizens in Kansas and Nebraska. I hope to send word of their apprehension in the next few days, and meanwhile await further orders."

A good report, the general told himself, the kind that makes a situation plain and at the same time takes it in hand. He liked the conception of a war department that was concise, orderly, and strong in action, like a great map on a wall, a lot of colored pins, and then a lot of threads that one man could hold in his hand. That was the main thing, to have all the threads, to know where every pin was every instant, day and night. Of course, there are exceptions; great men make exceptions. His march from Atlanta to the sea was an exception. He remembered turning from his desk once and seeing one of the children behind him, wide-eyed with a fixed stare, and demanding:

"What are you staring at?"

"You, sir."

"And why?"

"Because you're the greatest general in the whole world, sir."

"Am I?"

"That's what they say, sir."

"Who?"

"Everyone, sir."

But the works would fly apart if you had everyone marching from Atlanta to the sea. Such a thing could be done once in a lifetime, once in ten lifetimes. No more.

To cut loose—that was a great thing, if you had the man to do it. Only, there weren't many men like that.

He was dreaming into the past. Hot and cold, twisting around the sunlight; there was no other place like a cellar to work, no other place with the same combinations of heat and coolness, currents of air that caressed you. A good place to work, only now he was dreaming more than working, thinking of Lincoln and how he had never really known about Lincoln—or Lincoln about him. He less than anyone else had known how Lincoln managed to keep such a cool face all the time, cool and long and ugly, when he certainly knew no more than anyone else. Or less: and look what it meant to him, to have his hopes and fortunes and tears—they said he cried, like a woman cries—lost somewhere in a hostile land with a man's army. Sherman and his sixty-five thousand were marching to the sea and carrying with them the fate of a nation and of a civilization, eating like pigs and living off the fat of the land: it was a picnic, not war, but the sort of a thing done only once in a lifetime—or ten lifetimes.

He liked it better when they were all colored pins with all the strings in his hand. As a matter of fact, if Lee had only known, Lee could have destroyed him, even then at the end when everything was as good as lost for the south, Lee could have swung around, forgotten Richmond, forged southward and destroyed Sherman. As Washington had done once, at Yorktown—and Lee should have remembered Washington. Let Grant have Richmond while he took an army, a fat army of sixty-five thousand. No, he liked it better with all the strings in his hand.

The general scribbled onto the report: "Copy for Department of Interior." Let Schurz see how final the pacifi-

94

cation was. In another year, Indian troubles would be a memory.

Then he wrote to General Phil Sheridan: "Dispatch troops on railroad east from Dodge City to cover path of three hundred Cheyenne Indians going north from—" Where was it from? He racked his brains again, and then finally reread the dispatch. "—Darlington. These Indians, having left their reservation in an outlaw fashion, must be halted and returned without delay. Military measures may be used to deal with the leaders. Colonel Mizner, at Fort Reno, is in possession of all the details." Then he underlined a sentence. "It is essential that these Indians be rounded up before they can do further harm."

He signed his name and went on with his reports. There was a thirty-six-hundred-pound shortage in flour. Why did they persist in bothering him with this rubbish, which should go to the quartermaster department and nowhere else?

"Why did everyone persist in bothering everyone?" thought Carl Schurz, reading a report that was copied from a report to General William Tecumseh Sherman, a report by an obscure colonel somewhere in Indian Territory to the effect that certain Indians had left their reservation. Why was it placed on his desk after his secretary had read it? Why was the whole government being turned into a bureaucracy? What was the use of a man trying to make a little decency out of a lot of rottenness, when he had to wade through a pile of petty, bickering reports, sky high? Sky high and further; everything, it seemed, was the business of his department. When a man took a cabinet post, he buried himself.

He read, "Mizner," asking himself petulantly, "Who is Mizner? What am I supposed to do? If I have it copied, I can send it to the War Department, to the Indian Office." The thought of having it copied again and again and again set him to smiling. That was government in a way; you could call it government. It almost appealed to him, it was so meticulously German; have everything copied innumerable times and send the copies everywhere. Something came out of it; at least, everyone read everything.

His pince-nez had rolled off his long, pointed nose and lay on the report now, distorting certain words. Schurz took out a handkerchief and wiped the glasses with one finger as they lay there. He mounted them on his nose again and ran stubby fingers over his beard, trying to think of something else that seemed to concern the same people, the same part of the wasteland called Indian Territory. Not that it mattered greatly, but his mind was orderly; he liked to have similar things nestling side by side.

He called for his secretary, and when the man came in, mentioned Darlington.

"Something from Mr. Nicholson, sir."

"Perhaps." The burr was German. When he said only one word, he tried to make that word as free from any accent as possible, but he never actually succeeded.

The secretary brought a letter, but it was the wrong one.

"Something about Darlington," Schurz insisted. He

even remembered how it was bound, with four other reports.

"That's the Cheyenne and Arapahoe agency," he explained carefully, rather proud of his knowledge of agencies and reservations in the messy wilderness of Oklahoma. He had learned five countries; and that was an achievement for a man, to have a great surface of the world planted in his brain, if it was the brain where such things lay. They lay there like a map with pictures and reliefs and distortions and wide gaps—and then with parts that were photographic in their exactness, as the scene out of his boyhood when he had crawled through a sewer in a little village in Germany—and came out to face the planted legs of a Prussian soldier. And if the Prussian had seen him and killed him, as so many others were killed in that revolution, where would all the map be with its wonderful impressions of Germany and Switzerland and France and Spain and the United States?

"Such foolishness," he sighed. Some men forgot their past; other men lived entirely in the past. Some men lived one life, and it was simple and even as a flowing river; he thought that was the best way: not like him, living so many lives that there was neither rhyme nor reason to bind them together.

The secretary came back, and this time it was the right letter, and after Carl Schurz had read it through, he laid it side by side with the one that had been forwarded from the war office. Now things were in order, and now the situation at Darlington would go into a single manila folder. And then filed with a thousand other folders of the Department of the Interior, it would gather dust.

"Maybe that way is the only way," he said to himself, reading through General Sherman's instructions to various generals, colonels, majors. There were so many of them in his life, so many thousands of pairs of boots stamping through dust and mud and grass and high fields of yellow, waving wheat. He came back to Mizner in the report, and again he was trying to place the man. Mizner—Mizner—they were always changing the regiments on the plains. He couldn't even place the band of Cheyennes; at least six bands had been brought down from the north in the past few years and replanted in Indian Territory. A troublesome people: thinking of the plains Indians always recalled the wild bands of Tatars and Cossacks on their lonely steppes. But the Cheyennes were wild and hard and bad, and the plains people who knew about such things said they lived for nothing but war. But that he was inclined to doubt: he had never made such an opinion even of the Prussians, whom he hated, deeply, silently, with good reason. No people lived to kill and only to kill—such people could not have children and wives, and they would die off the face of the earth.

And now this little band of Cheyennes, one tiny village of three hundred souls altogether, had gone away from the place the government had given them. They were going home to the north—a thousand miles. Their minds were like children's minds, and for that they would have to die.

"They'll die hard," he agreed with himself. "That's all those Indians seem to know, how to die."

But his curiosity was stimulated, and he wanted to know more. He was hardly aware of how much he resented Sherman's quick issue of orders. He had been a soldier himself and he knew the military attitude, but withal a bullet was not the cure for every ailment.

He began to pore through the Darlington records. For two hours he soothed his conscience, asking himself, who else but Carl Schurz would go to such pains about such an obscure matter? In the end, he knew he would do nothing.

"But there's nothing to do," he told himself. He decided he would see Sherman the next morning. Still there was nothing to do. First and last, Sherman was right. If a law was broken, you had to punish the people who broke the law.

But other things intervened, and somehow the next morning the matter slipped out of his mind. The Darlington reports lay on his desk in their manila folder, but he hardly gave them a thought until eleven o'clock; and then he had to rush off to a cabinet meeting. In passing, he noticed them and made a resolution to speak to Sherman, somehow.

The cabinet meeting dragged while they waited for the President. Hayes was late. McCrary, the Secretary of War, kept looking at his watch, noting the hours petulantly. Carl Schurz bit off the end of a cigar, but did not light it. The Postmaster-General dozed.

Lunch was served. There was a fillet of sole, some boiled new potatoes with parsley, fresh green peas, coffee and apple pie. For Carl Schurz, America was most lacking in its food: flat, tasteless, colorless—it just satisfied hunger, leaving everything else removed and untouched. He ate with the thoughtful detachment of a man who has lost temporary ease in an attempt to recall the whereabouts of some insignificant object. He left the apple pie untasted and lit his cigar over the coffee.

"We'll be here all afternoon," McCrary growled.

The ash on the cigar grew, and then abruptly Schurz located his nervous dissatisfaction. He asked Devens, the Attorney-General:

"You remember the Harney-Sanborn Treaty?"

The Attorney-General was pecking at his apple pie. He glanced up with the querulous resentment of a man questioned suddenly about something furthest from his thoughts. He didn't like Schurz; he didn't like his aggressive disregard for all forms of political habit; he didn't like his accent or his squinting, curious stare.

"You should remember it," Schurz said. "It was in sixty-five."

"An Indian treaty?"

"It was in sixty-five," Evarts put in. He was Secretary of State.

Schurz was reassembling his thoughts. He could remember most of the treaty, the gist of it being a guarantee to the plains Indians of the lands they occupied in the north, the whole stretch of the Powder River country, from the Black Hills and the Rocky Mountains in the west to the Yellowstone River in the east; it concerned the Cheyennes and the Sioux, but mainly the Cheyennes since the Sioux ranged further eastward.

Schurz went over it briefly, marking the pertinent facts with little jerks of his cigar, leaving a trail of ashes upon the tablecloth. His whole manner was condescending enough to put the Attorney-General upon the defensive.

"I want an opinion," he finished. "Of course, no detailed thing, just an opinion like you might put into a subject of conversation."

Devens shrugged. "The whole thing's a dead letter," he said.

"How?"

"I don't see either pertinence or importance in a treaty made thirteen years ago with a pack of savages."

"We made the treaty," Schurz shrugged.

"It has no legality."

"No?"

"A gesture," Evarts said, smiling. "Surely that's all any treaty with Indian tribes amounts to—a gesture."

"I could give you three legal counts to nullify such a treaty," the Attorney-General said.

Schurz puffed his cigar and nodded.

"Firstly, when a sovereign state makes a treaty with another sovereign state, that treaty remains in force only so long as both states remain sovereign. There's no need to go into the matter of sovereignty: even if those Indians once exercised sovereignty over the regions they inhabited, they don't today. The mere fact that they've been expelled from the territory they inhabited precludes any claim of sovereignty.

"Secondly, such a treaty is conditional upon a state of friendly relations. The moment the Indians declared war, the treaty was nullified. Of course—"

At that moment, the President entered. The cabinet rose, but Hayes said:

"Be seated, gentlemen, please be seated."

Most of the meeting was railroads, a tired, harassed

Hayes trying to see his way out of a welter of graft, deception, and broken promises. Again, Carl Schurz forgot the Darlington question; there was left in his mind only an idle desire to know the third of Devens' reasons; and even that was forgotten as he became hot and furious over the question of the meeting, roaring his objections louder, the thick, guttural German accent becoming more and more pronounced.

When he returned to his office, the manila folder had been put away.

It was Jackson, the *New York Herald's* Washington correspondent, who brought up the matter again, and that was after two days had passed, two days during which time the Secretary of the Interior had forgotten the matter completely. Schurz himself was a newspaperman; he read many papers, and he had ideas about what a paper should be. Sometimes, it made him almost sick with fear when he realized what a force in America the newspapers were, what a force they might be. And again, he could see that force distorted and corrupted, turned to the use of tyranny and falsehood and hate and prejudice. He often thought that native-born Americans were blind as to the possibilities and wonders of their own land; it was only one who, like himself, had come as a refugee, fleeing from persecution and tyranny, that could see these many things. They took a free press for granted; for him a free press was a flaming sword.

He liked to talk for the press, and he liked to talk to a man like Jackson, someone who knew that America was three thousand miles wide and broad as the whole world. Schurz admired the *New York Herald;* it had its faults and they were many; it gave its front page over to the worst type of quackery in advertising: but there was a certain quality of fearlessness in James Gordon Bennett's crusades and more than enough of truth. It was only Bennett who would send out reporters like Jackson and let them write out their whole hearts. It made for hotter reading as against colder reporting, and Schurz liked his reading warm and close to the flesh.

So he smiled when Jackson was admitted to his office, a tall, skinny, baldish man, ugly the way Lincoln was ugly and always bringing back to Schurz a heart-tightening memory of that man who had once been his friend.

"You can give me a story, Mr. Secretary," Jackson said. It was a habit of his to call Schurz Mr. Secretary, a habit Schurz liked, recalling as it did memories of the old country, where it was Herr Postmaster and Herr Policeman and Herr this and that. You wanted to forget everything, but sometimes it was good to have a little brought back this way.

"Can I?" Schurz smiled.

"I know you don't like talk of Indians on the warpath, but Bennett says there's a war brewing in Kansas."

"Then go to the War Department," the secretary shrugged, pleased at his small joke.

"I was there," Jackson said. "With them, there's nothing but peace on the plains, peace and drunken Indians."

"That's the best way."

"But it doesn't make news. I have a pretty authentic report of fighting between troops and Indians in Kansas."

"Nonsense!"

"Cheyennes," the reporter said, and then Schurz remembered the incident at Darlington.

"It's nothing," Schurz said. "Some Cheyennes ran away. They left their reservation to go home and some military police went after them to bring them back. That's all."

"How many?"

"Maybe three hundred, women and children and all, you know they move like gypsies."

"It's something," Jackson said.

"It's not a story. Why shouldn't you write about the thousands of Indians who live peacefully on their reservations? Write about how the government is trying to make a new way of life for a whole race, to bring them to civilization in one generation. Why should there be never a word about the Indians until some little cog in the machine slips? It's a big machine, and do you expect such a machine to run without ever a breakdown somewhere?"

"When men fight, it makes news."

"Fighting? There were less than a hundred braves. Two cavalry companies went after them to bring them back."

"When was that?"

"Two days, three days ago."

"Then it should be over by now—?"

"Why not?" Schurz smiled. "You hear war on the plains, and you think of great armies riding back and forth, maneuvers, skirmishes, pitched battles—no, I say, thank God. No more of that for America. That war between the States, and it's better not to talk about it—that was the last. No war for America. Because a few soldiers go after some stupid Indians who do not understand that the gov-

104

ernment is trying to make a life for them, that is not war. That is like policemen hunting down a train robber. They will be brought back and made into peaceful farmers, and that way is better, no?"

"Or to Dry Tortugas?"

"Ach, no! What is this business about Dry Tortugas? We are not saints here in the Interior Department, but we do not send every stupid Indian to prison in Dry Tortugas."

"Yet Indians have died there," Jackson said gently.

"And so have white men. It's a shame; don't I know what a shame it is to have such a hell spot for a jail? But can we cure every tumor by spitting over our shoulders? No, it takes time. It takes a bill, a resolution, a time in committee, a vote; that is democracy."

Jackson was smiling at the bearded, spluttering secretary. Schurz said:

"Light your pipe. I'll pour a schnapps. I know it's a shame to come in here with a story and go out with no story."

"I've been out there," Jackson murmured, and then drank down the whiskey.

"Where?"

"Indian Territory."

Schurz stared at him, and the reporter met his look evenly and curiously.

"In the summer," Jackson said.

"Yes?"

There was a long silence after that; then, finally, the reporter stood up to go. Schurz took off his pince-nez and polished them carefully.

"It would be a long way home," the reporter remarked. "Where were they from?"

"The Black Hills, I suppose," Schurz said, without looking up.

"I was there."

"You've been everywhere, no?"

"Here and there. I liked the Black Hills. Maybe I like mountains because I never lived in them. I said to myself, here is something good for America."

"Why not?" Schurz said, in a tone of voice that indicated the interview was over.

"Yes—they would be crazy. It's a thousand miles from Indian Territory."

"Maybe they were crazy," Schurz said evenly. "Sometimes you think that an Indian is crazy, the way his mind works. But can you have three hundred gypsies going where they please?"

The reporter turned to leave, but the secretary's voice followed him to the door. "I'm sorry about the story, but there is no war. It would be bad if you should write about a war. We are trying to do something for the Indians. The country should know that."

"I wonder if the country gives a damn?" Jackson said to himself.

After the reporter had left, Schurz sat and stared at the door. He was angry at Jackson and angry at himself for having lost his temper. Actually, it was all nothing, and the reporter was shooting in the dark. They made a habit of that, and if a man left himself open, he suffered.

In this case, there would be nothing to write about. It would all be over and done with soon enough. Yet when a clerk came into the office, hours later, Schurz was still sitting and staring at nothing at all.

"Will there be anything, sir?" the clerk wanted to know.

"Nothing—"

"Mr. Freeling from St. Louis is waiting."

"Yes?"

"You made the appointment yesterday."

"Yes, send him in. And make an appointment for me with General Sherman."

All the time he was speaking to Mr. Freeling from St. Louis, Schurz was assuring himself that the only reason he had arranged to speak with Sherman was to keep the rotten little business out of the press, to get it over with quickly and quietly.

Going down the narrow cellar steps to Sherman's office, Schurz chuckled again, as he had always chuckled, at the real simplicity of the man who was the conqueror of Georgia to so many, "Cump" to just a few, a military genius to the whole world. The simplicity was real; it was no affectation that made him keep himself and the command of the armies of the United States in the basement of the house where he lived. He liked cellars; something in stacked earth around you made for peace and quiet. As to whether he was a genius, Schurz didn't know; and often he doubted whether any military man, including himself, had anything of even real cleverness, much less genius. Yet genius was something of a meaningless word. His friend who had died so long ago in Ford's Theatre—that tall, ugly, fumbling, sorrowful man had not been a genius.

More of a genius was Booth, who had also been in Ford's Theatre that night.

As Carl Schurz came down the last of the stairs, Sherman went forward to meet him, and the old friends shook hands warmly. They lit cigars and sat down with the paper-piled desk between them, with the streaked sunlight dappling letters and old wood, creasing warmth into the cool, quiet air. They talked of this and that and old times, and they dropped their ashes on the floor.

Finally, Schurz brought the talk around to the reason for his call. He took out the copy of Mizner's report and laid it on Sherman's desk.

"That," Sherman nodded, smiling a little.

"There was a reporter to see me, a man not a fool, you understand, and he wanted to know if there was an Indian war in Kansas."

Sherman laughed quietly.

"It's all over, I hope," Schurz said slowly. "It should be all over by now."

"As good as over," Sherman nodded.

"Then they've been taken?"

"I suppose so. On the plains, you don't have a telegraph operator every ten miles. I had this from Sheridan today." And he handed Schurz the following dispatch:

"Gen. Pope to Gen. Phil Sheridan, Sept. 12, 1878—

"The following dispositions have been made to intercept the Northern Cheyennes: One hundred mounted infantrymen leave by special train tomorrow for Fort Wallace to head off the Indians if they cross the R. R. east or west of that post. Two companies of infantry leave Fort Hays this evening to take post at two noted crossings of

Indians on the Kansas Pacific R. R. between Hays and Wallace. One infantry company from Dodge is posted on the R. R. west of that point. Two cavalry companies from Ft. Reno are close on the Indians, and will be joined by the cavalry company from Camp Supply. The troops at Fort Lyon are ordered out to watch the country east and west of that post, and are ordered to attack the Indians at once, wherever found, unless they surrender . . ."

Schurz put the dispatch down and muttered: "It's like a mouse trap."

"Pope is thorough—"

"Yes. I could see them thinking there is a war in Kansas."

Sherman shrugged. "Men go bad when they have nothing to do. It will move some troops. We'll hear today or tomorrow that they're taken."

"I suppose so." Schurz added: "If any are left."

"They'll get what they deserve. If they kill a dozen troopers, the exchange is still long on our end. I don't have sympathy for Indians. If we had cleaned out the lot of them fifty years ago, the country would be the better for it."

"Perhaps—"

"I've given instructions for all the chiefs and every other male left alive to be sent to Dry Tortugas."

"Dry Tortugas?"

"If you pull a rebellion out by the roots, it's over and done with. It's a hard way, but in the end it's the best way."

"Yes?"

"Otherwise, the spark smolders."

"I suppose so," Schurz said softly. He was leaning back and regarding the end of his cigar quizzically. "It will be good if we keep it out of the papers, yet I suppose it doesn't matter a great deal. The Indian resettlement plan is an act of government, and three hundred foolish savages cannot be allowed to wander around like gypsies. Only—" He turned the cigar over and trailed a breath of ashes across the floor. "It is good to work in a cellar, better than for a man to sit in a tower, high up above everything."

"It's cool," Sherman admitted.

"Very cool. What was I saying?" He drew on the cigar. "You know, I love this land. Sometimes they say to me, will you go back to Germany? Ach, I put that thought away from me twenty years ago. They say, your fatherland. I say, a fatherland is where a man can be free. So I lie in my teeth, but that is still what I believe. When a man grows old with a beard, he puts away one good belief after another; inside of his head the desire for goodness and liberty becomes rotten."

"Or else age brings a little caution and a little wisdom."

"Perhaps. But I would not fight at the barricades to-day and you would not march through Georgia. This word freedom, do you know how it comes? From the old Anglo-Saxon, free and doom. So we think what that meant; it meant the right of any man to choose death to slavery. It meant that no man could be enslaved, because from no man could the power to die be taken away. If everything else was taken away, he still had his free doom left."

"Interesting," Sherman said. "But there were still slaves until a few hundred thousand white boys died."

"Yes—" He picked up his things to go. "I was hoping that we could settle this thing out in the Territory, that it wouldn't be necessary to send them to Dry Tortugas."

"There's no way to reason with an Indian."

"No? It seems to us that they are without reason, that they do things that are crazy, like trying to cross over a thousand miles of country when there are troops waiting everywhere to arrest them. But maybe it is because they are so foolish that they think without looking at every possibility. They want to go home, so they go home. They make a long journey to the north, but to them it is not impossible. It is not impossible for a man to do a plain thing like going home."

"This time it is," Sherman said.

Then they shook hands again, and Carl Schurz mounted the cellar stairs. Sherman went behind him, to show him to the door, and the general wondered at the slowness of the Secretary of the Interior's steps.

"I'll let you know as soon as they are taken into custody," Sherman said.

But Carl Schurz hardly heard him. Lost again in his own thoughts, he was wondering how a thing can be wrong in principle and right in practice.

PART FIVE

September 1878

COWBOYS AND INDIANS

THE TROOPER whom Captain Murray had dispatched to Dodge City was a tall, gangling New Jersey farm boy of nineteen. Carrot-topped, long as a horse in a face that was almost solid over with freckles, "Red's" given name was Ichabod. Trooper Vanest might have been one with the Vanderbilts and Astors, had his family not holed away on a little farm beyond Paterson. They were slow, hinterland Dutch, plodding, quiet, turning dirt for many, many generations, not given to travel any further than Paterson, liking hard money and always having enough of it for security. Ichabod was the first traveler, the first adventurer, and even he was bewildered by the unease that had sent him into the army and then out on the plains.

He was always homesick. He was homesick for quiet and security and heavy Dutch food. He was homesick for the smell of a ripe barn, for the feel of black dirt, for the neighborliness of back-country Jersey. He was homesick for a fat, blue-eyed cousin who became more and more beautiful as the months and the years passed. His loneliness took the form of a sullen pugnacity, and his long, flat muscles enabled him to lash out like a windmill. Sometimes he was beaten and sometimes he wasn't. He had red hair and he was expected to fight.

The chase after the Cheyennes was the first promise of real action that had come his way, and all the distance of that hammering ride the fear inside of him had grown. He didn't want to kill or be killed; he didn't want to suffer and bleed, and he believed only too well the Indian stories the older troopers had pumped into him. It was like a dispensation from God when Murray sent him off to Dodge City, and he was sure that when he returned everything would be over.

The ride to Reeder was the first bit of freedom he had had in over a year. It was almost like a new life beginning for him, to be plucked from death's teeth and sent cantering alone and free across the prairie. He had lied about knowing the way, but the lie didn't bother him; he was dealing in luck, and he was hardly surprised at the ease with which he picked up the cattle trail to Reeder. He rode hard and happily, and by the time he had reached Coldwater, his fear had disappeared. His uniform made him proud and aloof, and outside the Monarch Saloon he gulped a glass of beer and proudly related the details of the newest Indian war.

"But the army's with them," he assured the little group of loafers. "The army's with them—"

Coldwater was sleepy and dull. He wondered how they could sit on the steps of the Monarch and peel twigs that way and not even blink an eyelash if Indians were on the plains. It was a hell-bent war party by the time he drove his tired horse into Reeder. It was dark already, and a few ranchers were driving their buckboards into the country. They stopped and listened to him and then whipped up their horses. At the Freestate Hotel, they gave him the best of four rooms.

"The army's a mighty comfortable thing," someone said.

There was even talk of a posse, but it got no further than talk; and Vanest sat up until his head was nodding with weariness, telling them how things were.

In the morning, however, as he was leaving Reeder, he was joined by two red-eyed saddle tramps, who said they'd like to ride along to Dodge with him and see how things shaped up there. They were going to Dodge anyway, they said, and would the army mind?

"Hell, no!" Vanest grinned.

They said: "All right, Red. Three's better than one when it comes down to them red bastards."

They had been either paid off or fired from a ranch below Coldwater. Black, the owner, was a bastard; they both agreed on that.

The smaller saddle bum's name was McGrath; the other's, Sutton. They were both gunned, tight around the belly with big Colts, and they wore dirty overalls and half a week's beard. Vanest was a little afraid of them, but he didn't mind their coming along. Even saddle bums would respect a uniform.

"Dodge is a hell of a wide place," McGrath said. He said it three or four times. The other didn't say anything. They rode fast, and after a while they stopped speaking.

When they rested, before noon, Vanest offered to share his rations with them.

"Hell, no. I could stand a drink," McGrath said.

"I ain't got that," Vanest grinned. "Maybe you went it a little too strong last night."

"Maybe you got a God damned long nose, soldier," Sutton muttered.

Vanest kept grinning; he didn't want to get into a fight with the two of them. He didn't like their look or the way they wore their guns. He began to talk rapidly about the Cheyennes.

"I seen outfits that could take them," McGrath said. "Not the army. I wouldn't give a plugged nickel for the army."

Vanest shrugged. They would be in Dodge City soon.

"Let's go, soldier," Sutton said.

They struck the railroad in another hour, and followed it west toward Dodge City. It was a hot, sultry day, with low clouds building up in the south. As they neared Dodge, coming over a rise and down toward the town, it rose up out of the short-grassed prairie like a rickety mirage. The long line of unpainted, leaning, clapboard shells faced the railroad on Front Street. It was curiously different from other plains towns that Vanest had seen in that it made no pretense of being a place where people lived. There were no houses nor outlying farms, with this as the central business section; it was a blight, a blot, a lumped scar up out of the belly of Kansas. It hadn't grown from the beginning, not even the terrific unpaced growth of a frontier town. One day there was nothing, and then the railroad came and with it Dodge City, hurled together, flung up, populated.

The population came as if the news were carried on the wind. The place was big and high and handsome; there were no homes, but nestling shoulder to shoulder on the long line of Front Street were more saloons, honky-tonks, whorehouses, and gambling spots than any other city in the plains country could boast. There was no night and no day; you rolled it together at Dodge. It was a junction. Driving up from the south along the Chisholm Trail, the Texas cattle came by the thousands to be shipped east on the Sante Fé Railroad: and the Texas hands by the hundreds fought the Civil War over. They brought hate with them and spewed it out in blood and broken bones. They mingled with the dregs of the plains, from Canada to Mexico. The buffalo hunters came in with their stinking hides, and the whiskey peddlers made it their headquarters from which to ship guns and sugared alcohol to the Indians. Tourists found the west high and wide open at Dodge City. English lords and Russian grand dukes, they all had to see Dodge. To remember America. If they found nothing of men and women working and building, raising families, trying to make a future where there was no past, they still had enough to remember America by. They could hear the guns crackle and watch the funeral processions to Boot Hill.

From a mile away, the red-headed trooper smelled the place. The smell was close to the earth and thick, and it drove out the prairie smell. It was fat; you could cut it with a knife, that mingled odor of stale beer, bad whiskey, and flesh rotting off the thousands of buffalo hides piled twenty and thirty feet high alongside the railroad. It made Vanest cough and it started Sutton vomiting.

"Christ, I need a drink," he said.

Front Street was busy, and so were the saloons, though it was just after noon. Men on horseback rode in and out of town, raising the dust, threading past the clutter of wagons. Along the hitching rails, the horses were close as peas in the pod.

Vanest walked his horse and gazed in wonder. Hardly recalling the dusty, heaped miles he had ridden but remembering the dread loneliness of Fort Reno, he felt in another world, a world that frightened him and belittled him. He felt glad for the security of his uniform.

He lost McGrath and Sutton at the third saloon and he lost them with relief. For all he had heard of Dodge, the parade of saloons was like nothing he had ever imagined, the Long Branch, the Stockman, the Alamo, the Lone Star, Kelly's Place, Sugar's Place, Ann Flitchee's Place. His sense of released excitement returned after McGrath and Sutton had hitched their horses in front of the Alamo.

"See you, soldier!" they called after him.

Then he was like a kid, reining in at the Lady Gay Theatre and reading the poster, EDDY FAY THE ATTRACTION OF LONDON PARIS NEW YORK ORIGINAL SONGS AND DANCES, and thinking to himself, just one night's leave—and he would have some stories to tell, even if they brought back the Cheyennes. He felt no need to hurry. The whole business of the Cheyenne band would be over before a troop could leave here. Not that such a troop would be likely to find either the Cheyennes or Murray. He was doing his job; his job was to deliver a dispatch; but there was no need to hurry.

He left Dodge City with regret. It was four miles to Fort Dodge, the army post, and all the distance he was wondering whether he would be given leave that night or the next. There was the possibility that the troop Murray asked for would leave immediately, but he grinned with knowledge that in the army things like that were not done too quickly. There would certainly be some red tape. He walked his horse slowly. If he arrived at the post late in the afternoon, things might very well hold off until the following morning.

He managed to kill the better part of an hour, even though he quickened his pace at the end and rode into the post at a smart canter. He was of importance now, and he rode on his importance until it was pricked by the blunt information that at Fort Dodge they had already been given telegraphic information of the Cheyenne escape. The enlisted men kidded him about his Indians and his red hair, while his message was taken to the colonel. But they were infantry, and he strutted his boots and saber. At the mess, he unbent enough to ask about the Lady Gay Theatre.

"Is it sure enough?" he wanted to know.

"Hell, it's sure enough."

"That's a wide place, that Dodge City, ain't it?"

"Wide open and bent for the devil," they told him.

"Lord—" He whistled and asked softly: "Whorehouses?"

119

"You ain't seen places like that, soldier, nor so many. Red plush carpets."

"You don't say?"

"Sure enough," they told him. "Hell, not for two-bit cavalry—they run high."

"I carry my pay," he grinned. "Lord, I don't know if I got leave or not—I don't even know what command I got to report to. I'd sure like to see that fancy song and dance, though. I ain't been in a theater maybe two years."

"You ain't never been in one, sonny."

"I sure have," he grinned.

A sergeant found him before the mess was over, told him to finish his food and report to Colonel Leach immediately. He bolted what was left and dejectedly followed the sergeant to the officers' mess. They were just serving the soup there and the soup was done with before Colonel Leach decided to notice him.

"You brought the dispatch from Captain Murray?" Leach asked him.

"Yes, sir."

"Your name?"

"Vanest, sir."

"Were you given any verbal instructions?"

"No, sir. Just to come along to Fort Dodge."

"When did you leave Captain Murray?"

"Early yesterday, sir."

"Where?"

"I guess close to the Kansas line, sir—"

"That's all," the colonel nodded.

The colonel went on with his meal, and Vanest stood there and waited, shifting from foot to foot. The sergeant had gone, and the colonel seemed to have forgotten him. No one told him to leave. He stood there and watched the long table of officers, and resented the manner in which they ignored him. Suddenly, his whole being was whimpering with a desire to be home, to cross over the thousand and a half miles to back-country Jersey. He had forgotten the theater, the whorehouses, the bubbling, smelly life of Dodge City. He could think of nothing but desertion; he told himself:

"If they give me leave tonight, I'll desert. I'll desert and bum back east somehow, maybe catch a ride on a cattle train."

A captain at the far end of the table raised his voice suddenly to catch the colonel's attention:

"I've been thinking, sir—I don't like the looks of what's making at Dodge."

"Eh?"

"It's going to be bad all right, sir," someone else said.

"Murray must have met them," the colonel shrugged. "Otherwise there'd be word from him by now. They were headed this way."

"That's just it. Suppose they cut him?"

The colonel shrugged again. He was a large, slow man, not averse to hearing his junior officers. "I don't like to have civilians in it," he agreed. "But it would take two days to push a company to the Medicine Lodge. One way or another, it'll be over then. And there's the troops on the railroad west of here."

"Unless they've dodged the cavalry, sir," a stout, round-cheeked captain said eagerly. "Let me take my company south on the mules. We can head them off at least, even if we don't round them up. It would be a feather in our cap."

Others agreed. "I don't like to mount infantry," the colonel said

"But we've done it, sir. And you're keeping them away from Dodge. You know what a fuss it will make if a posse goes."

"It might be worth the chance," the colonel said slowly. "In any case, you might join Murray. He wants that, but God knows why. He has two companies as it is. You'll have to operate under his orders if you join him—unless he comes north through here . . ."

Vanest had listened without hearing. The thought of desertion had taken complete hold of him, and his heart hammered with fear at the decision to do it that night.

He was brought back with the colonel saying: "Trooper, you'll go along with Captain Sedberg tonight. He'll deliver you back to your own command."

At the bar of the Alamo, McGrath and Sutton ordered whiskey. They poured and gulped it straight, fifty cents a drink, three apiece without chasers before the nausea passed. Then they felt better, and they began to stuff themselves with red cheese and crackers.

"Hungry?" the bartender said good-naturedly. "I can fix some ham and eggs." He was a fat, slope-shouldered man with a bald head, pasty white and smooth as an egg. "Or cold chicken," he added. Beef was no specialty at Dodge City. "Ride in today?"

They nodded. They poured another round and stuffed down more of the crackers and cheese.

"That's on the house," the bartender explained.

"I seen better free lunch."

"Sure, but not in Dodge," the bartender said. "Ride up from Coldwater?"

"What in hell business of yours?" Sutton demanded.

"No offense."

"That's all right, that's all right," McGrath grinned. He was feeling better. They finished the bottle and munched at the cheese and crackers until the plate was empty. As the bartender bent down to restock the plate, he spoke from under the counter:

"I heard there was Cheyennes raiding down that way?"

"Maybe there was."

And as he straightened up: "I put some of that sliced white chicken in. Better put it down before the boss comes through."

Sutton said thickly: "Christ, I'd like to get a crack at them red bastards."

The bartender put another bottle on the bar, and McGrath took it, paid for the drinks, and started toward one of the tables. "I'll bring over some crackers and cheese," the bartender said.

Sutton lurched heavily into a chair, and McGrath poured again. Sutton drank with the slow obstinacy of a man who wants to get drunk and finds it difficult. McGrath drank one to his two and whistled along with the piano. He never took his eyes from the door and watched each person enter the place.

The bar ran the length of the Alamo, forty feet, merging into a tinny, upright piano. A small, bald man rocked on the stool, playing the same jig tune over and over again. A line of sticky glasses tinkled to his playing, and there was half a pitcher of headless beer waiting within reach. The tables sat in sawdust the color of mud, making a sort of fence around a sawdust-streaked dance floor. Two doors at the end of the room bluntly told the ladies and gents where to go, and an unpainted board stairs rose into obscurity between them.

There were half a dozen men at the bar and a dozen more sitting in two card games. At the further corner a roulette wheel and a dice table waited for night. At another table, a red gown, stringy yellow hair, and puffed arms lay in the wreck of an overturned whiskey glass. The smell was thick, rancid, unspeakable.

Sutton was getting drunk. He said: "It ought to be a white man's country, but it ain't."

"Sure," McGrath agreed. He always agreed with Sutton when the big man was drunk.

"All right," Sutton said, smiling stupidly. "Know what I'd do with a scalp?"

"What?"

"Sew it right here on my elbow. God damn, right here on my elbow!" He picked up the bottle and lurched back to the bar.

McGrath followed him. "Sit down," he said.

"The whole country lousy with them—"

"Come and sit down," McGrath said.

A tall, sandy-haired man glanced at the bartender, then touched Sutton's arm: "Sir?"

Sutton turned slowly and warily. McGrath backed away,

the fixed grin still on his face. The tall man had a red, splotched face and spoke with an anxious drawl.

"Where'd you see them?"

"Who?"

"Cheyennes."

"Jesus God," Sutton growled, "I didn't seem them. They're riding up toward Dodge."

"How do you know?"

"Jesus God, how do I know!"

Other men drifted along the bar. The man behind the counter was wiping a glass and watching Sutton anxiously. The piano tinkled away, the little bald man swinging around on the stool and pouring himself a glass of the stale beer. A stout well-set, well-dressed man, iron-gray in hair and mustache, a rancher or a gambler or an engineer, aloof, somewhat contemptuous, said:

"Mister, if you seen Indians, talk up."

The piano player sipped his beer and edged toward the group.

"We come in with a soldier," McGrath said quickly. "He told us."

"Cheyennes—how many?"

"A whole God damn tribe, raiding," Sutton said. He raised his voice and repeated hoarsely: "A whole God damn tribe!"

"Where'd you come in from?"

"Reeder, if it's any of your God damn say."

"Maybe it is," the stout man nodded, his blue eyes lingering all over Sutton without haste, on the worn overalls, the blue shirt, dirty, old, torn without the shame of patches, the cut face, shadowed with complete disregard for a razor, the whole big, topheavy bulk.

Sutton tried to stare him down and McGrath plucked at his partner's sleeve. The stout man met Sutton's eyes calmly and the red-faced one, thin in brown jeans and open shirt, a freight clerk or telegraph operator, took heart and said:

"Why the devil make trouble with that Indian talk?" his voice a soft protesting drawl, but with enough dislike to infuriate Sutton, who lashed out and sent him sprawling. The stout man didn't move, but never took his eyes off Sutton's face. The one with the brown jeans lay on the floor; he had no gun: then on hands and knees, pushing up and away, he got out of the circle.

The stout man turned his back on Sutton, deliberately, walked over to the fallen man, helped him to his feet and with him left the saloon.

"Jesus God," Sutton said, "how do I know about them Cheyennes—" He rubbed his knuckles.

"Like to get a whack at them myself," the bartender said eagerly.

The piano player cackled and slapped his thigh.

Outside, rubbing his jaw with a hand that trembled a little, the red-faced man said: "Thanks, Mr. Blake."

"Dodge is rotten with that kind of saddle bum. But it pays to ride them softly. They don't last."

"He was right about the Indians. It came over the wire this morning."

"A war party?"

"Something of the sort, I guess. Cheyennes who broke off the reservation. They're supposed to be raiding north, but nobody seems to know anything about them. I kept quiet about it. People go crazy when they hear Indian talk."

"Like hunting," Blake said reflectively. "Man's big game, and in this country it's always open season for red skins. Well, I ought to get back to the ranch—"

"They said three hundred. That's a lot of Indians."

"Not that it would be a bad thing to have a posse go after them," Blake reflected, thinking of his ranch, horses and cattle, a house that had cost six thousand dollars to build. "Which way were they headed?"

"That's it, I don't know. It's none of my business. There's a regiment of soldiers here to take care of that kind of thing."

"A lot of good the regiment's done for Dodge."

"Still, it's law, Mr. Blake. You got to admit that's what we're short of here." He rubbed his jaw and smiled wryly. "It's all right if a man can fight—if he can't fight—well, any law is better than no law. Suppose they start off to kill Indians. Well, it's just a mob, no matter how you look at it. What's the difference if a mob rides out to lynch a man or a hundred men, or three hundred?"

"Defending their homes," Blake said absently.

"Homes in Dodge? What homes?"

Blake shrugged. They started down the street, and when they were opposite the newspaper office the telegraph operator murmured something and turned away. Blake hardly appeared to notice his departure.

it was falling afternoon in the town, and Dodge was

gathering men to its bosom. They rode in singly, in pairs, in groups. A railroad gang humped in on their handcart, lifted it bodily from the tracks, and deposited it in front of Kelly's Place. A family of Swedes, piled into their small, flat, cluttered household wagon, made slow, wide-eyed progress along Front Street. Pianos were going in many places, making the sound and suggestion of a tinny carnival.

The rancher turned into the sheriff's office, a clapboard box with a cracked plate-glass window. The sheriff was there, leaning back in his chair, dozing. Earp, the United States marshal, was tearing paper from an old notebook, making sharp-nosed darts. Blake took out a handful of cigars.

The sheriff in Dodge City at that time was Bat Masterson, a stocky, hard, quick-shooting man who lived with the knowledge that most of his predecessors had died with their boots on and their guns in their hands. Sheriff at Dodge was not a position; it was a poor risk, a hope, a bluff hand in a rotten game. Each sheriff had spoken of cleaning out the town, making it a place where a decent person could feel secure; but Bat Masterson was the first who showed any promise of living long enough to consummate that purpose.

Now, hearing Earp pass the time of the day with the rancher, Masterson swung his chair carefully down to its four legs, nodded, took the cigar, sniffed it, bit off the end, each motion careful, considered—slow, appraising, motions of a man who lived by being careful, whose life was a delicate thing to be weighed from all angles at all times of the day and the night. He bent to Blake's match, but Earp shook his head and smoked dry. Earp was a stringy man with the alert, cautious air of a fighting cock; his fingers played constantly with his gun, the nails clicking against the metal.

"How's tricks?" Blake asked.

"Quiet."

"Quiet's good."

"Good enough," Earp said.

Masterson asked: "How's the market?"

"Up a dollar twenty cents."

"That's good."

"It could be better," Blake said. "You don't make a fortune in cattle today."

"It's a way," Earp drawled, flicking a dart. "I'm so God damn sick and tired of keeping the peace, I'd hire on for twenty a month."

"If I had a wife and kids," Blake mused, "I'd be hitting it hell for leather now. As it is, I can't make up my mind to be inside my place when it burns or to put up at Dodge."

"Indian stories got you too?" the sheriff sighed.

"I wondered if you heard?"

"Hell, yes," Earp said, smiling thinly. "You can't help hearing. Every wild and wooly saddle bum who can't find buffalo to kill, whiskey to trade or money to steal wants to play with a scalp."

"Fighting men," Masterson murmured.

"That's one way of looking at it," the rancher admitted. "Another way is to come home and find your house down and your stock run off, if you're lucky enough not to be inside your house."

"They ain't burned anything yet."

"That's a hell of a way to reason," Blake said.

"All right, all right! What do you want, a posse, a citizen army? Where are these Cheyennes? You seen them? God almighty, I don't even know how many there are loose, or where they're headed. I could go around with the rest, waving a gun, yelling kill the God damn Injuns, but what for? I never seen good come out of that. I'm trying to keep the peace."

"Maybe you'll keep it too long."

"Maybe. But I'll keep it in Dodge. There's plenty of soldiers out on the grass."

"There's plenty of yellow right here in Dodge," the rancher said.

Masterson stared at him. Earp whistled. Then Masterson said softly:

"I know you a long time, Blake."

Then they sat in silence for a while.

They didn't move as the chopping hoofbeats grated in front of the door. Masterson turned a little as the rider rushed in. Earp said: "Hello, Jimmy." The boy's face was vaguely familiar to Blake.

"They got the Fullers," the boy gasped.

"Who?"

"Take it gentle, Jimmy," Earp said.

"Them God damn Injuns!"

Blake smiled and Masterson said sharply: "Sit down, Jimmy! What in hell are you talking about?"

"You heard me! They got the Fullers, shot it out all day and burned the place on their heads!"

"When was that?"

"Last night."

"You seen it?"

"Jesus, no, but Lenny Rand seen it. He killed his horse and Jesus God, I killed mine! Lenny was riding over to the Fullers when he heard enough shooting for a battle. He didn't go into it, but he says there was a thousand guns all right. He seen it burning against the sky like a prairie fire."

"Where was that?" Blake asked.

"Down on the Medicine Lodge."

"It could be the Fullers' place," Earp admitted. "But why in hell didn't he have a look? They didn't need to make a battle to get old Pop Fuller. You sure he heard all that shooting?"

"Sure as God," the boy said.

"Those bastards," Blake said, "will get to shooting over nothing at all."

Masterson stood up tiredly, went over to the desk and buckled on his guns. "I'll walk around," he said to Earp. "You ride over to the fort and talk turkey. There'll be wild heads riding out sure as hell, and they might as well have a company or two with them."

The telegraph operator, still nursing his bruised jaw, sat in the newspaper office and listened as the editor dictated his editorial straight to the printer. In addition to his Western Union job, Stanly Garburg was Kansas correspondent for the *New York Times*. His position was not official; when he found a story, he sent it in and hoped they would use it. If the story developed, they put a regular newspaper man onto it. Still, he treasured the papers which carried his small notices.

Now, as he watched the bobbing, clothes-brush whiskers of Atkins, the editor, he was thinking of this, his biggest story, his best chance, yet hoping it wouldn't materialize, thinking of the dots and dashes that had brought him the story of the Indians' flight, the charges and counter charges, the unhurried marshaling of troops from all over the plains country into a net that was apparently without a loophole. He knew little of Indians, for all that everyone on the plains seemed to have their own personal Indian story; yet he knew that the Indian wars were a thing of the past, that the Indian case was settled, now and forever. This was something else . . .

He listened to Atkins saying: ". . . How long shall free Americans live under the shadow of this dread fear? How long shall this red menace keep their homes, their hearths, their loved ones in the valley of the shadow? We say it has been long enough! We say that no more of our loved ones shall die to feed the gaping maw of savagery. We say to free men, Rise up and destroy them! We say, Citizens of Dodge City, defend your homes, take up your guns in the cause of peace and freedom! Strike back! Strike them so that they will know that the wrath of the Lord has descended upon them! Teach them a lesson that will forever keep them within the confines of their reservations . . ."

Garburg listened, smiling a little. He had heard the same words, the same exhortations, the same curses applied to rustlers, buffalo hunters, gunmen, whiskey runners, Texans. Atkins never changed the context of his editorials; indeed, if he had, the good people of Dodge City might read them. As it was no one read them, except when they were printed in eastern journals to show the crusading tenor of the frontier press.

When Atkins had finished, he came over to the telegraph operator, grinning and chewing his ancient corncob.

"Told them, eh?" he said.

"Do you hate Indians that much?"

"Hate them? Never knew one, never spoke to one except halfbreed Micky. But they stand in the way of progress. Same as the gunman. Progress can't stop."

"Still, I wouldn't print that," Garburg said.

"Why?"

"There'll be trouble enough. Why make more? Those Indians haven't come near Dodge. There's no proof of depredations. Probably all they want is to go home, back to the north."

"And are we to remove from the land we fought for, say to them go, go in peace?"

"Why not?"

"Ayah!" the editor spat out. "Go away! The breath of cowardice is too hot! Take yourself away!"

The detail from Fort Dodge left the post in the darkness and rode due south in the direction of Whitman, instead of cutting south and east toward Reeder and the Medicine Lodge River. Sedberg reasoned that the troops from Fort Reno had either intercepted the Cheyennes or missed them entirely. That the Indians had escaped the cavalry after being intercepted, he did not consider at all; on the other hand, if Murray had made contact with them, word should have come to Dodge, so the probability was that the Reno troops had lost the trail entirely. If they had gone on, as it seemed, to the north of Sun City, they would cover the eastern flank along with the troops that were patrolling the railroad on flatcars. Nevertheless, some instinct might have driven the Cheyennes in a wide swoop to the west, perhaps a feeling that there, where the country was least populated, was their best road for escape. That was all he had to go by, and on that chance he took his mule-mounted infantry south through the night. As for the hundred rumors of Indian raids that had filtered into Dodge City that afternoon from all parts of Kansas, there was no making sense out of them and no co-ordinating them. South was the only chance, and south he went, with the intentions of circling widely to the east and picking up Murray's trail the following day.

He had with him as scout old Pete Jamison, a halfbreed Crow who knew southwestern Kansas as well as the lines on his own palm; and as further help there was a good moon and white, pointed starlight, the kind that is seen only over high mountain ranges, the desert, and the great plains. The men rode close together, not speaking much, somewhat uneasy on their mules, but nevertheless making good time. They were not tired, for they had had a two-hour rest after mess, yet the prospect of the shambling mules' gait all night long was not pleasant.

Trooper Vanest rode near the head of the column, a few paces behind Captain Sedberg, and Vanest at least was tired and worn already, played out inside of himself and all along the flattened length of his muscles. Even now it was difficult for him to realize that the pleasure of Dodge City had come and gone in a brief interval and that he was riding back to the Indians or to the hellish yellow and red monotony of Fort Reno.

He heard Sedberg talking to the scout and he hated them both, hated everything connected with this vast, flat, hopeless plains land. He hoped that if they did encounter the Indians, Sedberg would be destroyed, go out in the same sort of bitter pain he was experiencing now. He despised the dull voice of the scout, the sing-song Indian accent saying to Sedberg:

"Dem Cheyenne, by Got, dem one awful bad hombre. Dem fight lak hell, lak scratching cat. I tink we find dem, we go awful careful, careful lak mouse in dark wit scratching cat."

"You find them," Sedberg said. "That's all, find them. Let me decide what to do after that."

"Sure. Sure. But I tink we go careful, Mister Capitan."

They rode on and the hours passed. The grass was long and high and black and wet. Coyotes called a defiant challenge to the thud of the mules' hoofs, and once they blundered into a frightened cluster of buffaloes. They rode the sides of wire fences that were already subdividing the plains, and now and again they made out the shuttered black bulks of ranch houses and barns. Often through the night came the whinnying of horses, the stamping rush of range cattle, and once, coming over a hill they saw beneath them the sorrowful glow of a chuck fire, log-like forms of cowboys stretched out like the spokes

135

of a wheel. But though they rode with pickets spread out five hundred yards on either hand, they saw nothing of the Indians, no sign good or bad, no burning ranch house, no glow hanging in the sky to tell of a hundred camp-fires.

The night passed, and the troopers rode half asleep in their saddles, heads hanging, conversation muted to expressions of disgust, or else in silence black as the night, broken only by the ceaseless pounding of the horses' hoofs. They rode that way until the sky changed from an ink blue to an ink black and then to the cheerless, somber, un-relieved gray of dawn.

"I tink no use," Pete Jamison said; and then a moment later reined around, stood in his stirrups listening with both hands cupped behind his ears. Sedberg held up his hand for the men to stop, and the two pickets circled uncertainly back through the night.

"I tink I hear veree funny noise," the scout said, grin-ning flatly, twisting his head from side to side. "I tink I hear someting."

"What?"

"I don know—maybe nutin, maybe a lot ah men ride."

"Where?"

The scout pointed ahead, and Sedberg strained to hear. The horses whinnied nervously and the men shook them-selves out of sleep, clasped the cold metal of their rifles, and shivered in the cool damp of the prairie morning. Then it came out clear, so that hearing nothing one mo-ment, the next they were able to distinguish a sound like muffled drums rumbling a long way off.

"Dey not far away," Jamison said.

"How many do you suppose?"

The scout shrugged. "Maybe couple hundred, maybe more."

"It could be the Indians," Sedberg thought, "or it could be Murray and his men." He twisted around uncertainly and looked at his troopers, packed close, wretched after the night's ride, fingering their rifles and unable to keep their mules from milling like cattle. Now that he was close to his goal, he didn't know just what to do. His feeling, as an infantry officer, was to dismount his men and spread them out in a skirmish line. But then it would be too simple for the Indians, if Indians they were, to avoid his men. So he waited.

Vanest, crouched painfully over his big gray horse, rubbing his numb thighs, saw the Indians come out of the misty dawn, roll down a little hill, and come to a questioning halt about a hundred yards from the troops. In that moment, he realized that Murray had failed, that he had failed. Somewhere, all his companions were safe and here he alone was facing the Indians, as if a bitter and revengeful fate had fought with him and won.

"By gar," the scout whispered, "I tink we got dem—or dey got us."

Sedberg waved his arm and the mules pushed forward. The Indians were silent, motionless, blurred silhouettes. Then, with the effortless ease of flowing water, more than half the Indians were streaming away.

"That way!" Sedberg cried. "Trumpeter, damn you, blow!"

The bugle notes seemed to give men and animals a common desire. The mules heaved into a run. But the scout, standing in his stirrups, pulled at Sedberg's arm and protested:

"Mister Capitan, dem squaws—you go crazy to chase dem squaws an leave all dose dirty Dog Soldiers step on your tail!"

Sedberg saw it now; the women and children were streaming away southeast, in the direction from which they had come. The men, the warriors, nimble as clowns on their little ponies, were circling to strike him in the flank. He tried desperately to swing his men, and then as the mules milled into confusion he yelled for the column to halt.

A pink hint of sunrise was in the sky now. The squaws and children drove into it, robed themselves with mist and obscurity, and the men, aware that their families were safe, paraded defiantly in front of the mounted infantry. As yet, no shot had been fired. Sedberg, despairing of taking the mules into a charge in any sort of order, gave the command for his men to dismount and open fire. The Indians danced away.

The troopers climbed stiffly from their mules, hanging to the reins, dragging the beasts into an open order that would give them room to fire, cursing the tired, stubborn animals. Vanest remained mounted; he was enough of a cavalryman to know that the whole maneuver was awkward to the point of being suicidal. He alone anticipated the swarming charge of the Cheyennes, even while the infantry struggled with the mules.

138

He saw the Cheyennes wheel apart like a feather fan opening, come down on the troops like tumbleweed before a gale, shrieking, yelling, stampeding the mules, riding through them and leaving the whole spilled company in utter confusion. The troopers were firing, but it was like shooting wild pigeons on the wing to try to hit those whirling, dancing horsemen. The Indians did not shoot much, and their few scattered shots were more to stampede the mules than to kill the troopers. They rode off into the night, while the troopers fought with the mules, picked themselves off the ground, flung futile bullets after the fleeing Cheyennes, cursed, blundered through the tall grass looking for their weapons.

But Vanest had gone away. His big gray horse had bolted at the charge, and then he gave it the spur in front of the oncoming Indians. His head whirling, his back full of a knife-like pain from a bullet that had slid under his shoulder blade, a wild, unaimed, flung bullet from one of the troopers, he was aware of only one thing—that it was over, that he was escaping, that now he would go home, not turn, never stop riding, but go home.

That way, he rode madly in front of the Indians and then away from them as they turned to the east, to their women and their children. Vanest rode on alone, his big gray horse dropping to a canter, a walk, and then finally standing still while Vanest hung in the saddle. All his memories of green, warm Jersey hinterland were clear; and they remained clear until the weight of his body pulled his fingers from the pommel. And then there was night even though the sun rose like a bright angel over the prairie. And then the big gray horse began to walk and graze, Vanest's body dragging along through the tall grass, one foot caught in the stirrup.

In Dodge City, in the Lady Gay Theatre, when half the performance was over, Frank Henick, the interlocutor, stepped between the curtains and bowed to the audience. He stood in front of the sixty candles that burned in the tin footlights, and he assumed a diffident and humble expression. He clasped his hands and said:

"Fellow citizens of Dodge City, fellow Americans, it is not in the spirit of humor that I address you now. There is a time for humor, and when you pay admission to the Lady Gay, it is not wrong that you should expect humor, indeed the best of that and dancing and singing entertainment; but there is also a time for the graver things of life, and it is of that that I now speak. I speak of a red menace that rolls over Kansas like a foul prairie fire. I speak of the red savage who burns and kills and destroys. I speak of brave men who crouch in their barricaded houses, women and children praying on their knees beside them, while he pumps bullets out of the windows to repel the foul fiend who would destroy all that is dear to him. Can you sit there, my fellow citizens of Dodge City, and feel nothing of what he suffers? Or does wrath and horror rise in your true hearts? Can you sit there and feel no desire to take your guns in hand and go out and strike down this heartless monster of savageness, who doesn't know what love and Christianity is, but only how to scalp and torture a man to death. So how can you forget, not only the brave men who gave their lives under the brave General Custer only a few years ago, but the brave men and women like the Fullers and the Clancys and the Logans and the other brave men and women who are lying scalped and bloody. I am only a paid entertainer, so maybe my words mean nothing to hard-fighting men like yourself, but I know that if you lend me a gun and a horse, I will be the first to ride with you. I thank you very kindly for your kind attention, ladies and gentlemen."

The orchestra tried to play the Battle Hymn of the Republic, but the wildly cheering audience drowned out all sound of the music. Frank Henick bowed and bowed, but there was no use trying to quiet the audience or go on with the show. The men nearest the stage plucked out the hot footlights, and Frank Henick, riding high on the wave of emotion he had so ably launched, led the torch-light parade out of the Lady Gay, down Front Street and into the Long Branch Saloon. By now, the excitement had communicated itself to every corner of Dodge City, and men and women poured into the Long Branch until they were packed shoulder to shoulder, shouting, cheering, yelling for Bat Masterson.

Masterson climbed onto the bar and yelled: "Wait a minute! Wait a minute! I can't hear myself think!"

"Sure, Bat—we're with you, Bat!" they cried.

"All right! You're hot as hell to fight Indians now! Maybe I can understand that. You hear stories that they're plowing Kansas under, and naturally you get riled. But this isn't sixty-six or sixty-eight; the Indian wars are

over, and if there's a band loose and raiding, the troops
are able to take care of it."

(Hisses and catcalls—to hell with the fancy soldier boys!)

"All right, maybe you don't like the soldiers—but they're
the law!"

"You're the law, Bat! Deputize us!"

"Wait a minute! I don't want a wild-head pack of citizens riding herd and shooting everything they see! If
you're set to do this thing, it's still going to be done right
and done my way! Otherwise I'll say the lot of you be
damned!"

"Hell, yes! Deputize us!"

"All right—you're going after the Indians. You can't go
tonight. For one thing, if you ever started shooting out
there in the dark, you'd kill more citizens than Indians.
For another, we don't know where them Indians are.
From the reports, they're in twenty different places all
over the state. We got to wait until we get a line on them.
A company of soldiers went out on mules tonight to try
to pick them up; we got to wait until we hear from the
fort. Meanwhile, we'll have a citizen committee make up a
posse. And tomorrow morning, if you still feel the same,
I'll swear you in."

Masterson climbed down to a flurry of cheering, only
thinly interspersed with the grumbles of those who wanted
to start straight away. For the most part, the people were
relieved to hear that nothing definite would be done until
morning. The crowd in the Long Branch thinned out,
spilling into the Alamo and Kelly's Place. A Texas stockman, hating Indians the way only a Texan can, set up
drinks three times in a row. Rowday Case, the gambler,

set them up twice. Dancing started and a few card games. The citizen committee went into the back room and began writing down names for the posse.

The posse was restless, nervous, indignant. There had been almost three hundred the night before, and now in the morning it had dwindled to less than a hundred. Its character had changed; the small farmers, small ranchers, family men had disappeared. Ten hours had done that; it was one thing to go to fight Indians in all the heat of a few drinks, a few speeches, a common will to rid the land of vermin. It was something else to go out and get killed deliberately in the bright unshadowed light of morning. It was better to go home and stick to your own place, put the stock in the barns and put up the shutters. Then if the Indians wanted to come there, you could fight on your own ground.

Another consideration was the appearance of old Pop Fuller. Instead of being dead as rumored, he had turned up very much alive, armed with his ancient Sharpes rifle and hot to kill a few Cheyennes on his own. When asked about the battle that was said to have accomplished his demise, he agreed that there had been a battle between troops and Cheyennes somewhere on the Medicine Lodge River. He didn't know much about it, except that the Indians were said to be heading toward Dodge. So here he was.

That took the edge off things. If Pop hadn't been killed, then perhaps a dozen other deaths were equally false. There were more desertions from the posse. Then a group of Texas riders found Halfbreed Micky, an addle-brained, harmless Piute, hiding under the counter in Briggs' General Store. Micky was the result of a whiskey trader's brief passion for a Piute squaw, and he had come into the world with a lopsided head and a queer, beseeching grin. He was perfectly harmless, gentle as a rabbit, afraid of dogs, and willing to do any work from scraping rotten buffalo hides to cleaning outhouses. Not only was he as far or further removed in kind from the Cheyennes as white men, but he was afraid of blanket Indians and always avoided them.

Now the Texans dragged him out, tarred him with creosote that they stole from the loading station, and as a measure of contempt hung him by one foot from a telegraph pole, instead of lynching him as they would have lynched a white man. They rode their horses down Front Street and shot off their guns a few times, and then left the scene before a few decent citizens with a little more nerve than the rest of the posse, got a ladder and cut Micky down. He was half dead, and the rush of blood to his lopsided head had put him into a coma. He lay there trying to smile, while Bat Masterson, who had come on the scene too late to do anything and who had known Halfbreed Micky for many years, stormed about and swore to God that he would kill the Texans the first time he saw them. The Texans, for all their vaunted courage, knew Masterson; they drifted out of town, and some of the men managed to sooth the sheriff.

This furthered desertions from the posse. Wyatt Earp washed his hands of the whole affair and went back to fold paper darts in Masterson's office. The sheriff said that if they were still bent on going out and getting killed, he'd at least go along and see that they didn't kill each other.

That way, the morning wore on. The posse had narrowed down to a group of saddle bums who wanted to be able to boast an Indian fight or a scalp sewn onto their lapels, of hot-headed, scornful young Texas riders, of tin horn gamblers, faro dealers, and bartenders who were tired of dodging bullets in saloon brawls and wanted a shooting of their own. There were also a few grocery clerks, who saw this as a wooly and wonderful adventure; two rather unintelligent English younger sons, brothers who took the whole thing as a picnic and a lark; the sheriff and four regular deputies; a telegraph operator who wanted to write newspaper stories; and lastly a half-dozen stockmen who were for anything that would help remove the Indians from the grasslands.

The others, the small farmers and ranchers, the railroad workers, the stockyard workers, the lawyers, doctors, tailors and merchants, had disappeared. And those left were impatient, anxious to justify themselves. They milled in front of the Alamo, mounting and dismounting, breaking open their guns, counting their shells, demanding of Masterson that he lead them out to find the Indians.

Masterson had sent word to Fort Dodge, following his thought that if the posse was bent on going, it would be best to have some troops along. The answer he received was, in effect, a refusal; the colonel had no more troops to spare. The message went on to explain that a company of mounted infantry had left the night before in search of the Cheyennes, that two more companies were patroling the railroad on flatcars, and that a fourth company was detailed to guard the environs of Dodge City itself. Also, a garrison had to be maintained at Fort Dodge. If the citizens insisted on going out to look for the Cheyennes, they would have to go themselves.

"That God damned cursed filthy army," Masterson thought, not with hate but with resentment that he alone should be held responsible for this mob, this posse, this witless, accumulated desire to kill Indians. From nine o'clock to ten o'clock to eleven o'clock he put them off with one thing and another. By then, the ladies of more or less crimson fame had wakened from their night's toil, and they lined the veranda of the Alamo, telling the men of the posse in no uncertain terms just what they were. There was Lilly Arande and the whitish-blonde, magnificent Congo Grace, Mary Smith, Fritzie who had no other name, Jelly Green, used up but left with enough foul invective. There were a dozen more, mocking, laughing, singing: "Oh, what are you waiting for, oh, what are you waiting for, my hearty braves?"

"Either you give the word, Bat, or we're sure as hell going without you," a stockman told the sheriff.

About ten minutes after that, Cally Ridgewood, a rider for the Double Shell Ranch, came dashing up Front Street, his horse lathered, his arms waving. He reined up and shouted: "They were camped at the bend, west of Ford! Jesus God, they'll be here in an hour!"

Then there was no holding the posse, and Masterson

146

knew it. Yelling, whooping, emptying their guns, they streamed down Front Street, crossed the railroad and fanned out, heading south and east.

They rode hard for an hour, keeping in sight of the river, and then Masterson pleaded for a halt. He knew that if they didn't rest their horses they would be in shape for nothing, not to attack, to fight, to run or retreat. It was difficult to hold them down; they reined in on a bluff overlooking the river, laughing, yelling, a few of the grocery clerks white and sick-looking, some of the Texas riders tight-lipped with a sort of doubt on their faces, but the rest laughing and boasting, listening to a big, scar-faced saddle bum called Sutton tell of the Indians he had killed, their numbers legion, their souls black and cowardly—with assent from his small partner, "Sure as hell he did!"

They stayed there about ten minutes, and they were mounting again when they saw the Indians.

That came as a surprise, the impossible turned into fact; for deep in his own heart, no one among them had believed it. This was a picnic, a lark; how could they find one band of Cheyennes in the tens and thousands of miles of plains country? Even Masterson had banked on that fact, that they would never locate the Indians.

The Indians had come up from the south along the river, just as the posse had come down from the north; they came up over a fold of ground and materialized suddenly, as things do on the prairie. They were strung out,

147

moving fast, a bunch of warriors leading, squaws, children clinging like monkeys to little ponies, horses loaded with household goods, dogs running with the horses, another bunch of men bringing up the rear, and men and boys strung out alongside of the column. They saw the posse at the same time the posse saw them, but they didn't change their direction or their pace. Only, almost imperceptibly, the women and children were closed up, bound around with men like a ribbon binds a flat candy package.

Sutton roared: "Oh, Jesus God!"

The Texans began to yell, sound without words. The posse mounted like a pool of water stirred frantically. The two English brothers stared at each other, grinning sheepishly, and one touched the other's arm worriedly. The telegraph operator felt his stomach sicken, his mouth go dry and bitter. One of the grocery clerks began to vomit as he struggled with his rearing horse.

A stout rancher, contemptuous of the howling rabble, asked Masterson: "What about it, Bat?"

The sheriff shrugged and slapped his horse's rump. Already the posse was spilling down the hill, spread out, loose, firing from their saddles, firing wildly and hitting nothing with their rocking, waving guns, not even the broad target presented by the Indians.

The telegraph operator wanted to see. He had told himself again and again, "This I must see, remember, put down sometime on paper." Yet for all that he saw it in flashes, like dots and dashes coming over the wire, clear up to the moment the Indians slowed their ponies to a walk, blurred then. He didn't know afterwards how the

Indians waited, a line of men in front of their families, men with grim, tired faces sighting over old rifles, carbines, long-barreled, ancient Colts, men with flat, horn-backed bows bent, the arrows trembling slightly, men with primitive spears and feather-trimmed shields.

The Indians fired one volley, a single crash that set the posse's horses screaming and rearing and broke the charge. The posse milled back, together, apart, horses dashing away with riders none too eager to turn them back, horses rearing while riders tried to load again, horses crashing insanely onto the Cheyennes, so that Sutton lay in the grass with a broken spear through his chest, his face gentle, relaxed without miseries and wants, small hates and desires and repressions, without anything at all but the peace that came from the horrid tearing of a Dog Soldier spear; so that the English boy, hating no one, for this was his lark, rode through all the Cheyenne village with a barbed arrowhead cutting the back of his jacket, burning his lungs, rode on beyond clinging to his saddle and crying for his brother and dying. And some fell from their horses, like Blake, the rancher, who died quickly with a bullet in his head.

The telegraph operator began to remember again, to see, to place one fact after another, as they might be written down. He sat clenching one hand with the other, hiding a finger that was gone, staring after the Indians who were riding away, listening to the heaped curses of Bat Masterson, wondering:

"What else did he expect? How will it be for me, without a finger? How do you stop the blood?"

149

Masterson reined in hopelessly and looked around at the scattered, broken posse. In the direction of the Arkansas River, the dark, strangely indomitable mass of the Cheyenne village was already disappearing into the yellow-grass Kansas prairie.

PART SIX   September 1878

THE TRAP CLOSES

Murray had come up on the trail, and his men were dog-tired and dirty; there was something about them that had been missing before. Wint said to the captain, stopping in the heat of early morning:

"Have you ever hunted?"

"Hunted?"

"With a dog, I mean, say with a pointer after quail and watched the way he quartered the ground."

"I hate hunting," Murray said. "I always thought there was something bad about a man who had to hunt."

Wint shrugged and said: "I like it, but that doesn't matter. I was thinking of the men. Look at them."

"They're tired."

"They want to fight now—they didn't want to before."

"They want to find what they're looking for," Murray

said. "You get that way. You dream about those damned Indians. You feel that there's nothing else in the world."

They had quartered back and forth, trying to pick up a trail, asking people: "What about Indians?"

A ranch house in the night, with shutters up, dogs barking, stock milling and fearful; and then Murray shouting:

"In there! In there! Hello!" When the householder came out with his gun, only half out of sleep and annoyed, ridiculous in his long white nightshirt, he would be thinking, perhaps, "Why in the devil's name can't they ride in the daytime, sleep at night? I hate soldiers, I hate uniforms. Why don't they go away and leave me alone?"

"Indians?" Murray would demand.

"No—I said no! No Indians! God damn you for fools, I haven't seen Indians in five years."

And then sarcastic comments from the men, the big, nervous gray horses digging up pasture and front yard, property; the men assuring him that this was no picnic—to defend his kind they were fine-combing the whole country.

"I said no Indians in five years!"

Murray remarked to Wint: "I'd feel better with a scout. Maybe they don't know anything. I guess half the time they don't. But they seem to; they seem to know where they're going. I wish I knew where we were going."

"North."

"And if the Dog Soldiers are going north—"

Wint shrugged.

They rode into Greensburg before dawn, nightriders or ghosts and phantoms in the night, waking the town, stirring panic, fright, wonder, pulling a hundred heads out of windows, a long line of blue-black men on Main Street, stopping in front of the Sheriff's office, the men dismounting, sagging and squatting after Murray had called: "At ease!"

"Sheriff!" Wint yelled, not caring anymore whether the whole town or the whole world woke and cursed them. "Sheriff!"

The sheriff lived behind his office and came out with a gun in his hand, pants pulled over a nightshirt, a small man with a halo of rumpled hair around an egg-like skull.

"Put away the gun, Sheriff," Wint said.

"My Lord, you got no call to wake up a town of decent sleeping folk like that."

"Maybe if Indians woke you, you'd be pleased as the devil, Sheriff."

"Indians?"

"Let him sleep," Murray said with disgust. "Ask him for a scout and let him go back to sleep."

The men were already asleep; they squatted in the street next to their horses, dozing, heads hanging, arms limp.

"We need a scout!"

The whole town was up and awake now and the scent of Indians was in their nostrils. They didn't mind being awakened now. Like old times, it was, and they suggested barricading both ends of the street. "Fight it out and give them hell!" the comment ran.

"Just a scout—just a scout."

"There's Pop Filway," the sheriff said. "My word, he knows the country, up and down and sidewise."

"Where is he?"

"An old Indian fighter," the sheriff said. "Why, sonny, he was taking off their scalps when you were teething."

"Well, where is he?"

They were yelling for "Pop." The crowd gave way and they pushed through an old graybeard, scrawny, sleepy.

"Here's my grandfather," Gatlow grinned.

"Know the country? Ever scouted?" Murray demanded impatiently.

"Scouted—my good Jesus, youngster, what makes you so uppity?"

"We need a scout—our scout was shot by Cheyennes."

"You after Cheyennes?"

Murray sighed and Gatlow giggled. Wint said:

"Look, Pop, you want to scout for us? We're trying to pick up a Dog Soldier trail—about three hundred of them going north. We followed them up from the territory and lost them yesterday. They must be near here, maybe twenty miles away at the most. Three dollars a day, and I'll recommend you to the colonel for a bonus. How does that sound?"

Someone gave the old man a slab of tobacco; he bit into it and chewed thoughtfully. "Sounds good," he said finally. "But God damn, sonny, don't go giving me no orders. Christ almighty, if there's one thing I can't stand, it's a bastard in a uniform giving orders."

"Sure," Wint nodded.

"I'll get me a gun and a horse."

"It's a waste of army money," Wint said after the old man had gone. Sergeant Cambrun shouted at the troopers, pulled them to their feet and cursed them back into their saddles. Murray went off to find the telegraph operator, and Gatlow giggled and dozed and recalled bits of poetry and dozed again. Fifteen minutes later they were riding out of town, Filway chuckling to himself and telling the two captains tales of the days when the plains were young.

Murray swung his troop west, north and west again. The old man was no fool; he hung over his saddle and either by chance or skill found the trail in the early gleam of sunrise.

"Dog Soldiers?" Murray asked.

"Now, sonny, you tell me. There ain't no other Indians in these parts."

"How long ago did they pass?"

"Lord, sonny, I ain't no hound dog."

"Guess at it, Pop."

The old man dismounted carefully and puttered around in the broad wake of bruised grass and broken earth. The troopers sagged in their saddles and watched with glazed eyes. The scout felt the earth, picked stems of grass, scuffed at the hoofmarks.

"Maybe an hour," he said finally.

"An hour?"

"Maybe two hours," he shrugged. "Can't tell, except that it wasn't long past."

"We'll rest here," Murray said. "Then we'll go after them."

His first impulse was to push on immediately. It had

155

become an aching, hurting desire in him, to find the Indians again and to hit them again, to fling more and more
force against them; it was a desire that drew like a raw
wound.

It was better after the troopers had slept for a couple of
hours. Murray could understand why Wint had thought of
hunting-dogs. The men were on the trail now, and they
urged their horses. At first, the Indians had been simply
Indians, a reason why troops were stationed on the plains.
One had fought the Indians; and one would possibly fight
them again. Troops and Indians were like counter-weights
on a scale, and you needed one to have the other. But
there was no real animosity. In this case, at the beginning, there was even, among the men, a sort of grudging
admiration for the Cheyennes; call the Dog Soldiers what
you liked, red savages or anything else—still you couldn't
get away from the fact, the fact that a people would go to
cross a thousand miles of garrisoned country to be home
and free. That was something they understood; it was
crazy, but in a way it was admirable.

But that grudging admiration was based on the supposition that the Indians would be speedily caught and returned. An Indian might start a movement like that, but
white men couldn't let him finish it. These Indians were
too successful.

They were too elusive, like greased stoats. They had no
right to make fools out of two companies of U. S. cavalry.
And in proportion to the Indians' success, the troops'

anger rose. They told themselves that this time would be the last.

Pop Filway led them on the trail, the old man riding between Murray and Wint; and behind the officers stretched the long line of blue-clad men on gray horses, riding two by two. They took a good pace, driving miles through the long, warm morning. They passed over swelling grasslands into rugged, broken country.

"We'll reach the Arkansas soon," Wint said.

"Maybe ten miles," the old man admitted. He was growing sleepy, nodding, dozing a little as he rode. Wint said:

"Pop, keep awake."

"Sonny?"

Murray pointed to the trail.

"Lord, sonny," the old man said, "can't you follow that road? That's plain and bare and simple. I could follow that up to Canady border if I had to, eyes closed."

"Maybe you will—"

"No, no, sonny. Don't fret. My Lord, them Dog Soldiers are human, ain't they? They got to eat and sleep and rest. From what you tell me, they already run their horses half to death. Well, you just camp on their trail and maybe noontime, maybe sunset you'll come onto them."

His guess was confirmed by a lone herder who left his sheep flock to ride along with the column for a while. He was a Mexican in the employ of "Meestair Kent," voluble in a mixture of Spanish and English, crossing himself while he told of a cloud of wild savages who had obscured the horizon.

"How long ago?"

"Wan hour, I tink." He said, "You give dem planty hell, dem Inyuns, ha, solyer?"

Murray spurred his horse and the long blue line cantered forward, blowing dust like a train blows smoke. The Mexican fell back and waved after them.

It was not much later that they heard the firing. Shots a long way off can sound like splintering brushwood, or if the air is very clear like a man walking on percussion caps. Sometimes shots sound like a flock of strange birds chattering. Murray stopped the column and Filway cackled like a hen.

"There's your Dog Soldiers, sonny," he grinned, proud at his achievement, cocking an eye at the trail the way an artist looks at his work.

"A lot of shooting," Wint said.

There was none now, only silence that was threshed gently by a flock of crows lifting and swooping across the top of the grass and then spilling skyward like buckshot.

"Beat you to it," the old man cackled.

Murray called: "Gatlow, Gatlow!—take a detail up there and ride hard. If anything breaks, get back here. Don't get into anything—just take a detail of three men along with you and see what you can see."

Gatlow, flushed, eager to avenge Freeland, saluted, picked his men, and dashed away. The column went on more slowly, Murray shading his eyes to follow the detail's progress through the broken ground, the long grass and the stunted cottonwood. Presently they disappeared, and all of the men as one seemed to sigh and stiffen and wait. They loosened their sabers, took off their gloves and rubbed their wet palms on their thighs. They bent in their saddles, shaded their eyes, and licked their dusted lips.

They didn't relax until they came up with the broken, bruised wreck of the Dodge City posse.

Masterson told Murray: "Look here, Captain, seems you're a reasonable man—"

"That's neither here nor there. You're directly responsible for this crazy attack. What did you expect, to ride down a tribe of Dog Soldiers with *that* posse of yours?"

"There was no way of stopping it. If the army had given us troops, this wouldn't have happened."

A rancher, his cheek cut by a bullet and still bleeding, said: "Take it easy, soldier. It's our own God damn business how we do these things."

"It's my business to keep order wherever my troops are!" Murray stormed.

"Then why in hell couldn't you keep them damn devils back south where they belong?"

Murray said, thinly: "Mister, for two bits I'd put the whole lot of you under arrest."

Most of the posse were gathered around Masterson and the officers. They were hot and mad, now that the confusion and suddenness of their defeat were past; they were bursting with resentment of the soldiers, hatred for the Indians. They cursed Murray and piled their fury upon him. The troops had dismounted over to one side; they sprawled on the grass, easing their aching muscles, hands clasped under their heads, paying little attention to the argument.

Masterson said: "Wait a minute, Captain. There's a lot of loose talk here, but we're not making things any better by acting like a pack of kids. There's no martial law in Kansas, and you won't be putting anyone under arrest. Meanwhile, these hotheads aren't helping any. Your job is to get those Cheyennes. We'd like to go along."

"I don't want you," Murray said. "I don't want civilians, and that stands."

"We've got our own fight now," Masterson insisted.

"I can see what you've done with it."

"Still, we're going."

"Like hell you are!"

Masterson eyed the captain coolly. The posse had split into two almost equal parts. Half backed Masterson; the others withdrew slowly, a little shamefaced, quiet, staring curiously at the relaxed troopers, making little groups around the dead and wounded. The telegraph operator sat in the grass, his wounded hand clenched under the other arm. The English boy wandered around aimlessly; his brother lay with a shirt pulled over his face, the broken arrow still in his breast.

"Let them go along," Wint shrugged.

Murray was still staring at Masterson. He nodded abruptly, walked to his horse and mounted. The cavalrymen climbed to their feet. The old scout, who had not bothered to dismount, chewed tobacco and spit into the wind. Masterson went to his horse and about half the posse mounted and rode with him. Murray led his troops on the Cheyenne trail without looking back.

The part of the posse that was left on the scene of the

battle watched the troops and citizens disappear and then apathetically made preparations to return to Dodge City with the dead and wounded. The telegraph operator stood for a minute or two looking toward the troops, then, wincing with pain, ran for his horse, mounted, and rode after them. He heard someone calling, turned in his saddle, and saw the English boy following him. He waited for the other to come up, and then they rode on in silence.

It seemed to Murray that there was no longer a need for haste. What was coming was inevitable. The Cheyennes had gained for themselves perhaps another hour's lead, two hours altogether, three hours perhaps; it made no difference. They would have to sleep sometime, stop sometime. A dead pony, scaled with flies, lay about a mile from the battleground. They had no ponies to spare; some would have to ride double. God only knew where they got their food; killed cattle perhaps; but it took a lot of beef to feed three hundred souls. And women of any race were not made to ride eight, nine, ten hours a day; nor were children made that way. He didn't want to think of their pain; their pain was none of his business; his business was only to run them down.

"Today?" Wint asked him.

"It doesn't matter," Murray said. "Today or tomorrow."

They forded the shallow, muddied drift of the Arkansas River and headed north and west, toward the railroad. The old scout, cackling with glee, picked up the trail of the tribe, into the water and out of it. There was another dead pony then, two coyotes feeding ravenously upon it.

161

They stood their ground, barking, snapping, until the troops were almost on them, then retreated only a little way, hungry for the meat and made brave by it.

At about two o'clock, they made out four canvas-top wagons and some mounted men coming up from the west. Wint rode to meet them, and found the wagons loaded with troops. An officer introduced himself to Wint as Captain Trask of Fort Dodge.

"The pleasure is all ours," Wint nodded. "My name's Wint. Captain Murray's in command. We're two troops of the Fourth, up from Fort Reno."

Trask nodded. "I thought so. You must have missed Sedberg."

"Whoever he is, we've missed him."

The troops had come up now, also Masterson and his posse. Murray gave the order to dismount and fall out. The wagons stopped and the cramped infantrymen climbed down to the ground. The posse bunched to one side. With the almost leisurely pace the troops had taken, the posse's old contempt for uniformed soldiers was returning. They watched the cavalry and infantry mingle, bickering over cigarette paper, tobacco, and sweets. The men from Fort Reno were cheered by the sight of reinforcements. They stood on their laurels and told the story of the chase; it became better with the telling.

Masterson had joined the officers. He accepted a cigar from Trask and smoked it quietly, while Murray quickly outlined the train of events since they had left the reservation.

"Sedberg was sent south to meet you," Trask told him. "He had a mule-mounted company. I think he went due south. He had that red-headed trooper you sent along with him."

"We missed him."

"And probably he missed the Dog Soldiers. I left the fort this morning with orders to try to cut them off between here and the railroad. I didn't expect to meet you."

"Well, you got your Indians, sonny," Pop Filway chuckled. "They're just a mite up ahead. You get your boys back into them gocarts and come along."

"They're up ahead all right," Murray nodded. "Masterson here and a posse from Dodge City had a run-in with them back across the river. Half the posse stayed there."

"Dead?" Trask demanded incredulously.

"Three dead. The rest went home."

"We've got them now, anyway," Trask said. "There are two companies on the railroad and a third cavalry company coming down from Larned. We have three hundred men here, enough to take all they can give and more. It's your game, captain—I'll go along with you."

"Thanks," Murray said. They shook hands and in a few minutes more the troops were on the trail again.

At that time, Western Kansas was still a land of broad open spaces, stretches of ground where a man could ride all day without seeing a ranch house or a farm. It was a land of wide, undulating prairie, high grass, grass so high in places that a man bending low over his horse could be hidden completely. It was a land of many shallow rivers, dry a good part of the year, roaring sometimes, placid and muddy most of the time.

Such a lonely part of Kansas was the area in the elbow of the Arkansas River. Here the Pawnee Fork made the northern side of a triangle with the main river folding down to a southern point. From Dodge City in the southwest to Fort Larned in the northeast was a place where a man could lose himself or a thousand head of cattle. It was not to be that way for long; already the steel thread of the Sante Fé Railroad had bridged the gap from the east to the west bend of the Arkansas River, and already, almost at gunpoint, the homesteaders were pushing into the limitless domain of the cattleman. But in 1878 it was still largely virgin prairie.

With this land as the fixed center of his observation, an eagle flying very high might have seen the bunched flight of the Cheyenne village, north across the lowest curl of the river, north and west into the dropping sun, north again and north. He might have seen, with far-flung sight, the detachment of cavalry coming south and west from Fort Larned. He might have seen the two companies of cavalry and the one company of infantry driving north on the Indian trail. If he had swooped and flung himself southwest, he would have seen a mule-mounted infantry company fording the Arkansas at the Cimarron Crossing, bound north and east. He would mark the progress of a flat-car train east from Fort Dodge, a company of infantry and two howitzers poking their ugly snouts at the sky. If he had turned northward then in hard flight, he would have come upon a cavalry company riding fast, south and east from Fort Wallace, up on the Smoky Hill River.

That for the eye of an eagle; yet others sensed the restless movement on the plains. Men on lonely ranches had
heard the word Indian; they barred their shutters and
cleaned their guns. Range riders saw the dark mass from
afar and guessed what it was. Telegraph operators felt the
closing trap, and under the green eyeshades their faces
tightened with excitement. Men who had never bet on a
horserace found themselves giving odds and taking odds.
Long miles of wires hummed with the message, and the
message spelled out on a thousand clicking keys, some a
thousand miles from each other. Railroad conductors,
crossing the wide stretch of the plains country, imparted
the information to their passengers, and white faces were
anxiously pressed to window-panes. Night in a hundred
prairie towns was a matter of anxious concern. It was
asked a thousand times:

"Where are the Cheyennes?"

Murray would have been just as satisfied to go up ahead
of the infantry; he wanted to clash and have it done with.
The fear inside of him could not be lulled by running
away. He wanted to beat at the Cheyennes now, quickly,
hard; he thought of his long line of troopers as a blue,
steel-studded whip. He rode slowly, holding himself tight
as a steel spring. He assured himself, "Tonight—or tomorrow."

"I'll be glad when it's over," Wint said.

"Tonight or tomorrow," Murray thought.

"We've got the wagons," Wint said, thinking aloud.
"The infantry can march back to Dodge, and we'll load

the Indians into the wagons. That's the best way. I'll talk to Trask and have him consign the wagons to us."

They were making good headway, not too fast, a steady five or six miles an hour which was the best the lumbering six-mule wagons could do on the open prairie. The two companies of cavalry led the way, the wagons following, the posse bringing up the rear in black silence. They, the citizens of Dodge, had run too much of the long scale of emotion from the night before; the reaction had set in, and they were sullen, full of hate and frustration.

Murray told himself: "They'll run away—or they'll go wild and kill. I'll try to keep them away from the women."

He remarked upon it to Wint, and Wint agreed. "This whole thing," Wint said, "it's not real—it's like a dream. I'll be glad when it's over."

Old Pop Filway rode in the van, eager, nosing to the trail, pleased with himself. His endurance was remarkable, for all that his almost passionate delight verged upon the obscene. He had been in the saddle since early morning, roused out of his sleep then, yet except for brief periods of dozing, he showed no signs of fatigue. He was full of animal-like awareness, sniffing the air, scanning the horizon, bending low and fixing his eyes on the trail. Lieutenant Gatlow rode up beside him and asked:

"Nearer them, Pop?"

"Lord, sonny, their stink's in the air."

"You don't mean that? I've heard of Indians smelling—"

"Sure as God, I smell them," the old man said.

"You've been on the plains a long time, haven't you?"

"Long time?" The old man spat. "You know of old Jim Bridger, sonny? He's seventy-two; I'm four years past

166

that; seventy-six come October nine, and been on the plains forty out of them. And never killed a Indian, sonny—never had to. Lord, I seen a lot of killing, but never stained my hands. God calls, I come up with my hands clean."

"You won't fight?" Gatlow asked.

"Lord, no, sonny. Lead me not into sin, the Book says. But I can take care of myself."

"I hope so, Pop."

"You never mind, sonny. The Lord provides."

Later, when the men were resting, eating the abundant rations Trask had brought from Fort Dodge, Murray sent the scout up ahead. The troops were under way again when Filway returned, bursting with excitement, grinning, chuckling.

"They're there," he nodded.

"Where?"

"Up a ways—a little crick they call Osage Run. They're there and bedding down for the night."

"How far?"

"Three miles," the old man grinned. "Women, kids—you got a whole Children of Israel tribe there, sonny. Dog Soldiers!—a bitchy fight it'll be, sonny."

Gatlow said: "He's crazy, Captain. Senile decay. He says he's seventy-six years old."

"Sure as God," Filway swore.

"All right, Pop," Murray said. "You're sure they're there?"

"I got eyes to see."

The little army had stopped. The cavalrymen sat their

167

saddles limply, horses two by two, a long line stretching back with twisted slanting shadows. The sun was very low, dispossessed of strength. The men were able to look full into the painted orange disk. The prairie, rolling into low hills up ahead, had taken on the intense, mournful somberness of uninhabited open space at twilight.

Trask rode up to join Murray and Wint. The junior officers pressed up, behind them most of the posse. Wint looked at his watch. Masterson hummed under his breath.

"I don't think they're bedded down for the night," Murray said. "I think they know."

"You've got a lot of respect for them," Trask remarked almost with insolence now that he was in on the achievement, coming only a few miles, not the long, weary distance from Fort Reno. It had seemed to him that Murray held back. He was an older man, and now he felt that he had surrendered command too easily. He watched Murray, tall, angular, unshaven, dirty, a big worried man who appeared to grope at the situation without real comprehension. Wint was more delicate, younger, a type that Trask had always kept aloof from, half in contempt, half in wonder; delicacy had no place on the plains. Wint was almost womanish.

"Respect?" Murray appeared puzzled.

"They're Indians, you know," Trask said. "That's all."

"I know," Murray nodded.

"I'd get this over tonight."

"Tonight or tomorrow," Murray shrugged. Wint watched him narrowly wondering at how he had lost his eagerness.

"Be dark soon," Filway chuckled. "By God, it'll be one bitch of a fight—you just get in before dark."

"Tonight's good as any time," Masterson said.

Murray was thinking, "In the dark it would be too easy—or too hard. Christ, why doesn't he take his rabble and go back to Dodge!" He had the army mistrust of civilians in a fight; Masterson's riders were too quiet. He wondered why he didn't have the courage to order them back to Dodge City, at gun's point, if necessary.

"Getting late," Wint said. He was staring at his watch again.

"We'll go up," Murray said to Trask. "Bring along the infantry for support. We'll attack if they show signs of moving out."

Trask grinned.

"Mind if we go?" Masterson asked.

"Stay with the infantry," Murray said shortly. "You'll get your fill later, Sheriff. Meanwhile, I'm giving the orders."

"Not too many," Masterson said.

"Still, I'm giving them, Sheriff. Stay with the infantry."

The two men eyed each other; then Masterson nodded slowly. He was smiling just a bit, not in amusement, Murray thought. Murray barked orders and the cavalry filed away, the old scout in the lead, twisting back to look at the officers with tiny, dancing blue eyes. Wint rode in silence, but once he touched Murray's arm and nodded. Night fell; the blue column wound through tall grass, into little gullies. Murray advanced a thin spread of scouts, a dozen men fanwise before them.

169

"But not because they'll attack us," he explained to Wint.

Wint nodded, peering into the darkness that was not yet complete, the half night of the prairie that was like a song, the wind in chorus, the high bending grass, the twisted trees, the far shadow-line of horizon with the infinitely pale sky, lost of sunlight, unredeemed.

"I feel I know them well enough," Wint said. "Every move they make."

"I feel that way," Murray agreed.

"You don't get to know Indians," Wint said. "You don't get to think of them as people. Unless it's this way."

"They were wrong."

"I suppose so. Funny how they always find a creek or river."

"They know the country."

"I wonder. They don't have maps, nothing like it. I remember showing a map once to a Sioux chief. He couldn't grasp it, couldn't make anything out of it."

"They remember," Murray said.

The pickets were returning. "They're there," Murray was told, "camped across the creek, on high ground. Dug in."

The old scout chuckled with pride. "What did I tell you?"

It was quite dark now, and Murray could see for himself the trailing sparks, the increasing light of many fires. They weren't trying to hide; they lit a beacon each night for all the world to see.

"I wonder where they learnt about trenches," Wint remarked.

170

Murray said: "They won't escape this time. We'll attack in the morning."

"Trask?"

"To hell with him! Tell the men to make camp."

Murray didn't bother to say to Trask the many things he might have said to him, that the men of the Fourth Cavalry were near exhaustion, that they had been in the saddle for almost twenty hours with only short rests, that any sort of night attack was a military gamble, that he didn't trust Masterson's men to lay hands on the Indian women. He let Trask rage while he sat in stony silence; and when Trask had finished, he said:

"If you wish to put all that in a report, Captain, you're at liberty to do so."

"And I shall!"

"Nevertheless, we'll attack in the morning."

And Trask was forced to abide by that, or else go ahead in the night with his single company of infantry. He chose to wait.

Meanwhile, Murray's men slept soundly. Not even the rumbling arrival of twelve more wagons interrupted their sleep. Eight of the wagons were a supply train from Fort Dodge, the other four Mizner's caravan making the long trek up from Indian Territory. The wagons, coming into camp, woke Murray. There was whiskey in the medical supplies of his own carts, and he had a few drinks, but when he tried to go back to sleep on his own camp-cot now, he tossed nervously. He gave it up, saddled his horse himself, and rode past the sentries down to the Indian camp. Their fires had burned down but men were awake, shadowy forms moving in front of the feeble glow. He reined in on his side of the creek, not so far but that they noticed him; he had the curious impression that he might have gone on into their camp without being fired on, greeted courteously in fact, greeted in their baffling, rippling tongue. He sat there for almost fifteen minutes before he rode back.

He woke Trask himself before the first gray hint of dawn was in the sky.

Murray said: "I'm sorry, Captain—about last night." He was almost humble. He said: "I've been down to their camp—they won't go away. They must be very tired."

Trask, sleepy, uncertain, merely nodded. He couldn't make anything of Murray.

"We'll go in on foot," Murray said rapidly, eager for the other's compliance. "They have guns, most of them, not too much ammunition, but they know how to shoot. The chief, Little Wolf, he's not like any Indian I've ever seen; he's cold—"

"A cavalry charge," Trask began.

"No, no—we've tried that before. I've lost men, a lieutenant, a sergeant. The only way is to go in on foot. Even if horses got through, that place is full of women and kids. I want to keep it in hand."

"These aren't the first Indians I've ever seen," Trask said impatiently.

"I know—but these Dog Soldiers, they don't die easily. And they want to die. You have to understand that. They're not out raiding; they're going home to the north, back to the Powder River country. They know how impossible that is, and because of that they've lost fear of everything. They're dead already; you have to know Cheyennes to understand that. And because they're dead, nothing more can happen to them."

Trask shrugged. "You don't sound convincing, Captain."

"I'm sorry."

"Do you want my men to go ahead—or to support yours?"

"To support mine," Murray said slowly. "I'd like you to keep Masterson and his posse with you."

Trask nodded, and Murray walked heavily back to his own men, to awaken Wint, to awaken the bugler, to stand in the cold, wet grass while events he knew only too well repeated themselves.

They moved down to the creek with the wagons in the van. It was Murray's plan to get as close as possible, using the sixteen lumbering carts as a barricade. He had the wagons swung in a circle and then backed into the creek, side by side.

The Indians were waiting, crouched in the ditches they had dug, the women, children and ponies in the rear, protected by a fold of the ground. They showed their faces, some of the Dog Soldiers, nothing else, a glint of the morning sun on their rifle barrels, nothing else, no sound, no war cry. But their chief, Little Wolf, sat in clear view on the edge of the ditch, smoking a pipe. Smiling, Murray thought, only the distance was too great to know certainly.

If he were smiling, he would not smile long. He sat like

a raised-up lump of the earth, leathery, folded, curiously like a fist, old, old as the yellowed prairie hills behind him, and smiling—

Murray bunched his men behind the wagons, now in long rifle range. The men pressed close to the six-mule teams, making the animals nervous, making them pull at the drivers, who were hanging onto the front-team bits. The drivers cursed, complaining that either way the teams would bolt, once the shooting started. The cavalrymen swung their sabers behind them, gripped carbines with both hands.

Twenty or thirty yards to the rear, Trask spread his men in a skirmish line, and behind them were the remaining men of the posse, sullen, bitter, hating the soldiers as much as the Cheyennes, ready to break out, ready to become hysterical in either fear or fury. And off to one side, low on the twisting creek, was the morning sun, bright in alliance with the pale blue sky.

Wint was white-faced. Murray smiled at him and nodded, his heart full of sudden and strange compassion for the younger man. Wint touched the trumpeter, who began to play, calling as if by magic a swarm of birds out of the high grass. The cavalrymen pushed between the wagons and formed their thin skirmish line. Murray was ahead of them, Wint off to one side and a little to the front. Murray kept glancing back, motioning with his drawn saber for them to close in or spread out. Some of them were grinning, others biting their lips anxiously, others white with dead faces, others crouched and wary as animals. Behind them, perched high on one of the supply wagons, Murray saw the old scout, mouth open, excited, watching the thing as he might an unusual show prepared solely for his benefit.

The men advanced in good order, slowly, steadily, slashing a surf of bending stalks through the grass, which concealed them from the waist down.

Murray told himself: "Don't look back any more. It will happen soon—soon."

His heart was hammering wildly, swelling seemingly, like an angry pulse absorbing all of him; his mouth was dry, nasty; his eyes were wet. With every step he fought the desire to run, to scream, to do anything but advance steadily and calmly upon the Indian camp. Wint was a bit ahead now, and Wint glanced back, smiling; he appeared gay, swinging his saber carelessly against the grass. Murray looked ahead; they were so close now that he could see the swell of Little Wolf's cheeks as the old chief puffed on his pipe. The Cheyenne heads were coming up over the trench, sharp and clear in the new, slanting sunlight.

"Commence fire!" Murray cried hoarsely.

Wint must have signaled the trumpeter to play, but the thin notes were lost in the crackle of rifle fire. The men were running, bending low; and then the Cheyennes fired, all together. The old chief hadn't moved.

Murray stood alone, and Wint was yelling at him; he didn't know what words, if words at all. He was barely twenty yards from the Cheyenne trench, but he stood alone; his men were down in the grass. The chief had taken the pipe out of his mouth. Murray's wonder centered in his own existence; he walked back as a man strolls on an avenue.

175

"You fool, get down!" Wint was crying.

Murray, aware suddenly like a man waking from a drugged sleep, flung himself into the grass, rolling over and over and coming to rest against a trooper who did not move, a trooper bent bowlike with a strained face smiling up at the sky. Murray touched the man who was dead. Murray crawled through the grass, past other men who were firing, on until he came to Wint. Curled up, Wint was trying awkwardly to bind a wounded hand with his handkerchief. Murray said: "Let me—" Wint whistled as Murray twisted the handkerchief. Cambrun, from somewhere in the grass, called over the noise of firing:

"Captain! Captain!"

"Yes?"

"Shall we try to advance?"

"Keep up the fire!"

"Advance?"

"No!"

Murray raised himself carefully. Powder smoke lay over the trench. The old chief had disappeared.

Gatlow was calling: "Captain Murray?"

"Yes?"

"Captain Trask has sent a man up. He says the posse cleared out."

"Just as well."

Wint had raised himself. He said: "My God, the fools!"

Kneeling with his head just above the grass, Murray saw the posse cross the creek about half a mile to the east, sharp and silhouetted in the sunlight. He saw them scramble up the high bank, bunch for a moment, and then spill out for the flank of the Cheyennes' camp. Evidently, others had seen them too, for a detachment of Dog Soldiers appeared from around the shoulder of the bluff upon which they were camped. The Dog Soldiers rode in a wide arc; the posse drove full against them.

The fight took on the whirling, kaleidoscope frenzy that only Indians on horseback can give a cavalry charge. The posse fell back. The Cheyennes drove against them, like spinning, cutting knives.

"Tell the men to fall back to their horses!" Murray roared.

They met Trask's infantry down in the creek bottom. "Keep them in play!" Murray told him. "I'm going to support the posse. If we can draw more of them out, it will be over!"

As Murray and his troopers gained the shelter of the wagons, Trask led his men in a running charge against the trench. Murray felt sick and helpless as he watched the infantry cut down by the burst of fire from the Cheyenne trench.

His men were mounting when the mule wagons bolted. What was left of Trask's infantry ran after the wagons. The posse was broken, in flight, leaving dead and wounded behind, leaving a memory that would stay with Dodge City for many years.

Murray led his cavalry full against the Cheyenne trench, but this time the Indians were mounted, leaping onto their little ponies with incredible speed, spinning in front of him, giving back, shouting taunts and wild war cries. He topped the rise and saw that the Indian village was already in flight, leaving the thin line of mounted braves to hold him off.

One of the wagons, an ammunition cart, had over-turned a half mile down the creek. The little band of Dog Soldiers who had dispersed the posse dashed down on the wagon, loaded themselves with cartridges, and sped away.

Trask was attempting to re-form his men. Masterson and what was left of his posse limped back to bear Trask's bitter reproaches. One by one the mule teams were rounded up and brought in.

Trask rode up to the trench and stared moodily at the two dead Indians who lay there.

For the cavalry, the running fight stretched out until noon. On horseback, the Cheyennes were devils, hardly human, twisting, spinning, as difficult to hit as birds on the wing, fighting like savage wolves if the village was menaced, running otherwise in easy flight from the heavy gray horses.

At noon, Murray drew his men off; the Cheyennes camped on a boulder-strewn hump. The troopers dis-mounted, sweating, dirty, tired. Wint, the bandage off his wounded hand, was flecked with blood all over. Gatlow was hatless; a spear had rent his breeches from hip to knee. Baily, an Ohio boy, had an arrow in his lung; he had stayed with them, somehow, dying all the time; they laid him out in the grass, and afterwards they buried him there in the tall grass without a name for his grave.

They attacked the Cheyenne camp and were driven off again. They followed the Indians in a wide circle to the west. The gray horses were run out; they hadn't the stamina of the wiry little ponies. They held to the Cheyennes, sometimes a mile away, sometimes more, sometimes less, but they could not ride the Indians down. They slogged on, into the weary sunset, sullen, bitter men, holding the trail like a defeated old hound dog will. They reined in sometimes and fired their carbines in futile rage. They spurred on their lathered horses, cursing them, pleading with them.

The sun dipped, and the Cheyennes camped again. The cavalrymen dismounted, sank to the ground, rubbing their numbed legs. The gray horses stood and drew choking, rasping breath.

Murray said to Wint: "They're not human—not men."

"You'll go in again?"

"I suppose so—in the morning."

"They won't be here in the morning," Wint said with curious certainty.

And Murray nodded.

Half the night was spent when the Cheyenne village moved out. The bugle called the troopers to life, and they stumbled about sleepily in the dark, saddled, mounted. But they rode slowly now, with no assurance; and when Murray signaled a halt again, they listened where there was no other sound to hear than the sobbing of their horses' breath and the barking of a lone coyote.

179

MATTERS OF JUSTICE

Six men, coming into Fort Dodge on foot, told the following story. They told it slowly, haltingly, with the word-measurement of men who must reassure themselves of their own existence. The men were buffalo hunters, hide hunters as distinguished from flesh hunters; and that distinction must be understood. For one thing, the flesh hunters killed that men might be fed, and by the prodigious effort of their killing, some became a legend. Such a one was Buffalo Bill Cody, who performed for the railroad workers the task of slaughter-house expert. His work, except for the utensils he used, was no different from that of any slaughterer in any commercial meat-packing house: no more praiseworthy, no more heroic, no more blameworthy. He differed from other professional slaughterers in that he toured the world with a wild-west show, loaded his revolvers with buckshot, and gained fame as a great hero and a great shot and a great liar.

181

However, he and the other flesh hunters did not account for any appreciable number of the millions of buffalo that roamed the plains. The buffalo were destroyed, in unbelievably few years, by the hide hunters. The hide hunters were after leather, pure and simple, the flesh and bones be damned; they were placer miners, skimming wealth from the land, and in their wake they left a horrible trail of carnage. They followed the herds with their great, heavy-wheeled wagons, and with their big buffalo guns, they killed and killed and killed. They worked usually four to two, two to kill, four to skin. Skinning was a science, slit the belly, slit the legs, skin and rip. A good man could tear the hide off a cow in seven minutes; the hides were piled green in the big wagons.

In the lush sixties, there were fortunes in hide hunting. Companies were formed, hard men for the killing and harder ones for the skinning. With forty or sixty or a hundred wagons they trailed the herds, and morning, noon, and night, their guns thundered. For miles over the plains drifted the charnel smell of rotting flesh until even the gorged coyotes spurned the meat. Such killing America had never seen before; and it is doubtful if ever before in the history of man millions of pounds of edible meat rotted in the hot sun. Even the incredibly abundant buffalo could not persist in the face of such slaughter. When the railroads first spanned the continent, trains had to wait sometimes for a whole day while a buffalo herd was crossing the tracks; five years later the buffalo were rare; ten years later they were practically non-existent, only a memory perpetuated in a million bleached skeletons.

For the Indians, this was the one crime of many crimes which they least understood, which hit them hardest and most tragically. On the plains, from time beyond memory buffalo had been their life; the flesh gave them food, the hides gave them clothes, robes, tepees, armor; the bones gave them weapons and needles; the teeth became ornaments, the sinews thread, the entrails pots and sacks, the hoofs glue; and even the waste, the droppings, was precious fuel, buffalo chips that burned with a warm, even flame. There was no waste, and down to the last drop of blood the buffalo was absorbed by the wandering tribes who killed only what they could use and looked upon the herds as an eternal source of sustenance.

As the period of hide-hunting came to a climax, as the Indians saw the herds vanish and the plains littered with the waste flesh, they conceived an almost insane hatred for the hunters. For no reason they could comprehend, these men were destroying them and their way of life. Flesh hunting, even on a great scale, they could understand; but complete destruction and complete waste were the most evil of all crimes. For with the buffalo went all that had been of the Plains Indian.

It was against this background that the hide hunters told their story to the people at Fort Dodge. Six of them, bearded, dirty, stinking of their trade and of filth, they were not pretty to look at. They begged tobacco and chewed it and spat and talked.

They were working north from the Arkansas River with two wagons. Not like in the old days; now the game was played out. You had to fine-comb the plains to spot a herd, and when you did it was thirty, forty, fifty cows.

Nobody became rich buffalo hunting; the big companies had given it up; it paid for powder and shot and maybe a night at Dodge.

But this time they had been lucky. They had run a herd south of the Pawnee Fork. McCabe and Ward, the two who had been riding circle, searching for animals, spotted the herd and drove it back toward camp, shooting like mad and yelling at the top of their lungs. That gave the other four time to harness the wagon, pile into it, and intercept the herd. None of the herd escaped; there were seventeen cows and a bull, and they got every one of them. That was a big haul; for those times, a good haul and a lucky one. It was good, careful shooting too, with all the animals lying in a circle of less than a half-mile diameter.

They finished a quart of whiskey on that, and then they skinned without even reloading their guns. They had plenty of flour and bacon, and as with most hide hunters, they had an aversion for buffalo flesh. So they only took two tongues from the meat, nor did they bother to move the carcasses.

Indians were the last thing in the world they thought of. As far as they knew, there were no Indians within a hundred miles. They built chip fires, set the tongues to slow-roast, mixed dough and put it in the sun to sour. It was about three o'clock in the afternoon then, and they lay about the fire, smoking and finishing another bottle of whiskey. They talked of one thing and another, mostly of how good their luck had been, but not of Indians. They still had no thought of Indians—not even when they heard the hoofbeats. If they speculated about the

hoofbeats, they passed it off as some ranch outfit returning from the range.

Then, when the Indians came over the lap of the land,
through the yellow grass, breaking like foam, a tribe of
three hundred souls, of men and women and children,
the buffalo hunters galvanized into action, clawed for
their guns, to load, to do something. The tide swept over
them and around them; they stood helpless, while the
guns were torn from their hands; it spilled like water, the
braves leaping from their ponies, the children rolling off
and clawing between the feet of the men, the women
pressing close to see something of it, the little ponies nervously pawing the ground, the dogs barking.

The six hide hunters stood in the center of a milling,
storming mob. Anderson, a big, slow, dull-witted man,
understood some Cheyenne; so did McCabe, who had
once kept a store and traded with the Arapahoes. Both
agreed that in those few tense moments they had been
closer to death than ever before in their lives. The
eighteen carcasses were scattered about in plain sight,
dumb proof along with their hide-loaded wagon. The
Indians were lean, famished, haggard; the rage poured
out of them the way water pours from a broken dam.
Anderson's shirt was torn off, his skin scratched by the
women; the others were similarly handled. The children
cursed them and bit at their legs. Then, when the men
finally made an arm-linked circle about them, forcing
back the women and children, the hide hunters considered it only a reprieve, perhaps only a prelude to some
awful form of torture.

Ward was a little drunk; his nerve went almost instantly. He began to cry like a baby. Anderson said to him:

"Damn you, Ward, shut up!"

McCabe said afterward that Ward only made it worse; the Indians were smiling, either with contempt or amusement. They didn't appear to understand English. Ward tried pleading with them, but they didn't seem to understand anything he said; or perhaps they didn't want to.

The braves had made a circle about them, and now they pushed back, leaving a cleared space with the six buffalo hunters huddled in the center. Once the women realized that the men were going to do things their way, they went off to butcher the meat.

"They must have been hungry," McCabe said, "starving."

The way they went for the meat proved that. They broke up the wagon for fuel. They roasted the meat in thin slices, so that it would do quickly. The children came first, chewing and whimpering while they ate. It takes a lot of hunger to make food something painful.

Meanwhile, the chiefs had taken the situation in hand. McCabe, telling the story at Fort Dodge, drew a picture of Little Wolf. "Not a tall man," McCabe said, recalling the impression of height Cheyennes gave—"not a tall man, but seldom—seldom. I didn't reckon to be tortured then. I figured to die, but not torture."

Little Wolf came forward, and the Indians watched him the way they'd watch a father. But there was an older man there, "—old and dried like an old apple," McCabe said; and Little Wolf kept that older man by his side, as if he were the father of Little Wolf.

"It might have been Dull Knife," McCabe admitted. "He was big chief, all right, and they never talked his name like they talked Little Wolf's name. I guess it was Dull Knife."

McCabe made something of their talk when it wasn't fast and furious. A lot of hate and bitterness; Anderson agreed with that—the rest knew no Cheyenne. The rest were waiting for their deaths, but for Anderson and McCabe a word here and a word there made their doom take shape and form. There was cold hate in the young men, not hot and wild, as you would expect from Indians, but controlled, purposeful! The six buffalo hunters knew no more about the Indians than that they had come over the lip of the ground, a tribe moving, a village taking its tepees from here to there. But where from and why, none of the six knew.

The chiefs held them back. Anderson didn't know why, neither did McCabe; but they were alive to bring the story of what happened back to Fort Dodge. The old chief whose name was Little Wolf had taken out his pipe, stuffed it full of coarse tobacco, walked to the fire for a coal, come back puffing. And the buffalo hunters, even Ward, knew that they would live while the old man wandered in the circle, puffing his pipe, building a wall of his strange presence between the Dog Soldiers and their prey.

It was a curious pipe. "A corncob," McCabe said. "Not one of them damned heathen things, but a ten-cent corncob."

Little Wolf smoked anxiously, thoughtfully, his broad, leathery face perplexed and wrinkled. And he went on

187

walking and smoking, carrying the lives of six men in the folds of his old, tattered blanket, impervious to the wolf-cries of his bitter people. They wanted death; they stood in the circle, chewing half-cooked meat hungrily, and demanding deaths between bites. They told over again how a million and more buffalo had gone from the plains—

Men like these, hide hunters.

McCabe didn't know what kind of a hold the old chief had. "He was a seldom man," McCabe said.

Because he kept the wall raised between death and the hide hunters—because his strength was the passive but iron will of a man who couldn't bear to be crossed. All the buffalo hunters agreed with that; the braves were afraid to cross the old chief, not afraid with common fear, but with something else.

"He was seldom," McCabe insisted, as if that one word said all that could be said. The officers, listening to the story at Fort Dodge, said that Little Wolf was bad medicine, very bad medicine.

The storm of demands, abuse, rage, white-cold anger broke over Little Wolf, but he ignored it until he had smoked his pipe and thought of the thing. Then he knocked out his pipe, pointed the blackened stem at the hide hunters, and went into a talk. Silence gathered then, and even the women and children gathered close and respectful to hear Little Wolf's talk. It was hard for any of the white men to catch the drift of his speech; in Cheyenne, a word is a word, but a sentence is also a word and ten sentences can come off like flowing water, all a word. The tongue is strange and rippling, pitched like music, with all the shadings, renderings, variations, and complexities of primitive speech. So McCabe got only a little of what he said, and Anderson even less. The others waited for death.

"I was listening like a man crazy for a drink," McCabe told them at the fort. "Can someone give me a drink?" They gave him a drink; he wiped his mouth and said: "The talk was a matter of justice."

"How did you make that out," they asked him, "if you didn't sabbe his talk?"

"I didn't sabbe," McCabe admitted. "You got to be a God damned breed to sabbe Dog Soldier. But I got the drift—"

But McCabe didn't know, and none of the buffalo hunters standing in that circle of death knew where the Cheyennes had come from, how they had come, or where they were going. They sensed some of it, but only sensed the abstract in justice—or injustice—a people, a nation, a fragment of all that walked the earth in human form, harried by great forces, ringed in and driven like wild beasts, a people whose intrinsic right was cause for death and only death.

And here, within that people, within the circle of their hot, lusting bodies, six miserable, filthy buffalo hunters . . .

The Dog Soldiers began to turn away, their faces fixed in a reflection of their own ultimate doom. Little Wolf had finished speaking, stood with his eyes on the ground and with much of the stony strength gone out of him. He said to the hide hunters, in Cheyenne, slowly:

"Leave this place—"

The circle opened, and the six hide hunters ran, not

understanding, thinking this only a beginning of the torture, the Indian way, the Dog Soldier way. They ran like mad, their hearts pounding, their breath sobbing out; they lost their strength, walked, ran again. But they were free, alone.

That was the story they told at Fort Dodge.

There was another story old "Cump" Sherman told the reporters, gathered around him in the basement office of his Washington home. "Cump" was fifty-eight, virile, potent, a legend alive. When he became excited at a press conference, he often rose and stamped around like a shaggy lion. The reporters called that "marching through Georgia," smilingly but not with disrespect. You couldn't laugh at Sherman's adoration for the country he had fought for, cut in two that it might exist, scarred it so brutally that the scar would last forever perhaps, yet healed it too. Sherman was sincere; he lacked imagination and brilliance, but he was sincere.

So when they gathered around him, firing questions, demanding: "But about this war, General?" his answer was simple and earnest.

"Gentlemen," he said, "you do more harm than good with that kind of talk."

"But there is a war in Kansas, General?"

"A war? No!"

"But surely Indian raiding, General. The reports are coming in every hour, from Dodge, from Coldwater, Greensburg, Medicine Lodge, Pratt. We've a listing of eighty civilians murdered, twelve ranches destroyed, troops fighting all over the state, Indians on the warpath."

It was then that the general rose, paced angrily, and told the reporters: "You understand, gentlemen, this is not war, not even something to be dignified with the word rebellion. Don't call it war. These savages are murdering, and rest assured, gentlemen, every murder will be avenged. This is the last Indian raid this country will be made to suffer . . ."

Then, when the reporters had gone, Sherman wrote the order that placed General George Crook in full command of all operations on the plains, with orders to bring down the Cheyennes the way one brings down a marauding wolf.

Crook superseded General Pope, and Crook, as a seasoned Indian fighter, was under no illusions as how to proceed. He had fought Cheyennes before, in their native Wyoming, on the Powder River, in the Black Hills, on the plains. He knew the Plains Indian, and he did not make the mistake of considering it good military strategy to oppose a hundred Dog Soldiers with a hundred troops, or with two companies of cavalry or with three. In this matter, where there would be so little glory, he wanted not glory but results, a game bag, a prize; so that he could write to his commander-in-chief, in a matter-of-fact way: "I have laid hands on Little Wolf's Cheyennes, as requested, and am sending them south in irons and under guard."

So Crook drew a circle on the map. The circle swept through Kansas and Nebraska and took in part of Colorado; and within that circle, somewhere in the vast sweep of plains and rivers, hills, gullies, grass and sand were the Cheyennes, probably near the center, certainly not too distant from the center. And it would be days, weeks before they could drive out of that circle. Here there was no need for haste, only for thoroughness.

The thoroughness began with a review of his forces. All told, nearly twelve thousand troops were now under his command, either within or close to the edge of that great circle. General Crook drew careful arrows in towards the center of the circle. Then, writing neatly on slips of paper, he translated the arrows into words. The words became electric impulses clicking under the fingers of men with green eyeshades, and the impulses became movement.

The movement stirred in the north, at Fort Robinson, where five troops of the Third Cavalry saddled and filed out from the wooden gates.

The movement stirred in the deep reaches of Dakota Territory, at Fort Mead, where the Seventh Cavalry was stationed. These, the Seventh Cavalry, were Custer's old regiment, the same regiment that had gone down in bitter defeat more than two years before at Little Big Horn. Two years don't wipe out such a memory, the loss of two hundred and sixty-five men killed and fifty-two wounded, nor do two years lay the rumors whispered all over the plains country—that the Custer massacre was revenge for Custer's own cruel treatment of all Indians, that Custer, left for last by the Sioux and Cheyennes, left alive that they might even old scores, took his own life in the end. For the Seventh, the memory was a carefully stimulated desire for revenge, and now as ten companies of them rode south from Fort Mead, they looked eagerly ahead to three hundred Cheyennes. It would even the score, nor would they make prisoners.

Major Thornburg, at Sidney, Nebraska, put his men on flatcars. He put a howitzer on a flatcar too, and the artillerymen made a pool of four bits each for the first shell.

From Fort Wallace, the Nineteenth Infantry set out under Colonel Lewis.

Colonel Lewis marched his men south and east, on a direct line between Fort Wallace and Dodge City. According to Crook's plan, the operations were not to be directly against the Indians, but in the form of concentric circles tightening. In this case, the Nineteenth Infantry was to be the western fold of a series of loops, a fence more than a barrier. Lewis and even Crook suspected that the Cheyennes were about fifty miles to the east and certainly far to the south. Nevertheless, Lewis took with him six Pawnee scouts and kept them flung out ahead of him as vedettes.

The Pawnee scouts were mounted, as were the officers and a small detail of cavalry which accompanied the infantry. The marching men, four by four, a snake-like line undulating over the prairie, were made slightly more mobile by eight supply wagons. The men had only their guns to carry, and under good conditions they could do thirty miles in daylight. Altogether, it was a good, solid little force, and Colonel Lewis was not worried concerning the issue if they should intercept the Indians.

But about other things, his concern was greater; his

furrowed brow was a shield to smaller worries. It bulked large and bothered him persistently that he had not written to his sister. He was careful about that, and letters went out with studied regularity. Now as he rode, he composed the letter he had forgotten, explaining his money troubles, the argument he had with Major Clair, all the petty jealousies that combined in a plains command, the lack of security, the deadly monotony—

There was something wrong with his back, sharp darting pains that converged at the base of his spine. He put in the imagined letter a long dissertation on kidneys and liver; his sister would understand the plaintive fear that came over him—two days in the saddle, and racked with pain already, old, tired. He glanced up, almost with resentment, at the three Pawnee vedettes dashing back with all their barbaric flare and stimulated excitement. He didn't like Indians; he was a fastidious man; it made him wince even to shake hands with one of the Pawnee scouts.

He asked sharply as they reined alongside of him, grinning so broadly and childishly:

"What is it now?"

"By Jesus, God damn Dog Soldier!"

"Why," he wondered, "do they learn to swear first?" He felt there was something notably obscene in meaningless blasphemy from the lips of a savage.

He asked casually: "You sure?—you see right?"

They grinned and nodded and spilled out in broken English the story of a fortified camp some miles ahead, on Famished Woman's Fork, a little creek Lewis had never heard of before. Several of the company commanders and Captain Fitzgerald, in command of the cavalry detail, had

194

gathered around. They expressed amazement and disbelief. The Pawnee scouts described trenches, and Fitzgerald said he had never heard of any Indians digging trenches. The others agreed.

"It sounds incredible," Lewis said. "Better take your men over and have a look." Actually, he didn't believe they were Indians, not with trenches. He mistrusted the Pawnee scouts, looked upon them as children mentally, capable of inventing fantastic tales. After Fitzgerald and his cavalry had gone, he went back into his reverie of self-pity.

He was startled and uncertain when Fitzgerald returned and reported that there was a band of Indians up ahead, dug in as the Pawnees had claimed, not doing much, resting, cooking, sitting on the lip of their trenches with just one or two mounted men out and watching.

"They don't seem disturbed," Fitzgerald said. "Not even when they saw us. Didn't pay any attention—stayed there like cocks of the walk."

"Dog Soldiers?" the colonel asked incredulously, feeling like a surreptitious lottery player who finds himself with the winning ticket.

"The Pawnees say so."

"Can't understand it, unless they have wings. They were east of Dodge last thing I heard. Why would they dig trenches?" he said tiredly. "We'll go over and round them up—take them along to Dodge in the wagons."

The company commanders gave orders; the long column turned its head toward Famished Woman's Fork; the cavalry spread out like bees on the honey-covered face of a dull bear. Colonel Lewis tried to remove his thoughts from the far east, the beautiful, clean, civilized east, to an annoying band of murderous Indians. His one positive feeling toward the Indians was of resentment, that they were where they should not be, that they had dug trenches, that they flaunted their outlawry in his face, in his thoughts. He resented them the way a police officer at the end of a hard day resents a dirty, obstreperous drunk.

He gave orders to quicken the pace of the infantry.

As they neared the creek, Lewis made out a line of mounted Cheyennes, spread out, twenty men in all perhaps, motionless on their ponies, watching with their faces lit by the descending sun, like masked actors in the footlit glory of a finale. The Pawnee scouts began to whoop and wave their guns, but the Cheyennes didn't move.

"Tell them to come in with their arms up," Lewis called to Fitzgerald, straining his eyes meanwhile to make out the trenches. He heard Fitzgerald's voice, careful, repetitious, saying the same thing over and over again in an effort to bridge the gap of language. The Pawnees rode in circles, whooping, screaming insults in their own impossible tongue. The infantry spread out in a double skirmish line. The Cheyennes still sat motionless, big men with dark, impassive faces; and behind them smoke rose from their camp, smoke gracefully tinted with the peaceful colors of sunset.

Fitzgerald rode back, and Lewis realized how impossible and barbaric the whole situation was. "No English," Fitzgerald explained.

"The Pawnees?"

"No, they don't sabbe Cheyenne. Too excited—there'd

196

be hell and the devil to pay if I told them to go up there
and make signs."

"Take your cavalry and round them up," Lewis said in
the matter-of-fact tone of a police sergeant who dispatches
an officer to run in a gang of adolescents. Fitzgerald
nodded and rode forward with his detail of eighteen men.
The Pawnees gathered the situation, whirled their horses,
and dashed shrieking toward the Cheyennes. Fitzgerald
spurred his horse to overtake the scouts; he had drawn his
saber, as had his men.

The Cheyennes leaned forward in their saddles, aimed
carefully, lazily, it seemed, and fired. Three of the Pawnees
went limp, fell from their saddles, rolling like bundles
of brown rags. The cavalry recoiled back on the troops.
One Pawnee drove on and impaled himself on a Cheyenne lance; the others raced off to one side.

The Cheyennes rode back to their camp. They dismounted in plain sight of the troops. Women led their
horses away, and the men joined others in the long trench,
still impassive, still waiting.

Fitzgerald's men, dismounted now, joined the infantry.
The captain's face was dull and still white with surprise.
Lewis' face twitched in little jerks of anger, but his fury
was controlled and indignant rather than hateful. He had
dismounted, and now he walked in front of the infantry,
each step painful and causing a spasm of agony in his
back. The troopers were watchful and wary, crouching as
they advanced.

Colonel Lewis, sword in hand, advanced as a discipli-
narian, intent upon his purpose. His purpose was to chas-
tise and punish, and he had no admiration for the old In-

197

dian chief who sat on the piled earth in front of the trench, smoking a dirty old corncob pipe, weaponless, smiling slightly with a smile that held more of pity than amusement. Colonel Lewis was leading a charge of trained veteran soldiers; he had neither fear nor respect for the Indians. That way, intently, he led his men into a blazing maw of fire.

The Cheyennes had fired all together, volley fire, directed by the waving arm of the old chief who sat on the edge of the trench. The troops tried to stand up before it, come into it, but it beat them back like an iron lash. They tried to shoot the old chief, but he sat and smoked and nothing appeared to disturb him.

They fell back, bitter, bloody, leaving their dead behind them, leaving their colonel behind them. He was on his knees, pressing up from the ground, a bullet in his belly, dreams of the east in his blurring intelligence, indignation, no hate but resentment, wonder too as he fell over on his face and let the pain go out of him.

Fitzgerald himself went up for the body of Colonel Lewis. It was a very brave thing for him to do, not with any effort at concealment but walking boldly up from the sprawling ranks of his men. He walked up close enough to see the lines on the old chief's face. The Cheyennes were watching him, but they held their fire. The old chief was no longer smiling. As Fitzgerald straightened up, his colonel's body in his arms, he thought he could detect something of pity and deep sorrow in the brown, broad countenance. Then he turned his back on the Indians and returned to his men.

As evening came on, the Nineteenth Infantry gathered

behind a semicircle barricade of wagons. The junior officers were without purpose or animation, and often they glanced uneasily at the wagon which held Lewis' body. They put out sentries in case of an Indian attack, but no attack came.

And then, later on in the night, the sound of hoofs told them the Cheyennes were leaving, going off into the north and the darkness.

Driving north, they made a winding, jagged track that couldn't be surmised. Twelve thousand men, almost a division of United States troops, seasoned veterans of old Indian-fighting regiments, were trying to take the three hundred. And of the three hundred, only eighty and odd were men, and of those only half were braves in the prime of life.

The armies in blue were scouring Kansas. The long blue columns, cavalry, infantry, trainloads of artillerymen with snub-nosed howitzers, ranged back and forth. Sometimes they fought, and then the wounded and dead lay on the yellow-grass prairie.

Sometimes, cornered, the Indians broke up into groups of two and three. They stole a herd of two hundred and twelve horses; they left their own wiry little ponies behind them, used up, run to death. They cut cattle out of herds, ate, dashed on.

The riders of the Eagle Bar D ranch, twelve strong, coming in from the range with their chuck wagon, topped a rise of ground and saw the two Indians skinning a buffalo cow. The riders splashed forward, and the two Indians, glancing up, seeing them, ran for their ponies. One Indian reached his saddle with a long, running leap. The other fell with a bullet in his leg. They closed on the wounded Indian who was twisting desperately to reach his gun. Mark Ready, the foreman, kicked the gun away. Axel Green laced his spurred boot into the fallen Indian's face.

The other Indian rode off about three hundred yards before he turned his pony and halted to watch them. The range was too long for any sort of revolver practice and there were only two rifles in the party. Kling and Sanderson, both of whom were good rifle shots, had a few tries at the Indian, but without any success. Green wanted to go after him, but Ready said:

"No, we got one—to hell with the other."

Sanderson agreed. "That's a Dog Soldier," he decided, nodding at the Indian who lay on the ground with a broken leg and a bleeding face. "Maybe the whole herd's hereabouts."

The Indian who had escaped rode off slowly. The other lay on one elbow, motionless, not even looking at the riders, murmuring a strange, minor-key tune.

"What's that?"

"That's a death song," Sanderson said. Marcy, whose grandfather had been killed by Indians, who felt it incumbent upon himself to hate Indians a good deal more than most others hated them, grinned widely.

"What about him?" Green demanded.

"The dirty red bastard," Marcy said good-naturedly.

"Let him be," Ferguson said. Ferguson was the cook. "It's no business of ours."

The Indian kept his eyes on the ground, lying on his side and supporting himself with one elbow. He was a young man, under thirty, clean-featured, with a long, powerful body that swept into a barrel mass of chest and shoulder. If his lacerated face or broken leg gave him pain, he showed no sign of it. He lay perfectly still in his old dirt- and blood-stained buckskins.

"We'll find a tree," Ready decided— "give him a Christian finish."

"Hell, no!"

"Look, Ready," the cook said, "we got no call to lynch him. Maybe he's a Dog Soldier, maybe he ain't. There's nobody here knows that much about Injuns. But we got no call to lynch him."

"The hell he ain't—look at the moccasins!"

The moccasins, worn through at the soles, frayed and tattered, still showed signs of former glory, beaded all over with infinite care and patience.

"Dog Soldier moccasins," Sanderson agreed.

Ferguson glanced from face to face; half of the party were young, under twenty, lithe, brown-faced boys. Ferguson had grouped them and separated them during long nights of gentle ribbing; that was right; every range outfit ribbed the cook. And Ferguson had seen each of those boys in human display, the lonely selflessness of men who live simply.

"Don't lynch him," Ferguson said. "Christ, leave him alone here if you want him to die."

"Shut up, cookie," Marcy said.

201

No one else offered anything. They stood in a circle, looking at the fallen man but not at the cook. Ferguson went to the chuck wagon, got a dipper of water, and held it out to the Indian.

"Drinkee—you um drinkee?" Ferguson asked.

The Indian raised his eyes, stared at Ferguson a moment, then took the water and drank. He said something in his own tongue.

"Hell, tie him and put him on his horse," Ready snapped, driven by the fact that he had made his decision, that all of him the men knew was in making decisions and carrying them out.

Ferguson shook his head helplessly, turned around, and climbed into the chuck wagon. They tied the Indian onto his own horse and then proceeded stolidly for about two miles before they came to a tree large enough to hang a man on. It was a big, mottled cottonwood dipping over the edge of a creek. They looped a lariat over a branch, stood the Indian up with the noose on his neck, and tied the other end to the bone pommel of his pony's saddle.

Somehow, the Indian managed to stay erect on his one good leg. Dignity was the only thing he strove for; his face was impassive and without fear; his eyes were closed.

"I wish to hell he could say something," Sanderson murmured. "I sure hate to see a man die without saying something."

Then Ready lashed the pony away and the Indian hung in the air.

Ferguson bent over, starting his horses, saying: "We got to find a place to camp. I got to get chuck going."

At Fort Wallace, Murray and Wint and their two bearded, weather-stained companies of troopers changed horses. Back-tracking, riding across half the state of Kansas east to west, almost all of it north to south, they had driven over more than five hundred miles of country. They had taken the flesh and the heart from their horses. And they themselves were not in much better shape.

At Wallace, Murray and Wint had a bath and a shave; their men slept. Murray pored over maps, filed a report for Colonel Mizner, another for General Crook, and drank himself into a stupor at the officers' mess. Colonel Lewis had gone off with the infantry; the captain in command, Goodall, watched Murray with scarcely concealed contempt. When Murray said that Lewis was a fool for going off that way, only Wint's eyes kept Goodall from answering one insult with a better one. Wint put Murray to bed himself, only to be awakened two hours later.

"Have the men saddle," Murray said.

And Wint didn't argue, didn't reason, knowing something of what went on in Murray's soul, the aching pain that couldn't be satisfied until the prey was dragged down. Murray, still blurred with drink, mumbled:

"When a man sells himself, he sells all of himself."

They saddled the remounts, and Murray, slumped loosely on a white mare—for now they had whites and roans and browns and blacks to replace their big gray cavalry mounts—led the way from the fort. He led them all night, cursing, angry men, half asleep; and in the morning they slept, then went on again.

They quartered back and forth. They found a rancher who reported twelve beefs missing, and riding circle on

203

his range they picked up the trail. They found a place where the Indians had dressed the stolen cattle. They came to a creek where a rope hung from a cottonwood tree and near by there was a fresh dug grave.

"Open it," Murray said grimly, but not prepared for the sight of a lynched Dog Soldier whose body the troopers lifted out.

"I wonder who did it?" Wint asked.

They buried the body again, and Murray thought: "One less—how much can they stand?"

"We should be near them now," Wint said.

Murray drove on, cursing the motley lot of remounts that had none of the stamina of their regimental grays, but driving the horses without love or mercy. The next day, noontime, they found the place where the Cheyennes had recently camped.

"A long camp," Sergeant Chambrun said. "They kept those fires burning for hours."

Wint picked up an abandoned buffalo hide shield; it had a bullet hole close to the edge. "They lose faith in a shield when that happens," he explained to Murray.

They came on the Indians toward nightfall, and Murray raged and cursed because the weary horses could not overtake the fleeing village. Wint said:

"We have to rest. The men can stand it, but you'll kill the horses."

And Murray grudgingly called an hour's halt, an hour during which he paced slowly back and forth in the darkness. Wint came to him, placed an uncertain hand on his arm, and said:

"Look, Murray—we've been through a lot these past weeks."

"Yes?" Murray was suspicious, hostile.

"Can I tell you how I feel?"

"You can tell me," Murray said.

"This is routine—you're in the army. It doesn't matter how it began, why you went to the Point, why you became an officer. The thing is that you're here and this is a routine matter. When it's done, we'll forget it. There'll be other routine matters."

"Yes?"

"Only it's under your skin. You're letting those damned Dog Soldiers do something to you."

"They're doing it to all of us," Murray said. He couldn't tell Wint how it was to become empty, to lose faith in everything, the cause you served, the uniform you wore, the things you believed in.

He had the men up at the end of the hour and they were off again in the night. And that night, sometime, they caught up with the fleeing village, fought in the dark with bare sabers against a rearguard of the Cheyennes.

A strange, wild black fight that achieved nothing. The village fled away again and the cavalrymen slid from their saddles and fell asleep beside their mounts, without lighting fires.

The *Herald* reporter, Jackson, had come a long way and was tired, uneasy, lonely, in complete accord with anyone who expressed hatred or contempt for Oklahoma, soured inwardly by this knowledge of how lost he was away from the things he loved best, soft beds, good beer, talk, good talk, not the talk of a Quaker missionary, his wife, a schoolteacher, agency handymen. He had not come as far as another *Herald* reporter, the Stanley who had gone into Africa to find Doctor Livingstone, but he had come far enough. Once before, he had been in the territory, and now it amazed him that he should have ever forgotten the mental and physical torture of a sixty mile stage-coach ride. He was leaning back in a wicker chair in Agent Miles' parlor at Darlington and listening to Aunt Lucy say:

"But really, Mr. Jackson, this is not summer heat, but Indian summer, it's so much hotter in the real summer."

"Hotter?" Jackson said.

"Dry heat, you know," Agent Miles explained hastily. "Not so unpleasant as your eastern seaboard heat."

Jackson nodded and wiped his brow. They were such simple people, so plaintively on the defensive, so tremulously apprehensive about what a New York City newspaper might do to them, stretching its long, clawing fingers across two thousand miles of the land, that he hadn't the heart to beard them. He had long since come to the conclusion that there were no real villains; he had never encountered a subjectively bad man, the printed personage of evil, power, and brilliance. Stupidity, selfishness, smallness, fear—that he had found in plenty and everywhere, as well under the domed ceiling of the capitol as anywhere else. But real evil—

He asked himself: "What else was I expecting, Simon Legree?" They were two simple white-haired people who had their living out of the agency. If that were taken away from them they would be as lost as he if he were never again able to write a line in his life.

"The heat in the summer is unpleasant," Aunt Lucy said in a burst of confidence. "That's why we have so much trouble in the summer."

"I suppose so."

"People in the east are so ready to find fault," she said.

"Of course, they don't have much idea how it is out here," he temporized.

"It isn't nice. We don't complain, but there are so many things we could complain about."

He nodded; he supposed there was more than enough to say on their side. "But it couldn't have been only the heat to make them go off like that?"

"It's difficult to understand why savages do things," Agent Miles said. "Sometimes they're like children—"

"You really believe that?" Jackson asked curiously.

"Of course," Aunt Lucy said. "Why, I was just pointing out to John last night, about the windows. You see, they can't understand that windows are to look out of, not to look into. Whenever they pass the house they stop and press their faces against the windows. And you can't make them realize how wrong it is."

"Just like children in so many ways," Agent Miles said.

"But not just the heat," Jackson insisted gently. "After all, they did know that summer doesn't last forever."

"They were obstinate. Some Indians can be reasoned

with, but the Cheyennes are stiff-necked people, haughty and proud. Tell them to do this and they will do that. Tell them to live in the south, where the government takes care of them and they answer, no—we will live in the north."

"They had always lived in the north, hadn't they?"

"Yes—but so had other tribes settled in the territory now."

Jackson said: "Look, Mr. Miles, I'm trying to get at the bottom of this, not to involve you in unjust blame, but to make it clear to the readers of my paper why a minority group in this republic of ours cannot legally occupy the land they have lived on for hundreds of years. Don't you see that the problem goes deeper than your responsibility or mine, or this agency's. We're a nation of a hundred minorities held together by the simple principle that all men are created equal—politically, so that we won't quibble on the word. Right now, every armed force the United States controls in the plains country is devoted to the single object of destroying an Indian village whose only crime is that they wish to live in peace in their own land."

"Hadn't you better take that up with the Indian Office?" Agent Miles said uneasily. "I'm an agent—it's not for me to say whether it was right or wrong to bring the tribes into the territory."

"But I must know why they left here, why they chanced this crazy, impossible dash to Wyoming. If all you say is true, if you fed them and schooled them—"

"They are savages," Agent Miles said listlessly.

"Then I must ask to see your account books," Jackson said coldly, decided now that if he must browbeat Miles, he would. "If you refuse to answer the simplest questions—"

The two of them, the old man and the old woman, stared at the reporter foolishly. Miles shook his head wearily. Aunt Lucy, nervously clasping and unclasping her hands, said:

"But surely you don't believe—"

"I believe what I must. I told you my paper would be just with you. And we're not without power, as congressmen and senators and even presidents have had reason to know."

There was a long moment of silence, broken only by the ticking of a clock on the wall and the short, nervous creaks of Aunt Lucy's rocking chair. Then the old woman said:

"Tell him, John."

"Yes, it would come out anyway."

Aunt Lucy began to cry. "I thought it was wrong. But how does one know the difference between right and wrong? I told John, but how does one know?"

"Please," the reporter said—"I'm sorry."

"Three men ran away," Agent Miles said.

"Cheyennes?"

"Yes, the same village. That's against the agency law, and I realized that if they weren't punished there would be no stopping the thing. So I sent to the chief and told him to give me ten men to send to jail at the fort as hostages—"

"But the three men couldn't be captured or returned?"

"I don't think so," Miles said.

"Would the ten be sent to Dry Tortugas eventually?"

Miles nodded.

"That was when they went?" the reporter asked.

"The troops went to their camp for the ten men, with a howitzer."

"And that was all?"

"Almost all," Miles sighed. "The rest you must know, not enough food, malaria, no quinine, no medicine. I had to feed some, choose. Is it right to make a man choose who shall eat and who shall starve?"

The reporter said nothing, only sitting hunched forward staring at the red dust lines already engraved on his shoes. Miles rose, went to the table and took up an account book.

"These are some of the shortages," he said. "Beef, seven hundred thousand pounds, coffee, thirty-five thousand pounds, sugar, seventy thousand pounds, bacon, thirty thousand pounds, flour, three hundred and forty thousand pounds—"

"Shortages?"

"Just shortages," Miles said helplessly. "When you put that in your paper, I will no longer have the agency, but the food situation will be the same."

"Yet men starved," the reporter said coldly.

"Some starved and others died of malaria and others went out to hunt buffalo where there are no buffalo. But what could I do? I had to say who should eat and who shouldn't; I did my best. The Christian Indians, those even half civilized, I had to favor them over the savages who made nothing but strife and trouble."

"I suppose you had to."

"Don't be hard on us," Agent Miles said, as the reporter rose to go; and he nodded, not trusting himself to look back at the two old people.

PART EIGHT   October–November 1878

THE VICTORS AND THE
VANQUISHED

To GENERAL CROOK, the Indians were never lost—as they were lost to Murray, to Fitzgerald, to Trask, to Masterson. For Crook was a man who sat over a map, and on the map a hundred miles were an inch, and even ten inches could be contained within the converging lines of his twelve thousand troops. Crook sat like a man in his own backyard watching an ant make frantic efforts to escape. The ant never escapes, though his world is his own where he lives unconscious of the man.

The converging southbound troops from Sidney, North Platte and Kearney were executing a pincer movement. Three long arms, stretching south, they contained the Cheyennes comfortably and securely. And up from the south, Murray and his two cavalry companies drove like the piston of a pump.

The only exit was in the north, and this exit General Crook proceeded to close. The exit was a hundred and fifty miles wide, stretching from North Platte to Sidney along the Platte River, and Crook set out to close it so tight that a mouse could not crawl through. Between the two towns, the Union Pacific Railroad paralleled the course of the river, and Crook dispatched two troop trains, one moving east from Sidney, the other west from North Platte, both of them mounting howitzers. The trains, steaming like impatient dragons, crawled back and forth, night and day.

In addition to the trains, he stationed two cavalry companies at Ogallala, the geographical center of the exit; these cavalry companies were in constant telegraphic communication with Sidney and North Platte and at least half a dozen way stations along the line. They could be rushed immediately to any point where the Cheyennes might appear.

On the north side of the railroad, where the fork of the Platte River made an eastward-reaching point of land, infantry was spread out in an almost constant skirmish line. In the daytime, their patrols intercepted one another for a distance of almost a hundred miles; by night their fires burned like ancient warning beacons, over hill and valley and prairie and sandhill. Citizens of Ogallala and Sidney joined to augment the patrols, to keep the fires going, to be in on the finish fight.

Up from the south, the coming of the Cheyennes was spoken on shining webs of wire. The men in the green eyeshades took note from a wandering rangehand, a Mexican sheepherder, a lonely saddle bum, a rancher peering from shuttered windows; and under the green eyeshades, under the yellow light of oil-lamps, their nervous fingers tattooed the news, a fight on the Smokey Hill, an Indian camp on the south fork of the Republican River, cattle entrails to show where they had cut food out of a herd, twelve horses stolen from the Tent Circle Ranch, a broad trail in the soft bottom of a river-bed, smoking fingers across the sky, a drum of hoofs in the starry prairie night.

Lost, an Indian village dashing across the wasteland of northwestern Kansas and southwestern Nebraska, they were nevertheless followed by the eyes of a whole nation, men in Washington prepared to write finis to an unpleasant affair, editors prepared to swing one way or another, travelers prepared to see the Cheyennes range alongside their transcontinental train, newspaper readers prepared for the culmination of all thrills, Custer avenged, the nation freed from even a memory of the red men who had once called it their own.

The world knew when they crossed the north border of Kansas and the world knew when they forded the Republican River in southern Nebraska with two cavalry companies hanging on their flank. And then, when Murray and his two cavalry companies lost them, they themselves were not lost to the other men in blue.

Major Thornburg, at Sidney, wired Crook: "IT IS BELIEVED THE CHEYENNES WILL ATTEMPT A CROSSING OF THE PLATTE RIVER IN THIS VICINITY SOMETIME TOMORROW."

They crossed that same night, not at Sidney nor at North Platte, where they were most expected, where the troop trains ranged ceaselessly, but in the dead center of the trap, scarcely two miles from Ogallala, where the beacon lights burned like a chain of bright beads on the sandhills.

Afterwards, when the Cheyennes had passed through the net, when they had filtered through Crook's mouse-proof trap, the story of their crossing was pieced together. They came up through the night leading their horses, approaching the Platte River nearly opposite Ogallala. They must have been so close that they could see the lights of the town, the watch fires with the shadowy shapes of men passing before them. They had spread out in a long, thin line, in groups of two and three, walking beside their horses, soothing them, whispering to them, quieting them. A white man may know a horse, but a Cheyenne is part of his pony, able to impart desires with a touch of the hand, a caress, a whispered word.

That way, in little groups, leading their horses through the fine sand, they crept up to the railroad track. A boy on a troop train, a boy leaning back in a picnic mood, humming a song, delighting in the endless jockeying ride, broke off his song and said that he heard something like a horse's whinny. Afterwards that was remembered, but at the time they listened without hearing anything more. A dog at one of the watch fires barked warningly, but a dog will bark at a coyote; afterwards, that too was remembered. And there were tracks to tell a part of the story.

They must have moved their horses across the track as daintily as a circus performer treads a tight wire. They left a sluggish trail between the watch fires to show how slowly they had crept. Coyotes barked, and perhaps that was the way they called to each other. Here and there were depressions in the sand to show how they lay and waited with infinite patience. A dog came nosing up to one, not twenty yards from a watch fire, and the next day the dog was found strangled. The Dog Soldier must have crouched there, the still warm body of the dog against him, and listened to the men at the fire calling:

"Billy! Billy! God damn you, Billy, where in hell are you?" And then, helplessly: "That dumb hound won't find his way back before morning—" And in the morning the dog, his long, silky fur hardly rumpled, lay with his tongue out, telling his part of the story.

They must have gone on that way, slowly, patiently, silently for more than a mile, and the next day the ranchers, the Ogallala storekeepers, the troopers, shook their heads at the cunning of savages. But after the mile, they mounted and spurred into the north again . . .

Crook, in a royal fury, told Major Thornburg what he thought of the major's military astuteness, and Thornburg, burning with resentment and hatred, set out after the Cheyennes.

Murray, tied to the trail like a man burdened by a cross he must bear forever, crossed the North Fork of the Platte and plunged into the waste of sandhills that had swallowed the Cheyennes. A dozen miles north of the river, he met Thornburg's sullen cavalry. From that point, the little army of almost seven hundred men followed the trail together.

Thornburg's cavalry were fresh, neat, well-set soldiers. They stared in wonder at the worn, battered remnant of Murray's command, bearded, hollow-eyed men led by a lean and dark-faced specter.

And even Thornburg, suggesting, "Don't you think, Captain, that we can carry on from here? Your men need a rest and you're a long way from your post," saw the look in Murray's eyes and said no more.

Toward evening, they came to a place where the trail split, part going on to the north, another part branching westward into the vast, lonely domain of the sandhills. Just before the break, there were camp signs.

Thornburg looked at Murray, who decided: "I'll go on to the north, Major—if you don't mind?"

Thornburg shrugged; he ranked Murray, but he wanted no arguments with a madman. Wint sighed wearily, but said nothing. That night the two troops from Fort Reno made camp apart from the rest, and in the morning, Thornburg was not sorry to see them depart.

Thornburg followed the trail into the sandhills. The going was hard and progress slow. The horses' hoofs sank deep into the powdery sand, and when the wind blew, it sent a hail of fine, sharp grit into the men's lungs. They rode on grimly, trying to shield their faces and mouths. When they made their camp late in the afternoon, they had come barely twenty miles. They camped in a little hollow where a bulky pillow of low knolls protected them somewhat from the rising wind.

The men were strangely silent and apprehensive as they watched the blood-red sun munch into the sparsely grassed hummocks. The place was lonely and silent, not a desert and not a prairie, a domain where there was no life, not even the flight of birds, not even the chirp of crickets. If anything, it was like a wild, forsaken beach where the sand dunes went on forever.

That night a wind picked up the sand and sent it running like a river, and in the morning the sand was still spilling in little whirlpools; the men coughed and spat and tried to shake the sand from their clothes and boots. But it was everywhere, in their food, in every tiny crevice and fold their skin made. And the horses were nervous; they had to be spurred on the almost obliterated trail.

Lieutenant Brady suggested to the Major: "Don't you think, sir, we ought to do something about water? We're running low."

"So are they," the major said shortly, nodding at the trail.

By noon, the trail was gone, washed out in the spilling sand.

They went on for the rest of that day in the direction the Indians had taken; they made a silent camp, at which time the officers went around and collected the canteens. There was precious little water left. They doled out a cup apiece to the men; the rest of the canteens lay in a pile, guarded by Sergeants Rain and Morrisey.

At dawn, when the bugle sounded, the sun was lifting itself in a weary haze. Sand and mist mingled in a low-hung curtain. The men took their water rations sullenly, seeing their canteens loaded in rattling heaps on the pack horses. Major Thornburg walked to one side with Captain Alexton; the other officers gathered in little groups, watching the two bend over a map.

Alexton knew something of the sandhill country. Until a month ago, he had been stationed in the north, at Fort Robinson. Now Thornburg asked him:

"Do you know where we are, Captain?"

"Going in this direction," the captain said, "we should have reached the North Fork."

"It seemed so from the map. It's west of us?"

"I think so—then it bends north. We can't miss the river if we go south."

"The Dog Soldiers wouldn't go south—"

"No."

Major Thornburg was thinking of the hundred and fifty miles that lay between them and Fort Robinson. Men had died in less than a hundred and fifty miles of desert. "If there's a waterhole near here, they'll make for it," he said.

"There's one, Crazy Rider's Well—I don't know if I could find it."

"You could try," Major Thornburg said.

They turned north and west, the major hunched over and riding with set lips and a bitter memory of Crook's reprimand. They continued to spur their horses to make the beasts move at better than a walk; they went on into the sand while the haze rolled up and hid the sun. The grit of fine sand crusted on their lips and on their lashes. The world rocked with the horses' sliding steps, and the dunes shimmered into fantastic shapes.

At midday, it was barely half a cup of water, not enough to wash the dirt from their parched throats. The men growled thickly and the noncommissioned officers cursed back in a whisper. No one raised his voice.

Night, and the waterhole was anywhere or nowhere. The sand blew like sleet, and there was nothing to build fires with, not even the buffalo chips that lay like manna everywhere else on the plains. They fed on cold rations, dry salt meat, dry pilot biscuit that lumped in their throats and gave them an agony of thirst.

By the next morning, the horses were suffering acutely from thirst and hunger; yet more from thirst, so much so that they forsook attempting to graze on the parched dune grass. By noon, Thornburg, desperate, gave orders for the men to dismount and lead the horses.

That way, they stumbled on, dirt-crusted seekers in a horrible dream. They sought in eternal disappointment; behind each dune were other dunes, behind each hill a waste of sand.

When they found the waterhole, an alkali pool of bitter white liquid, they drank and drank and then became sick. And that night, eight of the horses died.

And still, there was no sign of Indians.

The following day Thornburg gave up and turned south. Now the sand was in their backs rather than in their faces, but the wind had turned icy cold. At night, without fires, the men suffered miserably, and more became sick. More horses died, and those left could only proceed at a slow walk, dragging their raw hoofs.

Their progress was the progress of an unholy funeral party, coming back from some forbidden land. All of their thoughts might be summed up in what Axelton croaked to the major: "If they're back there, then God pity those Indians—"

They camped, went on, camped again, dragged on again,

guided by compass, driving the horses and leaving dead horses behind them. They ran out of food, and some of the men babbled like children.

They left three of the men dead behind them before they reached the North Fork, river-water, grass, and even a house on the horizon with a flow of blue smoke from the chimney.

On one hand, Murray drove on, following his trail deeper and deeper into the great, wind-swept Dakota barrens, always with reports of his quarry ahead of him. But on the other hand, after the trail had split, the half of the Cheyenne village that had plunged into the sandhills vanished as completely as though they had never existed. Proof was abundant that the Cheyennes had separated into two parts; a French-Canadian fur hunter, bound into the Black Hills with his line of traps, reported seeing Cheyennes, men and women and children, worn from long travel, but not three hundred, not more than a hundred and twenty or so. Two Sioux scouts, attached to Fort Mead, also reported seeing Cheyennes, giving the same count.

Yet of the others, those who had gone into the sandhills, there was no sign, no word, no trace. The expanse of dunes had taken them in, given them its fierce shelter, swallowed them completely.

Not even Crook, the Indian fighter, Crook who had cleaned the plains with acid and lye, could raise the missing Indians from the earth. There were the five troops of the Third Cavalry ranging south from Fort Robinson, tracking back and forth, pushing their sand-crusted horses over the dunes and through the shadows of the tall and sunlashed buttes; they laced the country, returned to Fort Robinson, were sent out again, fine-combed the sandhills. From Sidney, column after column drove north from the Platte River and tasted the alkali spread of desert.

"No trace of the Cheyennes," dot-dashed over the wires, again and again. "No trace of the Cheyennes—" Monotonous enough to lay the country's blood lust; and the country was beginning to forget. Indians were not so important —unless they were hunted or were themselves the hunters. The fact that they existed meant nothing; the fact that they were in the Nebraska sandhills was no more important than the sandhills themselves. Let them stay there then.

Kansas took count of itself and discovered that there was not one case, not one single solitary case of a citizen being murdered or molested by the Cheyennes, not one case of a house being burnt by the Cheyennes: horses had been run off, some stock slaughtered for food, and that was all.

But in the outlying army posts, the Cheyennes were not forgotten. Under Crook's constant prodding, the search went on, and from Fort Robinson, party after party went out to continue the fruitless combing of the dunes and the dry plains.

It was such a party, a company of the Third Cavalry with Captain J. B. Johnson in command, that left Fort Robinson late in October and rode slowly south. For two days they pushed their search to the south, cutting carefully back and forth, investigating every valley, every rock cleft, every bit of wretched timber that might shelter a few persons. In early afternoon on the second day, a cold wind sifted down from the north, bringing with it an ominous cloud bank, a chill promise of the first winter snow. Captain Johnson reined in his horse, put his cheek to the wind, and shrugged.

"Going back, sir?" Lieutenant Allen asked him.

"I think so," he decided.

"I think we're ghost hunting," Lieutenant Allen said. "I think there never were Cheyennes—"

Sergeant Lancy, red-faced, bearded, rode up to them with his palm laid against the wind, his breath cloudy, his shaggy head nodding agreement. "She'll snow," he decided.

"Ghost hunting," Lieutenant Allen repeated, fascinated with the idea.

"I took my bath." It was the sergeant's boast that he never bathed once the snow had fallen.

Johnson was looking at something ahead of them. Lancy, his horse uneasy and skittish, had nothing but scorn for the line of cavalrymen he faced, their figures hunched, their collars turned up against the wind. "Aah!" he boomed. "Aah, she ain't cold yet! She'll be cold!" He found their misery a matter for laughter. "Send them home to the fires, sir," he told the captain, chuckling to himself.

Johnson had seen something; he walked his horse ahead with intense concentration, motioning with his arm for the column to follow; he shaded his eyes against the hanging sun.

"What is it, sir?"

Johnson didn't answer and the column moved on slowly into the sunny west. In the south and the west, the sky was blue; north and east, gray that melted into a black band with the earth; the heavens had divided with cold melancholy and winter flirted on the knife-like edge of the wind.

They all saw it now yet no one spoke, as if in accord that this was something first to be proven. It drew them the way a grotesque in a dream draws the dreamer. But they didn't hurry. As it emerged into shape and form, their progress became even slower, and presently the column halted.

And someone asked: "What is it?"

A thought of all, but not a question, rather a reflection, an echo, an expression of horror uneasily expressed by men who knew the good things of comradeship, the warmth of fires, the security of numbers bound together with the uniform they wore, the easy-going man-to-officer relation of the plains troops. They knew what it was; they knew before any proofs had been stacked; they knew that their search was over.

They saw it come out of the west and toward them, such slow movement as that with which a dying animal drags itself back to its lair. There were men and women and children, almost a hundred and fifty of them, but at first they seemed to be things, and you wouldn't call them men and women and children.

There were about fifty horses in the group, but not

horses; on four legs, but not horses to cavalrymen who curried their own steeds every day. They were caricatures of what had been lithe ponies, bones with hide stretched over the bones; and on them were objects that had been children once, bundles in rags with tatters streaming on the knife edge of the cold north wind.

The rest of the column walked on foot and their rags streaming in the wind gave a macabre effect of gaiety. There were women and men, hollow-eyed, hollow-cheeked, skinny as scarecrows. They wore articles of Indian clothing, and the cavalrymen could see that this had once been a buckskin hunting shirt and that had once been a buckskin dress and these had once been moccasins, the gay, beaded Cheyenne moccasins that were like no other footgear on the plains. And they could see a tattered thing that had once been a trade blanket, striped merrily in red and yellow and green. They could make out what the sand-crusted rags had been.

But there was no knowing what the people had been. Dead eyes hold their secrets, and the eyes of these people were dead though the people walked. Their black hair hung loose in the wind, ribbons of black hair, just as their clothes were in ribbons. Many were barefooted, and on others the moccasins were bits of ancient leather. They walked slowly because it was the only mode of progress left to them, and they walked because there was no place of rest in that sandy, cold expanse from which escape was hopeless. Their mute tale was of hunger, privation, thirst, suffering, but their tale was without boast: and the pride of their hopeless, shattered selves communicated itself to the troops.

They came nearer and as they approached there was movement in their ranks, a slow swirl of defiance. The women, bunched around the children on horseback, were falling back; the men came to the front, forming themselves into a protective half-circle. They held weapons in their hands, guns and revolvers, and they faced the white cavalry with courage as pitiful as it was defiant. Their progress, which had been slowing down almost imperceptibly, stopped altogether.

And Lieutenant Allen said: "That's what we've been hunting." Lancy shuddered; he was a big, healthy man, and he couldn't look at something like that easily. Captain Johnson said, as if forced to establish a fact he was already certain of:

"They're the Dog Soldiers?"

No one answered him; there was wind with its tired wind sound, but otherwise silence; even the horses, two by two in rank, stood without moving and among the Indians not even the children made any noise. The trumpeter, at the head of the column and just behind Sergeant Lancy, turned his tight-rolled bugle over and over, polishing its brass surface on his sleeve. The men sat erect in their saddles, unconscious of the cold, unfeeling of the wind that had chilled them so before.

Johnson had to do something; he was the commander; it was incumbent upon him to think and act. He had accomplished what the army of the plains, twelve thousand strong, had failed to do; he had met the Cheyennes and they were his prisoners, unable to run away, unable to resist. He pressed joy and achievement into his brain and he urged his horse forward; but there was no reward, and when he stopped halfway between his men and the Indian band he felt as lonely as though he stood by himself in that desert of sand. The wind was toward the Indians, but still his men would hear him; there was only a space of about twenty yards between the two parties.

He said: "Hello, there, hello"—lamely, asking: "Who's chief—head man?" He looked at their faces, hollow, sand-encrusted, black eyes set in wells of dry parchment. They didn't move; apathy or defiance or weariness or stupor; they leaned in a bend of grotesque bravery.

"Hello!" he said. "You sabbe English—you sabbe white man talk?"

"White man talk!" he repeated. "Make talk!"

He turned his horse half around. Sergeant Lancy was watching him. The trumpeter still polished his bugle. Lieutenant Allen shook his head.

"I'd be careful, Captain," Sergeant Lancy said.

His horse took a few steps back to the cavalry line. Johnson dismounted.

"Careful," Lancy warned.

Allen dismounted too; he felt an instinctive need to support Johnson, to share the burden of horror and futility. He went over to the captain, and they stood together and watched the Indians. The sun was dropping, small, cold, cased in the icy pack of the north wind; and the black rim of clouds hungered for the rest of the sky.

"They don't know English," Johnson said hopelessly.

"No—"

"They may be playing dumb, but there was no report that they knew English. They're tepee people."

"If we took them in?" Allen suggested.

"You don't need strength to pull a trigger. I hate to lose men over something like this."

"You'd think they would understand how insane it is to put up a fight."

"I don't know if anything is insane to them now," Johnson said. "When people are so far gone—" He shrugged and walked to the troop. He went down the line asking if anyone knew Cheyenne. Some knew a few words of Sioux, but there was only one, an Omaha boy, who put any claim to Cheyenne. He said he knew a little, really not anything at all, just a little; some things he understood and he could speak a word or two. Back in Omaha, there was a halfbreed who had claimed to know five Indian languages and would instruct in any one for the price of a drink; but that didn't make him a talker. He told Johnson he'd be glad to try, and they walked back toward the Indians.

"Surrender," Johnson said.

The boy wasn't sure. He thought he knew how to say, become slaves or prisoners, not exactly surrender. He had a vague impression that in Cheyenne the word was one thing concerning the surrender of a white man, another thing concerning the surrender of an Indian, and thus changing to fit numberless objects—a funny language. He had known a range cook, a Chinaman, who claimed to understand Sioux words, lots of them.

Johnson shrugged impatiently. "Go ahead and try."

The boy went forward uneasily and yelled something at the Indians. He repeated the word under his breath, called it out again. The sound fled on the wind, archaic, foolish, humorous. The boy kept edging away from the Indians.

"Try something else," Johnson suggested. He felt an almost frantic need to break down the barrier of speech; he felt a need for haste, as if their bare, crusted skins were capable of transferring chill to himself and his men. The storm was coming down quickly.

The boy spoke a few words more, and this time there was movement among the Indians, reaction. They were speaking among themselves, just a hum, barely sound as the wind carried it away from the troops. Then the noise stopped and their ranks parted and an old man came up, an old, old man, such an old, withered, tottering man that his very existence in that tribe of misery was unbelievable. He came right up to the boy, so close to him that the young soldier backed away, and he spoke softly and slowly and painfully, the effort being supreme and insistent.

"What is he saying?" Johnson demanded.

"I don't know," the boy reflected uneasily. "I think he's telling us to go away, but I'm not sure."

"Surrender, make him understand that."

"Yes, I think he sabbed that," the boy nodded. "I think he wants us to go away and leave him alone."

The old man went on talking. Sometimes, he pointed to the men behind him, sometimes he pointed over the troopers' heads to where the storm was brewing; sometimes he shook his head very sadly.

"He wants us to leave him alone," the boy decided, an uncertain grin of achievement breaking his freckled face.

230

"Something about them going home, just going home. We should go away—"

"Tell him—" And then Johnson realized the futility of the boy attempting to tell them anything; the barrier was there, and it was more than a barrier of words, it was an era, a history, an aching gap between the past and the present. Johnson shrugged and told the boy to go back to the ranks. And then the old man stood alone and curious and ancient, cold, tired, purposeless with all the sorrow of old age, seeing too much, knowing too much, suffering too much.

"What are you going to do?" the lieutenant asked obliquely, harrying himself more than the captain for an answer, watching the men, the sergeant, the fading sun, the approaching storm.

"Do?"

Lancy snapped: "Trumpeter, damn you, stop polishing that Godforsaken horn!"

Johnson said gently: "Sergeant Lancy, go back to the fort and explain the situation to Colonel Carlton. Tell him just how it is. Say I suggest he send two companies down and enough wagons to bring those poor devils back. Meanwhile, we'll stay with them. Maybe we can get them to come in by themselves—"

"A howitzer, sir?" the sergeant suggested.

"What?"

"I said, a howitzer, sir?"

"Tell him what I said."

"He'll want a howitzer, sir. I'm not meaning to talk out of turn, but you know how he is about guns when it comes to Indians. Shall I say you don't want a gun?"

"Say what I instructed you to say," Johnson muttered. "If the colonel wants to send a gun down, that's up to him, not to you, Sergeant."

"Yes, sir."

"Better get going," Johnson nodded.

The sergeant rode off. Allen had removed his gauntlets and was warming his hands with his breath. "Cold," he said.

"Yes?"

"It's getting colder—I think it'll snow."

Johnson said aimlessly: "Back east it has to warm up before it snows."

The Indians were moving. They made no attempt to go away from the troops, but instead filed directly past them. The men, still holding their guns aggressively, made a pathetic fringe along the scarecrow group, and as they passed the troops the men fell back, so as to constitute a rear guard. Johnson watched them pass on, their pace the pace of the old chief who led them. Then he nodded to Lieutenant Allen, who swung the cavalry around and after them.

There was no need to do more than walk the horses, and even that way Johnson had to signal a halt again and again. It took all of the Cheyennes' little store of strength to fight their path into the biting north wind, and sometimes, leaning against the cold blast, they hardly moved at all.

In front of them, the horizon was black, heavy clouds forcing their way into the blue sky like smoke from a sprawling factory town; behind them, silhouetted against the sunset, were blue-uniformed men wrapped in sheep-skin-lined coats, riding strong, well-fed horses.

Only once, Johnson spoke. He said: "The fools, the poor, damned fools—"

A while later, the Indians camped. About half of their men crouched over guns, facing the troops, while the rest helped with the business of settling down for the night. The children were lifted from the horses tenderly, caressed constantly, treated as a beggar might treat one precious possession left over from better days. All this the troops were able to see easily, for the Indians permitted them to approach within a dozen yards of the camp before they menaced them with guns. And the soldiers could also see what the children were, skinny grotesques with bloated bellies, children who no longer laughed, no longer smiled or chattered, no longer whimpered even, horrible gnomes wrapped in a welter of all the rags their half-naked parents could spare.

Braves and squaws limped around, searching for bits of brushwood, dry grass, anything at all that might serve for firewood. They found the small rubbish that even the dreariest waste-place will give up to patient searching, and they heaped it together and made little fires glow in the twilight. They had no food, for they made no effort to cook anything over the fires, nor did they go close to them, piling the children around instead, and trying to make a wall of their bodies to shield the children from the north wind.

Johnson stood all he could and then went to a pack horse and pulled out two bags of hardtack. He took the two bags and walked toward the Indian camp, almost up to the guns of the watching men. He had no physical fear that they might shoot him or leap at him or do anything; his fear was something else, fear generated by their close proximity, by the very fact of their existence. He set down the bags, peering at them meanwhile, unable to avoid the horrible fascination of their misery. He opened the bags and took out a few biscuits, held them up a moment, then dropped them back. It was getting dark rapidly, and in the dark the hunched, wasted figures of the Indians took on a woeful dignity. Their rags healed together and the sand-crusted parchment of their faces mellowed in the tones of dusk.

Johnson backed away, and when he brushed against something, he jumped inadvertently. It was Allen, who apologized:

"Sorry, sir."

"All right, Lieutenant."

"It's terribly unreal, isn't it, sir?" Allen said, feeling that he had to say something.

"Too damned real for me."

They stood together, a little way in front of their men, facing the edge of the wind and trying to make out the Indians in the dusk.

"Do you suppose they'll take the food?" Allen asked.

"I think so."

"If you'd like, sir, I'll set a can of water up there?" Allen suggested eagerly.

"If you care to."

Allen hurried away and returned in a few minutes with two heavy canteens slung over his shoulders. "Just go up and put them down?"

"It's safe enough," the captain nodded.

Now complete darkness had come. The funnel of black clouds spun themselves across the sky, leaving only the faintest thread of subdued brilliance on the western horizon. A few steps, and the lieutenant's figure merged out of form and sight; the wind, rising almost to howling pitch, absorbed the sound of his footsteps. Johnson was startled when he returned, appearing suddenly from the night.

"Allen?" he realized that he had been nervous; he laid a hand on the lieutenant's arm. "All right?"

"They took the bread," Allen grinned; he was excited, trembling with cold and nerves. "It was too dark and they saw me too quick; I heard a breechbolt go." He sighed. "They didn't shoot, thank goodness; I put the water down and came back here."

"What about tonight?" he asked after a while.

"We'll sleep around them," Johnson decided. "I don't think they'll break for it, but just to be sure. Put out every third man on a two-hour watch."

Allen nodded. "Maybe it will snow tonight," he said.

Waking, Lieutenant Allen lay in the darkness listening, and then crawled to his feet, holding the blanket tight across his shoulders. It was very dark, too dark for him to see the face of his watch. He tried to strike a match, had several go out in the rush of wind, and then got one to prick out the hands and numbers. It was a little after two.

He felt his way past sleeping men, saw a figure, said: "Hello, there?"

"Lieutenant?"

It was Gogarty, one of the sentries; he mumbled about the cold and cursed the Indians.

"Where's the captain?"

Gogarty didn't know. Allen stumbled on, guided by whispers and grunts, fell over a sleeping man who grumbled into wakefulness.

"Captain?"

"What is it?" Johnson asked wearily.

"There's something going on over there."

"Why don't you go to sleep, Allen?"

"It sounds like digging—"

"Don't be a fool! Why would they be digging?"

"I don't know."

"Then go to sleep."

"But why would they be digging?" Allen asked. He lay down and fell asleep asking himself that, why would they be digging?

Dawn came in a bottled world with the lid down tight. The snow hadn't started yet, but the whole arc of the sky was blanketed with heavy clouds. Johnson, waking from uneasy sleep, stiff, cold, found grateful comfort in the strong smell of boiling coffee. Charcoal fires provided a breakfast of thick-sliced bacon, hardtack soaked in grease, and strong coffee.

Moving to the cook fire, he glanced at the Cheyenne camp, rubbed his eyes, and realized that Allen had heard digging during the night. It was impossible but it was a fact that those bags of skin and bones had spent the night throwing up a circle of breastworks, digging a rifle pit for their women and children. The fact was proof;

236

the dirt lay piled up, fresh-dug; but the accomplishment was nightmarish in its conception.

Eating breakfast, the troopers stood and stared, the way men stare at a sideshow. Johnson walked in a circle about the Indian camp, trying to realize why, when their position was so obviously hopeless, a hundred and a half starving savages would spend the night digging entrenchments and preparing for a fight. He returned to Allen, who said:

"I've never seen anything like it, sir."

"No—"

"Will you try to make them surrender again?"

"I suppose so. We have to do something until the troops come down from the fort." Then he went off to find the Omaha boy, to persuade him to go up to the breastworks and talk to the Indians in the few words of Cheyenne he had. The boy was reluctant; he stood close to the charcoal fire, warming his hands and watching the Indian camp suspiciously.

"I don't like to go up there unarmed, sir," he complained. "They're crazy people. Only crazy people would dig themselves in like that."

"It's safe enough."

"Well, I don't know, sir. I don't think they know what I'm talking about." Then he went with slow, dragging steps, after Johnson had laced him with contempt and agreed to go along with him. He went up closer and closer to the Indians, shouting out surrender in the guttural speech he supposed was their tongue.

A rifle cracked, and a bullet threw up the dirt at their feet. The boy scrambled back, but Johnson had to be what

237

he was, the one man to make decisions, to know; he couldn't run, and he turned his back on the Indians and walked calmly away. It cost him all the strength left in his thin-worn nerves, the trembling expectancy of a bullet in his back, the knowledge of death that didn't come. Lieutenant Allen and some soldiers ran out to cover him, and when he reached them, his face and hands were wet with perspiration, in spite of the cold.

Without speaking, the captain went to the fire and poured himself a cup of coffee. He drank it down in a few quick gulps, sighing with relief as the hot liquid seared his throat.

There was nothing now to do but wait for the troops. The charcoal fires weren't much good for heat, and Johnson sent two men off to find some brushwood. They came back with enough to make one roaring blaze, and as the flames licked up, the snow began to fall. It fell with the slanting hiss of sand, and the flakes were small and dry; the wind continued to howl, whetting its knife edge, and it drove the snow into the sand, mixing it with the sand. And altogether, it was punishment, even for the detail of well-clothed troops, pressing close to their fire.

For the Indians, it was something else, and the white men didn't know, nor did they try to know. Sometimes they looked and saw without speaking, ragged bundles hiding their heads from the icy torture.

Toward evening, the first detachment from Fort Robinson arrived, a company of the Third Cavalry with Captain Wessells in command. He had with him Sergeant Lancy and three Sioux scouts, all of whom could speak and understand some Cheyenne. He told Johnson that two howitzers and three supply wagons would come up sometime before morning.

Wessells was not an imaginative person; when it snowed, he sheltered or clothed himself, and when he was hungry he ate, nor was he capable of subjective speculation upon cold or hunger in others. Everything apart from himself existed in another world; his selfishness was primitive and direct, instinctive rather than calculated. He was a good man when it came to carrying out orders, but his manner took on fumbling uncertainty when he was forced to consider the complexity of desires and directions in other human beings. His solution was to make a pattern for men, never troubled by the vagrant thought that one man was somewhat different from another. He had one good quality in an army man; he never doubted himself.

Perhaps he oversimplified; he said to Johnson: "We'll go in there and round them up and have them ready when the wagons come." He stood in front of Johnson, licking snowflakes from his mustache and breathing out clouds of steam.

"It won't be easy," Johnson considered.

"You said they weren't in any shape."

"They have guns. You don't need to be in shape to pull a trigger. I thought that if we sat around them a while longer, they'd come out by themselves. If we go in there, we'll lose men."

"You can't fight without losing men," Wessells said in

a matter-of-fact way. "If this snow keeps up, we'll have a hell of a time getting back to the fort."

Johnson shrugged. "I figured that once they saw the howitzers they'd come out."

"Maybe—"

"I'll take one of your Sioux and talk to them," Johnson said.

"It's no good talking to Dog Soldiers."

"I'll try," Johnson said.

He went up with Anxious Man, a Sioux scout who made no bones about being afraid. He explained to Johnson, in broken English, that there had once been a deep friendship between the Cheyennes and the Sioux. They might kill him because he had been a friend; Johnson was an enemy and thus much safer. It was a simple thing to be an enemy.

"Talk to them," Johnson said. "You're a dirty, yellow Indian. Talk to them."

Anxious Man crouched against the wind and pressed close to the captain. When they were within a few yards of the rifle-pit, some of the Cheyennes stood up, among them the old, old man. They swayed like weeds in the driving curtain of snow.

"Tell them it's no use fighting us," Johnson said. "We have them entirely surrounded by troops and they can never escape. If they surrender, we will feed them and take them to the fort, where they will be warm and have houses to live in. But if they fight, men will die."

The Sioux spoke, his hands crossed nervously on his chest, his singing speech a wailing part of the wind and the driving snow. And the old man answered, courteously, gently, his voice out of the dying, shriveled body an insult to reason and sanity.

"Dey already dead, dey say," the Sioux translated. "Dey go home, go home, go home, go away—" Somewhere behind his words was poetry and motion, the complex beauty of a primitive and musical speech. "Dey dead, go away."

"Damn you, make them understand that big guns are coming up, big guns that will blow them to pieces!"

"Dey dead, go away," the Sioux shrugged.

Wessells organized the attack. Half of a company would come in on foot from one side only, so there would be no danger from their own cross fire. The men had to take off their gloves to handle the carbines, and they stood in the snow, their hands turning blue with cold. Wessells blew his whistle and they ran in, crouching, slipping in the snow, trying to peer through the matting of flakes. They never saw the Cheyenne trench, so heavy had the snow become, but the Cheyennes must have seen their blue figures bulking from the white lacework. The shattering volley of rifle fire hurled them cursing and bleeding back toward Wessells.

They fell back because it was impossible to lie in the snow and snipe at an enemy they couldn't see. They fell back and Wessells confessed to Johnson:

"That's no good. We'll wait for the guns now."

He had tried something and it had failed, and Johnson couldn't reproach him. To Wessells wounded men were as much a part of the army as uniforms. He stolidly made a man comfortable who was shot through the thigh and he helped set a broken arm. When they crawled back and brought in a young trooper, Jed Hurley, shot through the head, Wessells mutely made the entry in his notebook. Nor did he hate because of what had happened.

"Those red bastards," he said calmly, "will keep us here until morning." And added thoughtfully, "They'll freeze."

Toward midnight the snow stopped falling, but the wind continued to blow, piling up great drifts. And a little after midnight, the wagons and the two howitzers arrived. Wessells had waited up, and before he went to sleep, he saw that emplacements were made for the two guns and that they were aimed and loaded.

When Captain Johnson woke in the morning, he found Wessells already up and engrossed with the artillerymen. Wessells explained his plan, to have the men form in a circle around the Indian camp and come in slowly while the howitzers dropped shells on the Cheyennes. The men would not attack, but would be ready to receive the Dog Soldiers as the shells took effect.

"The place is full of women and children," Johnson said. "There aren't more than forty or fifty men."

"They asked for it," Wessells shrugged.

"They haven't any food. In another day they'll come out willingly."

"The colonel's orders were to bring them in."

"He didn't know—"

"About the women and children?—he knew. He said, bring them in. This is the safe way. Why should we lose more men—if we don't have to, if the shells will bring them out?"

Johnson agreed reluctantly.

The troopers took their places in a wide circle around the camp. The camp itself was quiet, a little heaped mound in the vastness of snowdrifts. The wind had died away; it blew only fitfully now, feminine bursts that sent curling handfuls of snow dancing before it. What movement there was in the Indian camp had no purpose, a white, sheeted figure rising and stumbling from one place to another, a man advancing a little beyond the entrenchments, then returning.

Wessells took his place with the artillery, watching the troops through his glasses. Johnson remained with the troops. Wessells waited until all the men had taken their positions and then he let his upraised hand fall. One of the howitzers belched smoke and flame, recoiling in the snow. The shell screamed and burst just beyond the camp, snow and dirt unfolding like a flower in the morning sun.

The lieutenant in charge of the battery called corrections. The other howitzer roared, this time arching its shell directly into the center of the camp; and the camp came alive with moving, nervous figures who, even at the distance, managed to convey their hurt and pain and surprise.

Wessells said: "Fire," and a howitzer roared again. In its flowering burst now was flesh and blood and human eagerness distending into nothing.

"I think that's enough," Wessells said.

The old, old chief came out first, his arms raised, his courtly defiance lost with the bursting shells. The circle of

243

troops closed in, but not too close. Johnson and the Sioux scout, Anxious Man, went up to meet the old chief.

Then two others, tall, haggard Indians, half-frozen, half-starved; it was hard to tell what they might have been once. They helped the old man through the snowdrifts and they stood next to him as he faced Johnson. And even with all their broken defeat, there came to Johnson so strong an intimation of what they had endured, that he said softly, almost humbly:

"Even brave men must surrender when there is nothing else to do."

The Sioux translated and the old chief nodded, tears running down his cold-chapped, leathery cheeks.

"He say, dere women an' children under dat shell."

Captain Johnson found it difficult to speak. "I'm sorry," he said.

"Dey go 'long wid you now. Dey don't go home no more."

"Ask him his name?" Johnson whispered.

"Dull Knife. De odder Old Crow—de odder Wild Hog. Dey great chiefs."

"Great chiefs," Johnson nodded. "Ask him where is Little Wolf and the rest of his people?"

"Dey go home. Dey break in two pieces fust, maybe den a better chance one part run away from troops. One go dis way, one go dat way. He go in sandhills, but Little Wolf take young men an' go nort—way nort—way nort—" He pointed out into the snowy north. "Way nort—maybe over du border."

"Canada?"

"Maybe lak dat, maybe by Powder Ribber."

244

"Tell him," Johnson said, "that he should bring us his guns, all his guns, and then we will feed his people."

Wessells, counting the guns, said: "There are only thirty here, and no revolvers."

"Perhaps that's all they had," Johnson suggested.

"I don't like it. They must have had revolvers."

"Indians don't favor revolvers."

"Still, they must have had revolvers, some revolvers. We ought to search the women."

"The women?" Johnson asked quietly.

"They're Indians."

Johnson turned his back on the other and walked away. Wessells shrugged and stared at the guns. Alone and in command, he might have searched the women, but with Johnson there—

He dismissed the thought and gave orders for the guns to be labeled and packed. Then he walked over to where the Cheyennes were being fed under the watchful eyes of armed sentries. It didn't disturb him too much to observe the wretched half-starved, half-frozen huddle of brown-skinned people. They were something outside of him, of a different world. Even their pain was alien and away from him. If he noticed the hollow-cheeked, large-eyed faces of the children at all, it was to conclude that Indian children were that way, the fact and nothing beyond it.

When they had finished eating, he gave orders for them to be loaded into the wagons; and then the whole caravan set off through the snow to Fort Robinson.

PART NINE   November 1878–January 1879

FREEDOM

For CARL SCHURZ, it meant
only the stroke of a pen, the matter of saying, "They have
won—or they have lost." And signing his name in the ca-
pacity of government. Government was that, a bill, an
order, a receipt. And then forces came into being and
little men were moved over a vast chessboard. Government was constitutional and democratic because the people voted, and you couldn't have a meeting, a discussion,
a session, a conference without that word being all over
the place, the people this and the people that. The people
elected a president, a congress, the president appointed a
cabinet; nobody elected a lobby, but they got things done,
and the people elected Grant and never smelled the cor-
ruption. Nobody knew about the people, who existed
somewhere apparently, unless you sometimes shook hands
with one of them. But government was an art and a science and a profession, which the people never understood.

247

He was government, the Secretary of the Interior, a scientist, a professional, a man who had stood behind barricades once. And recently he had said to a friend:

"Barricades are a youthful frenzy. It annoys me that everyone should remember what I desire to forget." He hadn't yet arrived at the point of declaring, "Minorities are a nuisance. And since every majority leaves a minority, democracy is cumbersome and foolish—"

He might have said to himself, finally signing the order returning the Cheyennes to the south, to the far-off Indian Territory of Oklahoma, across a thousand miles where their blood had marked a trail:

"There are only one hundred and forty-nine of them in a country of so many millions—"

Or perhaps: "It is over now and it must not occur again," although sensing something of a future where it would occur again and again and again, where the trail would not be the trail of three hundred primitive horsemen over a thousand miles of green prairie, but of thousands and millions across the blackened and tear-wetted face of the earth.

At Fort Robinson, late in December, Captain Wessells as Post Commander received the message from Washington. The ever-shifting policy of Western Army Headquarters had split the Third Cavalry, detaching Colonel Carlton and the major portion of the regiment, and leaving at the post only two full companies and one below-muster company. Johnson had gone with Carlton, leaving Wessells as senior officer, the next in command being Captain

248

P. D. Vroom. Lieutenant George Baxter was in command of the below-muster company. Lieutenant Arthur Allen remained at the post, taking over the field duties of Wessells' company.

Wessells' first reaction to his first senior command was deep satisfaction. An acting post commander could look forward to a regimental commission, and ambition was an urgent and instinctive part of Wessells' being. While he rarely doubted himself, he lived for the time when he could destroy all doubt. He lived in an orderly world, and he loved the army because there a man could take a hand in making the world even more orderly. Most of his rare outbursts of temper came from very minor causes, a button hanging from a uniform, a rust mark on a saber blade, a spot of dirt at dress parade. His lack of imagi nation made him take things as they were, but as they were, he desired them perfect.

It was at his suggestion that Colonel Carlton had confined the one hundred and forty-nine Cheyennes in an old, unused log barracks building, drafty, mice-ridden, its sixty-foot length warmed by only one ancient stove; not out of malice, but because the old log building was the most convenient place and the easiest one to guard. Robinson was not a stockaded fort; it was a conglomeration of barracks and storerooms sprawling on a hillside above a wooded creek. Its defenses consisted of some rifle pits, gun emplacements, and one heavy barracks building that could be used as a blockhouse. To have given the Indians any sort of freedom of the place would have meant a constant chain guard. This way, only a sentry at the barracks door was needed.

After Colonel Carlton had departed with most of the regiment, leaving Wessells in command, the captain's policy toward the prisoners did not change. Deliberate cruelty played as small a part in his character as deliberate pity. The Indians were Indians, and he was keeping them under guard because at the moment there was nothing else to do with them. The long barracks building was bitterly cold and the ancient stove supplied almost no warmth, certainly none that could permeate the whole dark length of the log building; as the winter wore on, the temperature dropped to the zero level, veering only slightly above and often far below. But there were no stoves to spare at the post, and it did not occur to Wessells to put in a requisition for additional stoves simply to aid the comfort of a rebellious band of savages.

Language was a barrier; the Indians suffered dumbly, animal-like in their obstinate existence. They wore their tattered rags, and even if they had demanded clothes, Wessells had no clothes to give them. Certainly, he would not draw upon his regular army replacements, and as for trade goods, he did not consider that he had the authority to spend government money to clothe Indians. Food, which had to be brought by wagon or packhorse the whole long distance from Ogallala, was scarce enough, and when the men went on short rations, the Indians went on no rations.

The deadly monotony of winter life at the post did not make for kindliness or amiability. Wessells, perhaps, stood it better than the other officers; it left him substantially as he was, absorbed in the hundred small duties of inspection, supply, seeing that enough wood was brought in, seeing that the buildings were repaired, drilling the men, digging out of the mountain-like winter drifts, exercising the horses—all that was grist in his mill, the life he had chosen for himself, the tight, neat, orderly life that encased his world in the army pattern, that gave it limit and shape and form which otherwise it would never possess.

But for the other officers, the short days and long nights dragged by in horrible monotony. At Fort Robinson, there were no women, no music, no books, no form of amusement save the endless penny poker, the interminable whist games. Among the enlisted men, a dark sulkiness became blacker day by day; among the officers there were bitter arguments over the most inconsequential of things, bursts of rage, moods, day-long and week-long fits of silence, and not too infrequently blows exchanged, fights which Wessels had sense enough to ignore. He had seen hate and sullenness flare into murder at lonely army posts; and that, disturbing as it would the orderliness of his rule, he dreaded more than anything else.

He tried to stagger the officers who went out with wood parties, but beyond that, his imagination failed. At the mess, he spoke so little himself that he hardly noticed whether the conversation was gay or sullen.

And meanwhile, the Indians stayed in the guardhouse, an ominous, dying miscellany of what had once been the proudest nomads on the great grass-oceans of America.

The message from Washington came as a welcome interruption. It promised a sort of action, at least something to plan and act on. Wessells announced it in the mess room.

"They're going back," he said.

"Back?" The talk had fallen off; they raised their eyes at the captain's announcement.

"The Dog Soldiers?" someone surmised.

"I thought they'd be sent back," Allen said. "Almost seems a shame."

"A long way down," someone whistled. They were all sick of winter, of the post, of the deadly procession of days; they all hoped to have the assignment of escorting the Cheyennes back to the territory, back to sunlight.

"Who takes them and when?"

Wessells shrugged. He didn't care a great deal; for himself, there was the task of seeing the winter through at Fort Robinson as post commander, and that was enough. Vroom or even Baxter with the under-muster company could take the Indians down the line to the territory. After they had gone, life at the post would be simpler.

"This week, I suppose," he said.

"They won't like it."

"No—"

"Do you suppose they'll make a fuss?"

"They'll go," Wessells said. "What else is there for them to do?"

James Rowland, a halfbreed Cheyenne, the son of an Indian mother and a white father, had heard about the Cheyenne imprisonment, and had come over to the post from Pine Ridge, hoping to find some employment as an interpreter. Carlton had taken him on at half-pay and rations. Now Wessells instructed him to go to the barracks and tell Dull Knife and the other chiefs to come to his office for a council. Wessells asked Vroom and Baxter to join him, and in his office the three of them smoked cigars and waited for the chiefs to appear.

The office window faced on the parade ground, and across the snow-covered parade, the long barracks building was clearly visible. Beyond that, the snowy ground folded into stunted pines, which lifted with dark green undulations into the hills. The sky was gray and heavy, the sun lost in an ocean of hours. A storm was making in the trackless reaches of Dakota, and Vroom said dismally:

"Snow again."

"It looks like it," Wessells agreed, studying the end of his cigar.

"Suppose it locks us in?"

Wessells shrugged. "I like a clear Havana," he said, still studying his cigar.

"If I go down, I'll send back some good smokes."

"I was thinking of sending Baxter," Wessells said, testing the inch of ash. Vroom rose and walked to the window; he was a big, ruddy, blond man. The hand with which he wiped a pane was a mat of pink flesh and wiry yellow hairs. He wiped the pane clear and told Wessells:

"Here they come."

Baxter said: "It's a long way down—" He was listless and thin and young; he peered past Vroom at the snow as if trying to conjure up a thousand miles of white-blanketed space.

"Three of them," he said. "I don't understand what keeps that old fellow alive."

"Indians don't die until they want to."

253

Wessells wasn't very interested; he glanced once at the three ragged chiefs following Rowland across the snow, an armed trooper on either side, and then he went back to contemplation of his cigar.

"Anyway, they don't feel cold the way we do," Baxter decided. The old chief wore moccasins, but one of the others was barefooted. "Surly brutes," Baxter said.

"You could start off soon," Wessells said. "If we snow in, it'll be a damned job."

Vroom turned back, rubbing his fleshy cold hands together, going close to the stove. Baxter kicked the door open and threw in another stick of wood. Wessells smoked calmly, taking sensuous pleasure in his cigar. When Rowland knocked, the captain said: "Come in—come right in." Baxter opened the door and Rowland came into the office uneasily, fumbling with his fur cap. The three chiefs shuffled behind him, wincing at the heat, their eyes tearing, their heads bent slightly. The old man walked a little to the front of the other two, his hands pressed together and clutching a rag of blanket he wore over his shoulders. The others, tall, skinny wrecks, never took their eyes from the old man.

The two guards remained outside.

Wessells sat in an old rocking-chair, his legs crossed, the cigar clouding the room with blue smoke. When the chiefs entered, he nodded at the stove and said: "Go ahead, warm up," and to Rowland: "Tell them to warm up."

They were filthy and conscious of it, uneasy with all the subjective horror of a clean race. They tried to put pride into their rags, and pride kept them from warming their shivering bodies over the stove. They stood in the center of the room, shifting from foot to foot.

Wessells rose and offered them cigars, which they refused. He said: "This is council, so we shake hands. Shake hands all around? Right?"

Rowland translated, and the old man, his eyes still teary, tottered about, shaking hands with the three officers. The other Indians didn't move, nor did they ever take their eyes from the old man, regarding him with compassion and sorrow. They wore no blankets, and their tall, gaunt forms were hardly concealed by the ancient remains of buckskin shirts and trousers.

Wessells settled back in his rocking-chair and resumed his cigar thoughtfully. The chiefs waited. Wessells rocked back and fixed his eyes on the ceiling. He hardly knew how to begin; for all that he was not a sensitive person, he reacted to the chiefs. He recalled other days on the plains when he had seen the Cheyennes in all the glory of feathered horse and bonnet, shield and spear, life in dancing colors and barbaric pride. Not that he regretted what was now gone forever, but he had to reconcile this with his memories. Still staring at the ceiling, he said:

"We will be friends now—we will all be friends." It sounded inane, even in his own ears. "We will be friends," he repeated, and waited for the interpreter.

The old chief answered sadly and Rowland said: "That was what he wanted, to be friends, he's so old. Look at him and you'll see why, he's old, he wants to live in peace, that's all. He says he didn't lead his people away to fight a war with the white men, just to go home and live in peace."

255

"Yes," Wessells murmured, glancing at Baxter who was smoking, insolent and proud of his youth and health and the color of his skin, at Vroom who was regarding the pink splay of his palms intently.

"Yes," Wessells said. "We shook hands, we talk council now, we're friends." Even through an interpreter, he could not get away from what he regarded as the correct form of conversation with Indians. "Tell him we talk council now—" The ceiling was split pine, smoky, milled on a traveling donkey, warped; the boards had been nailed green. Wessels reflected that you can peg green timber and keep it in place, but when you nail it, there's always a warp. "Tell him," he began—

He turned to the chiefs and spoke directly: "All this hasn't been good, not for you, not for your squaws and children. Now you see what comes of running away. There's a law, and you have to obey the law. The law comes from Washington, where the Great White Father lives. He is the president, and he says this and that, and when he says a thing, it's the law. You must obey the law. Now he says you must go back to the place you ran away from. You must go back to the Indian Territory and live in peace on your reservation. We will take you back in wagons with soldiers to protect you, and we will feed you on the way. We will not arrest any of you, but when you get back to your reservation, the agent will arrest those of you who have committed crimes, and he will give you a fair trial."

Vroom didn't like that last and he glanced warningly at Wessells, but Wessells had no subtlety; he had stated the thing as he saw it to people who had no choice of decision. He puffed his cigar and listened to Rowland's liquid Cheyenne. It never occurred to him that this was speech, nor was he curious about Indian talk. It held as little interest for him as the barking of a dog. Vaguely, he resented foreign language, the more so since it was native to his own soil; and back of his mind there was always a feeling that the Indians were interlopers. They had come from somewhere else and they didn't belong.

"They are sad," Rowland said simply.

"Don't tell me that—tell me what they said."

"If it was just going back," Rowland said, shifting his fur cap nervously, "it would be hard—they're in rags. The old man says how can they travel so far when they have no clothes, just rags? The old man says that the children will freeze."

Wessells shrugged.

"What is in the south for them?" Rowland demanded, working his face as he fitted the words to English. He wanted to please the white officers, yet his mind was crowded with memories, the tongue his mother spoke, her people coming to visit her on their wiry ponies, big, grinning warriors who gave him sweets they bought at the trade store, an uncertain kinship with something he desired to lose forever. He was white; his name was Rowland, not Big Bear or Walking Moon or something like that.

"In the south," he said, "starvation and fever will destroy them. They're afraid—there's only a few left. They want the tribe to go on."

"They have to go back," Wessells stated.

The old man looked at Wessells helplessly. The interpreter was not much good; he left an ocean of space which

257

could never be bridged. The old man groped across it and then retreated to the shelter of his two comrades. They spoke in muted tones, and then the tallest of the lot patted the old man's shoulder gently. The old man's eyes had filled with tears again. His words to Rowland took on a tone of complete bewilderment.

"They must die? The president wants that?"

The stage talk, the cheap dramatics of the whole thing annoyed Wessells. He rose abruptly and took a turn across the room. He planted his words with short, jerky motions of the cigar.

"They have to go back—that's all. Just make them understand that."

And Rowland tried to make them understand it. He spoke to them while the three officers listened and then he turned back and shook his head.

"They won't go back."

"The hell they won't! Tell them—"

"It's no use," Rowland insisted. "Their own land is only a couple of hundred miles from here. If they can never reach it, they'll die here. They say they were dead a long time ago; they say a man is dead when his home is taken away from him, when he becomes a slave in a jail. They say it's good of you to make a council with them, but if the president wants them to die, they'll die right here."

"They'll go back," Wessells insisted stubbornly. "In a few days everything will be ready, and then they'll go back."

More talk, and Rowland, in between, transferred meaning like a puzzled child. The talk was circular, impotent.

Across a gap of centuries, the three chiefs were formless shadows.

Wessells settled in the rocking-chair again. He said to Rowland, punctuating his words with the flaking ash of his cigar, "Tell them that an order is an order and a law is a law, and neither may be disobeyed. When they decide to go south in peace, then everything will be good and we will be friends again. Until then, they will receive no rations, no water, no food."

Rowland conveyed the message. The three chiefs received the verdict with impassive, conditioned faces.

"Take them back to the barracks," Wessells nodded.

After they had gone, Baxter said: "I would have held onto them, Captain."

Wessells shook his head. "You want their respect. A thousand miles south is a long distance."

"I agree with that," Vroom nodded. "Only starving them will be a rotten mess."

"They won't starve long. They'll come around."

"Something like this can make an awful stink if it gets out."

"Why?"

"Starving—I don't know. It can make an awful stink."

"My orders were plain enough," Wessells said.

"How can it get out?" Baxter wondered. "Christ, a rabbit couldn't get out of this hell hole."

As one day and then another slowly passed, the siege of the Cheyennes came to lie like a black cloud on the garrison of Fort Robinson. The first day passed silently, quietly, the news of Wessells' decision running through the ranks of the enlisted men and the old barracks building becoming a focus for all eyes all day long. The guard at the door was increased and a close chain beat of sentries put around the building. This meant that each sentry had a short beat which overlapped the beat of the next man, a measure hardly ever resorted to at an army post.

Among the garrison, the feelings of the men were mixed; a good part were entirely indifferent. Not given to over-complication of motives or purposes, they adopted the simple philosophy that the only good Indians were dead Indians; and they directed their resentment toward the Cheyennes rather than toward the measures taken to subdue them. Others of the men muttered that it was a dastardly thing to starve any people to death, even Indians. There were some who had children of their own and wives of their own, and it occurred to them that even a brown-skinned people might feel the pangs of starvation and thirst. Their feelings, one way or another, fed on the deadly monotony of the life they lived; and the sprawling barracks became an ulcer in their midst. They cursed it, glared at it, attempted to ignore it; they grew short of temper and short of speech, bickered constantly, and fought over the slightest matters.

Two of the men, James Lisbee and Fred Green, had a knife battle that left Green coughing out his blood on the snow. Angus McCull struck his sergeant and was put in the guardhouse in irons. That was open fury; underneath there was constant, sullen pettiness. And for everything, Wessells' only solution was to make discipline tighter and tighter. Top sergeants at the plains posts were hard men;

they hardened now almost to the point of insanity. Good-natured Sergeant Lancy used his big fists like hammer-heads on the slightest provocation, and Sergeant O'Tool became a dark mass of hair-trigger rage. On Wessells' orders, the post trader refused liquor to any of the garrison, and that made things worse.

On the second day, signs of thirst became apparent among the imprisoned Indians. They scraped every bit of snow from the window-sills and they opened the door and scooped up the trodden snow within reach. The sentries' bayonets would not allow anyone to even step from the doorway; the barracks began to give out the smell of a charnel house.

Wessells was adamant, yet he considered his methods reasonable. The Indians were a pressing source of annoyance, but he did not hate them. Three times a day, he sent Rowland into the barracks to talk with them and make them see the error of their ways. The first day, they had fuel for their stove, but on the second day he cut that off too. He didn't approve of half measures.

On the second day, Rowland asked not to be sent to the barracks. "It's bad in there," he explained. "It's like a hell—"

"Losing your nerve?" Wessells demanded.

"No, only—well, they're desperate, Mr. Captain. They're getting crazy. And I think they have guns."

"You're crazy," Wessells said. "Where would they get guns?"

"I don't know. Maybe they break down some carbines when you capture them and hide them on the squaws.

Maybe they hide some revolvers on the squaws. I think they got at least five guns, that's what I think."

"You're crazy," Wessells insisted. "You're crazy and yellow. I've never seen a breed that wouldn't go yellow."

"Well, all right—I go in again," Rowland nodded reluctantly. "I go in again. But it's like a hell in there. They never come out and they never go back. Sure as hell, they die in there."

Lieutenant Allen begged Wessells to do something about the children. "Those kids," Allen said, "were starving when we brought them in. I'm not arguing about your methods, Captain. You're in command here and it's up to you."

"I'm willing to feed all of them," Wessells said. "It's their own choice."

"How much choice did the kids have?"

"Indians—" Wessells began.

"Good God, sir, even Indians are human! You can't starve little children and pass it off by calling them Indians."

"I'll thank you to mind your own damn business, Lieutenant," Wessells said. But once implanted, the thought bothered Wessells, enough to make him point out to Rowland that the Cheyenne children were free to leave the barracks. "Tell them to send the children out," Wessells said. "We'll feed them and take care of them."

But Rowland came out of the barracks pale and shaking his head and declaring that it was like hell inside. "—Just like hell."

"They won't send out the children?"

"They say they will die together. They just sit around

262

and look at me. And Jesus Christ, it's so cold in there, so damned cold. They sit, everyone huddled up with everyone else, so they can be warm, and they look at me."

The thermometer was at six degrees below zero.

"They'll come around tomorrow," Wessells said.

But the next day they began to sing their death songs. It had been bad enough when the sprawling barracks was a silent tomb, an ominously quiet shell encasing the bodies and souls of men. Now a keening came out of it and drifted on the cold wind into every corner of the post. They had a flute in there, and sometimes its mournful minor-key music accompanied the wailing death songs. It was the last, primitive requiem of a doomed race.

It ate into the morale of the garrison. The troopers gave the barracks a wide berth and tried to avoid looking at it. Any smile now was a forced, twisted grimace; the men didn't laugh. And what was even more disturbing, they didn't fight so much. They were black and bitter and sullen, but a note of fear crept into their lives. They were tense, expectant, and nervous.

And even Wessells began to realize that it would need only a spark to create anarchy in that lonely, isolated garrison.

At mess, the officers would stop talking. One would say something and someone else would answer and then someone wouldn't answer, and a question would hang in the air along with the silence while they listened.

They'd go on eating, and finally, someone would say: "Why don't they stop that unholy keening?"

"Why?"

Someone would say: "They don't sing the death songs unless they know they're dying."

"Damn it, shut up!"

Still they would listen, and the forced conversation would sound silly, pointless.

"Snow—"

"It looks like snow."

"A norther—"

"Well, I don't know. It seems too cold for snow."

"I don't know about that. I've seen it snow in colder weather than this."

"It never gets much colder than this."

"The hell you say."

Their very words were encased in their insularity. They hardly ever spoke of the east any more; they hardly ever spoke of women, of families, of the good things they had eaten, the good plays they had seen, the good books they had read, the good, warm companionship of civilized places.

Even Wessells' lethargic nerves became infected. Whereas in the past he had been the focus of the post, a solid if empty leader, he now began to show signs of uncertainty and bewilderment. Two days of the mournful death songs had made him desperate. He was determined to settle the affair in one way or another. He got hold of Rowland and told him:

"You're going back in there, do you understand?"

The halfbreed shook his head.

"You're going in there if I have to kick you all the way."

"I don't come out alive," Rowland muttered.

"Damn you, you'll come out alive, you dirty breed! You've been taking army pay and army rations and doing nothing for weeks. You're going in there now and you're going to get the chiefs to come out with you for a council."

"They got guns," Rowland protested.

"I don't give a damn if they have a battery of artillery in there. You're going in and you're coming out with the chiefs."

And finally, Rowland went into the barracks. Later, Wessells learned what the interpreter had seen in there, the dying Indians, huddled on the icy floor, the death-mask faces, the children with their bloated bellies and withered limbs, the squaws whose beautiful, rounded flesh had sunk into pockets of angry bone, the old men, the young men, the wives and mothers and fathers and sisters and brothers all one in the cold torture, the shameful, sinking flame of what had once been a proud and happy race.

Rowland came out with three chiefs, not the old man, but the two who were with him and one other; as Rowland counted them off on his fingers, smirking even after the horror at his achievement, Wild Hog, Old Crow, and Strong Left Hand, great chiefs with foolish names—and no names in the world are as foolish as Indian names—but great chiefs.

"They wouldn't let Dull Knife, the old man, come out," Rowland told Wessells. "He's head man of the tribe, like a papa to them. They keep him there because they want to look at him when they die."

"Didn't you tell them for a council?"

Rowland shrugged. "They don't think these chiefs ever come back. They kiss everyone and say good-by. That's the way they feel now."

Wessells received the chiefs in his office, smoking a cigar and sitting in the old rocking-chair, and trying to bring into his face and voice an expression of impartial justice. The three dying grotesques stood in front of him, shivering, still trying to be proud in their rags, but looking like nothing within the pale of reason. Vroom was there, and two troopers. Vroom was sniffing a handkerchief he had soaked in anise. Rowland kept far away from the chiefs as he could get.

Wessells came to the point directly and said: "You see what stubbornness has brought you. Now you see that it is a very good thing to obey the law. I have no hate in my heart. Go back to your people and tell them to come out and prepare for the journey south. Then I will feed them."

The fear, the wonder of it came into Rowland's voice. "They'll never go south, you can kill them, but that's all—" as if he was trying to peer into his ancestry and discover what would prompt such mad devotion to the nebulous thing white men called freedom.

Wessells said to the two troopers, evenly, the cigar clenched in his teeth, "Put those red bastards in irons."

And the Indians, not understanding his words, watching him without hope, without curiosity, without anything but a somber, ancient pride, didn't move.

The troopers stepped back and raised their guns to

cover the chiefs. Rowland shrunk away. Vroom loosened the flap of his holster.

"Tell them they're under arrest," Wessells said harshly.

Rowland began to speak, but already the chiefs realized what had happened. From under his rags one of them, a giant of a man with a long scar across his sunken face, drew a knife. Another flung himself at one of the troopers, who struck him a sickening blow on the skull with the barrel of his carbine. Meanwhile the man with the knife, crying aloud in his own tongue, leaped at the other trooper. The soldier gave back, afraid to fire his gun in the whirling mass of movement the room had become. He fended off the blows of the knife with his arm, taking several bad cuts; and then Vroom was in behind the Indian, hammering at his head with the long barrel of his Colt. Wessells, drawing his revolver, tried to cover the other chief, but Vroom and the troopers were in between. Vroom's man went down, his head cut and bloody, and Wessells chanced a shot at the other chief.

The shot must have gone wild; it filled the office with echoing thunder and woke the post. Vroom turned on the chief, who swept him aside and with one superhuman motion flung himself through the window, taking away glass and sash and all. The man rolled over and over on the snow, came to his feet, and ran twisting toward the barracks. Wessells, bulking in front of the shattered window, emptied his revolver at the fleeing Indian, but the range was already long for pistol shooting and the man turned and twisted.

By the time the troopers reached the window with their carbines, the Indian had already gained the shelter of the log barracks, flinging himself past a sentry who tried to bar his progress and through the open door.

Now the whole post was awake, troopers running from everywhere. Vroom went out to quiet them, while Wessells gave instructions to handcuff the fallen chief. The Indian with the scar was just regaining consciousness. He groped for the knife, but Wessells kicked it out of reach and stood over him with his revolver while the other was being manacled. The wounded trooper, clenching his bleeding arm, stumbled away to the infirmary.

For Wessells, it was like coming up against a wall that stretched endlessly on either side, topless in height, a blank, oppressive wall that faced him without relief. The wall was there at mess that evening; he saw it in the faces of the men, though their eyes avoided his, in the way they ate, slowly, tasting each mouthful of food, staring at the food, drinking water and coffee with a sense of suppressed wonder and horror—as if they had never known before what it meant to have soft food under their teeth, liquid wetting the delicate linings of their throat, all the food, all the liquid they could possibly desire, coffee with condensed milk to turn it yellow and sweet, meat, potatoes, bread. Jam in four jampots down the length of the table, crackers, cigars.

They couldn't eat much. The food lay in their plates; it would be taken back to the kitchen and thrown away. Up and down the long table, captains and first lieutenants and second lieutenants with their regimental colors drooping overhead. Most were young; some were nearing middle age. None of them knew what it was to kill a hundred and fifty persons, starving them to death. Most of them tried not to think of what it was.

"They've stopped that damn keening," someone said.

And then they all listened. Then Vroom lit a cigar. Someone tried to tell a joke, labored through to the end of it, and left them immersed in silence as oppressive as before.

But nobody made any move to leave the table.

Baxter said: "They've barricaded themselves in. Jenkins tried opening the door."

Wessells nodded.

No one dared suggest that they might be fed. For Wessells to make the move would have meant the complete shattering of something basic inside of him, something that gave him reason to live. For the others, looming behind Wessells, there was the insensate bulk of "orders from Washington." Lost in a vast wilderness of ice and snow, they were still the outstretched finger of an illusion they lived by.

Morosely, Allen remarked, "It seems they have guns. Rowland's sure of it."

"If Johnson had let me search the squaws in the beginning—" Wessells thought.

"They can't have many guns," he said.

Everyone was thinking: in a day, in two days, they would begin to die. What difference would guns make?

"That breed's a liar."

"He was too frightened to lie."

Someone suggested poker. Vroom, without enthusiasm, tried to get a four for whist. Someone went to the door, opened it, and glanced at the thermometer. The mercury was at four below.

"Cold—"

Vroom still aimlessly sought his whist game.

"Tomorrow, we'll go in there," Wessells said, without conviction.

"Four below," someone said needlessly.

"How's Lester?" Allen asked, referring to the trooper whose arm had been slashed.

"All right—he got a bad gash though. He'll be all right if she doesn't fester."

They drifted around the mess, back to the table. Vroom gave up his search for whist. They sat there and watched the orderly scrape together the crumbs.

The moon rose that evening in all the white glory of completion. The cold snap had dissipated the clouds, and the sky was a black bowl hung with thousands of stars. At nine o'clock, a man could have sat in the open in the center of the parade and read a newspaper without straining his eyes, so strong was the moonlight and the reflection from the snow. The ring of hills and dark, snow-clad pines only served to enhance the scene, and the post houses lay like random blocks tossed into a spotlit amphitheater.

A coyote, caught in the intricate web of scent, food scent, man scent, horse scent, the old, familiar scent of Indians lying somewhere in the deep recesses of his little brain, sat back on his tail and barked sad frustration at the glowing moon. He barked until the cook freed two

270

mongrel dogs to send the coyote yowling back into his
dark pine forests.

The horses, wrapped in their own steam in the long,
cold stables, whinnied nervously.

The sentries, of whom there were many, sentries in a
chain guard around the barracks, sentries at the door, sentries at the stables, the sentries and other men whose business took them into the cold, trailed their breath in long
tendrils behind them and moved quickly and nervously.

The post trader closed his store early and tried to interest himself in an Omaha newspaper.

The enlisted men in their barracks played cards, rolled
dice, read ten-cent novels, polished bits of equipment;
and some of them went to bed, early as it was, for lack of
anything better to do.

Sergeant Lancy had a toothache, a great, swollen cheek
and red eyes. He hadn't slept for two nights.

Captain Wessells smoked a cigar and watched a listless
game of penny and two stud. Because they were short of
pennies at the post, they played with little blue identifica-
tion tags. Most of them were heaped in front of Vroom,
who was playing every hand and winning every other one.
Lieutenant Allen was writing a letter to his mother, a
carefully composed complete account of each day's twenty-
four hours, a habit he had kept since he first went to the
Point.

His letter was detailed and homey and rich in the thousand little things that construct life for a mother; he wore
his flannel underwear, he wore two pairs of socks, cotton
next to his skin and wool over that, yes it was cold, but
you didn't feel the cold here as you did in the East; it

was a dry cold, very healthy, underlining healthy with the first smile he had been able to manage in several days. They had expected snow, but tonight it was very clear with a beautiful full moon in the sky, and it seemed the full moon brought out the coyotes and made them bark. No, a coyote was not like a wolf and not at all dangerous, a little thing hardly any larger than a fox, and not much good for anything except to steal and knock over the garbage pails. Really like a furry little dog. She must not worry about Indians because there would never be any more fighting on the plains, and he had been talking with Captain Vroom about anise, which the captain believed in completely, a point for her, since she favored it so much; although he didn't believe it was much good for colds. You didn't catch cold very easily here, the air was so dry. . . .

The cook had finished with the dough for the next day's bread, setting it in wooden tubs next to the stove and covering it over with damp cloths. He and Captain Wessells' orderly discussed the French; neither of them liked Frenchmen, although neither had ever known a Frenchman. They had come onto the point from Chinese cooks; both had known Chinese cooks.

The sentries in the chain guard around the barracks jail cursed the cold and speculated upon whether the mercury was rising or falling. One claimed it was at least ten below. Another said that when it dropped under five, you lost all power to sense the difference in temperature. He said that five below or thirty below felt the same; he had a theory about the human senses being fitted for only a certain range of cold or heat, a decent range, not lousy, filthy cold. They all agreed on the last point.

That was at Fort Robinson, that night, at nine o'clock.

At ten o'clock, a sentry of the chain guard around the barracks where the Indians were confined, heard something curious. Afterwards, he said it sounded like a pistol being cocked. The night was very quiet, and the slightest sound carried a long way in the clear, cold air. The sentry, whose name was Peter Jafison, waited for his mate on the chain to approach him. They stood together for a moment, just in front of one of the barracks windows.

These windows were shuttered from the inside. Heavy shutters which swung to from the inside and could be barred without the inhabitants leaving the house, were a common thing on the plains, indeed anywhere on the American frontier where houses were built with the secondary purpose of being used as fortresses. When the chief, Strong Left Hand, had fled from Wessells' office back to the barracks, the Indians had barred the door and closed all the shutters, nor had they been opened since.

Now Jafison and his mate moved closer to the barracks, listening. Some of the other guards stopped to watch them. Jafison thought he heard the sound again, a pistol being cocked; also it seemed that inside the barracks many men were pressed up against the log wall, breathing hoarsely. His mate, Luke Purdy, poked the butt of his carbine through a broken window pane and pressed against the shutter. It gave a little, as if it were not barred but only held closed from the inside.

273

Jafison didn't like it; he said so. "There's something funny as hell going on in there," he remarked.

Purdy kept pressing the stock of his carbine against the closed shutters. Another sentry, at the end of the building, broke his beat and started toward them. The two men at the door were watching Purdy and Jafison with their backs to the door.

What happened now came with such suddenness that afterwards no one could tell a clear and coherent story. It was apparent later that under each window the Cheyennes had built steps of piled saddles and old rawhide parfleches, Indian packs. Now, suddenly, all the shutters and the door were flung open simultaneously; the windows, pane and sash, were knocked out, and through every opening Indians poured forth onto the snow, the men first, leaping from the windows with almost incredible nervous strength, the women and children behind them, crawling out, clambering down, helped by the men. At least the first ten Indians were armed with rifles and pistols; the others had whatever makeshift weapons could have been fashioned inside of the barracks, legs from the iron stove, boards torn from the floor, sticks, stones dug from the icy ground under the floor; many had knives the women managed to hide when captured.

Purdy went down immediately; he tried to fire his carbine, but a pistol roared in his face and left him dead in the snow in front of the window. Jafison killed an Indian with his first shot, was hurled aside unharmed, and then he backed against the log wall of the barracks and kept on shooting. None of the other sentries were killed; they

274

either leaped out of the way or went down stunned under the wave of Indians.

The Cheyennes poured out and streamed across the bright white expanse of the parade ground, running as well as their enfeebled condition would permit, the men and women carrying the smaller children and the old people who were too weak to run. Instinctively, they headed down toward the wooded creek-bottom, seeking both shelter and water.

The first burst of fire awakened the post. Wessells, just unbuttoning his coat for bed, grabbed his revolver and ran for the parade. The stud poker game was still going on; the officers leaped to their feet and flung out, leaving a trail of blue markers behind them. In the barracks, half the men were already asleep; they poured out in their woolen underwear, pausing only for their carbines and a handful of cartridges; the other troops, in all the various stages of undress, were already out on the snow.

Before them, like a set stage in the moonlight, was the brilliant white expanse of the parade ground, dotted with the fleeing Cheyennes. For the troops, for the officers, this was the moment of release, complete release from the brooding presence of the Indians, from the specter of an unholy people who put insane and curious value upon what they called their freedom.

They began to shoot, and their rage, their release into intangible, inhuman rage, made them cold as the searing white moonlight. They stood there shooting like men on a firing range potting clay pigeons. They fired until their frozen hands blistered from the heat of their rifle

barrels. And the Indians, dark against the white snow, top-
pled over, crumpled into baggy heaps, rolled aimlessly,
spotted the snow all over, left a polka-dot pattern of their
dead upon the snow. They killed without thought, without choice, without compassion, sending their bullets into
the hearts of five-year-olds and ten-year-olds and ancients
who had seen eighty long years flow past. They picked
off running women and sent their lead into wounded
women who crawled moaning through the snow. Forgetful
of the cold and snow, they ran barefooted after the Indians, pausing only to discharge their carbines at any
crumpled figure that showed signs of life or movement.

Meanwhile, the vanguard of the Cheyennes, those armed
with the few rifles and revolvers, had managed to reach
the creek; there they fell on the ice, flat, smashing the thin
center crust with their fists and guns, drinking and drinking, in spite of the crackling rifle fire behind them. Then
they crawled to the bank and made an attempt to hold
off the troops while others scrambled down to the creek
and rushed insanely for water. Altogether, about fifty persons reached the creek-bottom.

Wessells and Vroom led the flood of half-clad troops
after them. Wessells, waving an empty revolver in one
hand, a saber in the other, yelled like a madman as he
ran down to the creek. In the back of his fire-lit mind was
a vague realization that he had failed miserably in his
first command, that put in charge of a group of prisoners,
he had not only failed to carry out orders concerning
them, but had allowed them to escape. That realization
burst asunder all the delicate interplay of training, breed-

ing, learning, restraint, leaving him hapless and furious as a lunatic.

At the creek-bottom, they overtook an old man carrying a child. Wessells cut the old man down with a single blow of his saber; someone close behind him shot the child. They ran up the creek and saw in the moonlight two Indians armed only with knives, trying to stay the pursuit a little so that those ahead of them might better escape. The troopers rushed past Wessells, firing; one Indian went down; the other, bloody all over, somehow stood on his feet and waved his knife. Vroom spitted him.

They came on a wounded Dog Soldier, lying in the creek where the rim ice had broken under his body, moaning his death song. Wessells clicked the hammer of his empty revolver. Troopers behind him fired a dozen bullets into the body of the dying man.

They came on a little group of six women and two boys, lying against each other in the snow, too weak to go any further. One of the women carried a dead child in her arms. The troopers opened fire and kept on firing until the six women and one of the boys lay in an icy pool of blood. The other boy had managed to scramble into the brush. Wessells and the troopers went after him and found him, a dozen yards away, wedged into a cleft. One of the troopers threw up his carbine, but Wessells knocked it away. Another trooper began to vomit.

Wessells went into the cleft and dragged the boy out, a thin, terrified gnome of eleven or twelve, wasted, bloody, sobbing and whimpering hysterically.

The fit passed, washed out, used out, expiated in blood, leaving the Fort Robinson troops cold and tired and sick.

They stood around the child, trying to soothe him, trying to quiet his fears. Then they picked him up and carried him back to the fort.

Wessells, sick to his stomach, cold, trembling, walked across the parade. The sound of firing, long stilled, echoed in his ears. Now, at the post, the only sound was the moaning of the wounded.

All around him, soldiers, mutely, were picking up the dead Indians and carrying them over to the old barracks, where they were piled like logs against the wall. Others were carrying wounded children, helping wounded women. But there were not so many wounded as dead; by the dozens, the dead were laid up against the barracks wall, and still there seemed no end. More and more bodies were brought up from the creek-bottom.

Wessells went into the infirmary where Doc Clancy, the post surgeon, was trying to put broken flesh and bones together. The short, bald doctor had drawn a pair of trousers over his underwear; he worked in his slippers, arms and clothes stained with blood, a bottle of whiskey at his elbow. The Indians lay about with drawn and twisted faces, the men silent for the most part, the children whimpering with pain and the memory of a horrible dream, the women moaning and sobbing.

"It won't do any good to get drunk," Wessells said.

"Drunk?" the doctor glanced at him and then ignored him.

"I said it won't do any good to get drunk!"

"God damn you, Wessells!" the doctor said.

"Shut up!"

A stream of curses, filthy, barbed, tumbled off the doctor's lips. Wessells stood there for a while, listening, and then he left.

Wessells saw the wagon come back to the post. It had been sent down to the creek-bottom to follow the Indians' trail and pick up the dead. Wessells walked over and watched them pull down the frozen bodies.

Walking into the officers' messroom, Wessells saw Lieutenant Allen at the table, his face in his arms. Allen was crying.

"That's no damn good!" Wessells said.

Allen didn't move.

"Jesus Christ, be a man!" Wessells cried. "Jesus Christ, you're an officer, not a kid at school! Get up!"

Allen rose slowly. "Yes, sir—"

"Go to your quarters," Wessells said quietly. "Go to sleep. Get a good night's rest."

"Yes, sir," Allen whispered.

"You'll feel better in the morning."

"Yes, sir."

Wessells sat at the table and smoked a cigar and stared gloomily at nothing at all. Out of the cold, Vroom came, stamping his feet, pulling off his gloves, trying to build something out of his large physical strength yet giving Wessells the impression of a punctured and deflated bag.

"I saw Allen," Vroom remarked obliquely, eyeing Wessells, waiting. He accepted a cigar and sat down at the table.

"Christ," he said.

279

"How many?" Wessells asked him, leaving the question in the air yet knowing that it would be comprehended.

"Sixty-one so far," Vroom said evenly. "They're bringing more bodies in from up the creek. And I guess some of the wounded will go."

"Sixty-one," Wessells repeated.

Vroom puffed his cigar stolidly.

"Why couldn't they go back?" Wessells murmured.

Vroom continued to smoke.

"Sixty-one," Wessells said again, as if trying to imprint the fact on his brain.

"Mostly women," Vroom announced.

Wessells said, after a while: "That bunch that escaped—they've got guns. We'll have to go after them in the morning and bring them back."

"I suppose so—if they're not dead and frozen when we get to them."

"Either way, we'll have to go in the morning."

"I suppose so."

"You'd better remain at the post," Wessells added. "I'll take Baxter."

"It doesn't matter," Vroom shrugged.

They sat for a while in silence, smoking, and finally Vroom said: "Turning in?"

"Later—I want to get out a report."

He finished the report, went to his quarters, drank the best part of a pint of whiskey, and tried to sleep. It was no good. He lay on his bed, fully clothed, and the darkness before his eyes was full of pictures, too many pictures and too real. It was no good. He pulled on his mackinaw and stumbled out, driving the pictures before him; he went outside into the cold and the sweat poured from him.

He saw the wagon coming back to the post with another load of the dead. He stood there, watching the soldiers swing out the bodies, holding them by head and feet. He found himself asking them:

"How many?"

He walked past the yellow windows of the infirmary and the memory of the keening death songs was no worse than this. He felt an awful need for action, any sort of action.

He met Lieutenant Baxter, who said: "I can't sleep, sir. I tried."

"Yes—"

"Did anything come from headquarters?"

"Not yet—I don't know. I just sent in the report."

"Will the newspapers get it?"

"I suppose so," Wessells said. "They get everything."

"I suppose you had to mention my name, sir?"

Wessells nodded; for the first time in his life he reluctantly sensed the numberless packed layers of a man's soul. He didn't want to probe; he was almost afraid to discover what sequence of events might explode upon the linking of Baxter's name with the massacre.

"I had to," he said.

Baxter kept nodding; he was like a frightened child and he kept avoiding with his eyes the charnel bulk of the barracks.

"What are our casualties?" Wessells asked. He was almost frantically eager to discover some compensation; the weight of dead was already so great that more dead on his side would serve to lessen it rather than increase it.

"One," Baxter answered.

"One?"

"Just one, at the barracks, shot through the heart—that was Purdy."

"Just one," Wessells repeated incredulously.

"I couldn't sleep," Baxter remembered plaintively. "God, I'm so tired and I can't sleep."

"There must be wounded," Wessells insisted. They were unloading the last of the dead Cheyennes from the wagon. "There must be wounded," he said. "They fought us, they had guns."

"About five, sir. It looks bad for Smith and Everetts. They wouldn't go to the infirmary at first. They ran down to the creek, bleeding—" He was chattering, gushing eagerly with details.

"Oh, shut up!" Wessells sighed.

"I'm sorry, sir."

"Yes, yes—sorry myself."

"I thought—"

"Never mind," Wessells said.

Baxter couldn't stand still; he was jumpy, nervous. Wessells felt the cold seeping into his body. He said to Baxter: "We might as well get after them now."

"I thought, in the morning—"

"We might as well start now," Wessells said.

They trailed along the creek-bottom in the early dawn, Wessells' company and Baxter's under-muster company.

Wessells rode in front with a Sioux scout and Rowland; Baxter brought up the rear. The men were cold and sick and silent; they rode for hours without speaking.

Some miles from the fort, they found a Dog Soldier in the creek, half encased in ice. He had been shot in three places, once in the head; it was incredible that he had come so far. They stopped to bury him, to camp and cook their morning meal. Then they went on.

They found a place where three pairs of bloody footprints led away from the main trail. They followed this offshoot for three miles through the pines until the whip of a rifle brought them to a stop and left one of the troopers with a useless, broken arm. Then they dismounted and crawled forward, keeping up a heavy fire. The rifle went on cracking with dogged regularity, and they were there for two hours sending their lead into the pine thicket.

Finally, the rifle was silent; they crawled ahead, waited, closed in a little more.

"No ammunition, I think," Wessells said, rising. They came in behind him. The Indian was dead, his body shattered by at least a dozen slugs. He lay over his rifle and behind him were two squaws, their bodies frozen stiff. Apparently, realizing they were dying, he had gone off the trail to be with them at the end.

A sergeant pointed out the Cheyenne's wounds. "Christ, they die hard," he whispered.

That night they camped and it snowed, a light, feathery snow, not much, but enough to blot out the Cheyennes' trail. In the morning, they fanned out, walked their horses over miles of ground on either side of the creek, trying to pick up the trail. They had no success that day nor the next day; and after that, a thaw set in, one of those sudden, northwestern mid-winter thaws. The snow shrunk and sponged into slush; the ground softened until the horses' hoofs sank inches down, and the sun shone with all the delicious heat of early summer. They had come down from the hills onto the rolling prairie, and now Wessells headed for the Wyoming border.

There was civilization in a lonely rancher's cabin, sitting in its corral and sending a tendril of blue smoke seeking to the sky. There was civilization enough to make the column of blue-clad troops pause in almost religious awe. Their hands were bloody; they felt like errant children coming home.

Wessells led the way to the cabin and shouted for the rancher. He came out drying his hands on a dirty towel, smiling, two tow-headed children pulling at his legs.

"Howdy, soldier," he nodded.

His wife, a strapping, blue-eyed woman, emerged with buckets and drew water from the well.

"Nice weather," the rancher grinned.

"Like summer," Wessells agreed. He couldn't trust himself to say much.

"Just the nicest weather I ever seen this time of the year. Down from Robinson, soldier?"

Wessells nodded mutely.

"Had much weather up in the hills?"

"Cold," Wessells said.

"Sure, it was cold down here a while ago."

"Have you seen Indians in this neighborhood?" Wessells asked precisely. He couldn't stand being there much longer; he felt he would go mad looking at the rancher, the children, the woman.

"The boy who rides for me, he seen something down south a ways. It looked like the God almighty, from what he said."

"Indians?"

"Maybe you'd call it that. He didn't say it was nice to look at. And he wasn't drunk, mister. He said—"

"Never mind that," Wessells interrupted harshly. "How many?"

"Hell, mister, take it easy," the rancher drawled. "I ain't saying what I seen. The boy—"

"How many?" Wessells snapped.

"All right, soldier, have it your way. About twenty, he reckoned. Maybe more, maybe less."

"On foot?"

"Sure, mister, on foot."

They rode south, pushing their horses over the soft prairie. They drove on with all the cold desire of men who must destroy to atone for destruction. They crossed into Wyoming and struck the old Cheyenne and Black Hills Road, and toward evening they sighted a little log stage stop called Bluff Station. There, information was more precise. Two ranchers, riding in that afternoon, had seen a beggars' procession, a scene out of inferno.

Wessells listened and nodded. The troopers were loosening their saddle cinches. Wessells heard the rest of the story and mounted his horse. There was something silently terrible in the way the troopers tightened their cinches again and mounted.

They saw the light of the Cheyenne fire when they were only a few miles out of the stage station. Wessells was not impelled to hurry; in his heart, he felt that this was the end of the chase—and also the end of many other things. They rode forward slowly, their horses' hoofs making little sound on the soft prairie.

Still the Cheyennes must have heard them. When the troops came to the fire of buffalo chips, it was deserted. They waited there while the Sioux scout went ahead crouched over the trail; in a little while he was back.

"Where are they?" Wessells asked.

"Up dere, in buffalo wallow."

Wessells was very calm. He felt old and tired, and now he wanted sleep desperately. He called Baxter and told him slowly: "We're going to surround them—a complete circle, you understand. Put the men in their places and let them sleep there. Mud? I don't give a damn about the mud. Put the men in their places and let them sleep there. Keep a chain of twenty sentries going, behind the men; I don't want them killing each other. And let a few men get the horses out of rifle shot. You can keep your horse with you and I'll keep mine, but I want the rest unsaddled and out of rifle shot. You understand?"

Baxter nodded. Wessells was falling asleep on his feet. As soon as the circle was completed, he spread his blanket, lay down with his head on his saddle, and went off almost immediately.

Wessells woke before dawn and lay with his head on the saddle, watching the sun rise. Gradually, as the gray mist of morning lifted, the sloping edge of the buffalo wallow came into view; somewhere in there, in the mud,

286

were the twenty-odd Cheyennes; yet so still, so quiet, so peacefully deceptive was the whole scene that Wessells was almost inclined to believe they had surrounded an empty pit.

Far off, on the upflung curve of the prairie, he could make out the further edge of the circle, the small, black figures of the sentries on their chain beat, the huddled shapes of the sleeping men. It was hardly possible that anything could have crept through that.

He rose and flexed his cramped muscles. It was quite warm, more like early fall than winter. He walked down the line of men until he found the bugler, and a moment later the clear notes of reveille sounded out.

And still no sign from the buffalo wallow. While the men ate a cold breakfast, Wessells sought out the Sioux scout and asked him:

"Damn you, you're sure they're there?"

The scout shrugged. "Track go in—dey don' come out."

"We'll advance from all sides," Wessells told Baxter.

"Isn't that dangerous?"

"Tell the men to keep their fire low. The ground's too soft to stop a bullet."

"You don't think we could talk to them, sir?"

"Talk to them?"

"The breed's here."

"My God, they won't surrender," Wessells said. "They want to die—those red bastards don't want anything else."

"For the record, sir?"

Wessells ground his toe into the mud thoughtfully. Then he nodded. "I'll talk to them."

He went up with Rowland, who was afraid and making no pretense of not being afraid, who kept saying: "You do a foolish thing, I tell you, you do a foolish thing."

"Call to them," Wessells said.

Rowland shook his head, crawled forward, and then cried out in the strange, musical, plaintive tongue. He called, waited, and called again. Wessells was surprised when an Indian drew erect on the edge of the wallow; it was like a visitation from the dead, the tall, bony, half-naked specter, swaying, looking at Wessells not with hate, not even with regret, but only with somber wonder.

He didn't have to tell Rowland what to say, nor did he ask the halfbreed to translate the sighing words of the Dog Soldier. Only when Rowland reached him, he stood hesitating, and this time a bullet from the buffalo wallow plowed the mud at his feet.

He started to run back, but the waiting troops took the shot as a signal to charge. He stood waiting for them, seemingly unaware of the crackling fire from the pit. When he turned to go with them, he felt a hot, angry blow on his head. Then he was down on the ground with his face in the mud, trying to draw erect. Two troopers supported him to his saddle.

He lay with his legs thrown out, his eyes closed, while they dressed the wound in his scalp. The attack had been beaten back, and now Baxter stood next to him. The lieutenant kept asking him whether the wound was bad.

"No, no! Christ, Lieutenant, go back to your men!"

"Shall we go in again?"

"How was it?"

288

"We lost two—seven others wounded."

"Just keep up the fire," Wessells said. "Tell them to shoot low. The ground's soft."

All day long, the firing went on, incessantly, plowing a circle of mud around the buffalo wallow; and as the afternoon lengthened, the troops crawled in, closer and closer, always firing. Bit by bit, the return fire from the wallow slackened off, until at last it ceased entirely.

The sun dropped low in the west, and still the troops kept up their fire. Then, at long last, the bugle sounded and the firing ceased.

And then, of a sudden, the prairie was still with an incredible, unearthly stillness. A hawk, winging down from the heights, passed low over the buffalo wallow and then swooped up into the sky.

Minutes passed; the sun was close to the horizon now with a single fleecy cloud across its face.

And then Baxter stood up. And then other men, one by one, without any given signal—until all of the hundred and fifty were walking with measured steps toward the buffalo wallow, their carbines held tightly and expectantly.

And still nothing happened.

They gathered around the edge of the buffalo wallow in a tight circle. They stood there silently for a while, and then the circle loosened up as men pushed out and turned away.

Wessells came up, supported on either side by a soldier. The circle opened for him, and he stood on the edge of the buffalo wallow, looking down at the bodies of twenty-two men and women. He stood there while the sun set, while a cool wind rose up, while soft, gentle night came to the prairie.

PART TEN   January 1879–April 1879

THE END OF THE TRAIL

I**N THE** January 18, 1879, edition of the *New York Herald*, the attitude of the Department of the Interior was presented clearly and tersely. In fact, a single sentence told the nation:

"Secretary Schurz declined to speak on the matter."

Simply, so very simply, in such a matter-of-fact way was the incident filed in the dusty drawers of history; Secretary of the Interior Carl Schurz declined to speak on the matter—Carl Schurz who was born in Germany, who fought in the Revolution of 1848, who fled his country as thousands of other Germans fled it, before and since, who at one time or another saw the word *Freedom* burning in bright and glorious letters across the morning sky, who came to America when America was a young giant of promise and hope, who spoke to his countrymen in their own tongue with a message of liberty, who knew the raw man, Abe, who fought for Lincoln the president, knew him, called him his friend, who gave up the post of Minister to Spain that he might return and fight to preserve the Union, who saw the blood flow at Gettysburg. It was the same Carl Schurz, who when told that the ante-room to his office was filled with reporters, said:

"Send them away—"

And asked for a statement:

"I have no statement to make."

But the news from Fort Robinson:

"I have nothing to say."

Yet the attitude of the government?

"Send them away. I have no statement to make."

The secretary had read his copy of Captain Wessells' report over and over; he had read until the words lost meaning and became dancing lines of type. He had read until he no longer comprehended the meaning of insurrection, revolt, disobedience.

He sat there behind his desk while the afternoon waned, while evening came; and through the tall windows of his office he saw the bare branches of a tree blot out in the comfort of night. His clerk entered the room again and said:

"There's another reporter, sir."

"I told you to send them away."

"Mr. Jackson?"

"I can't see him," Carl Schurz said.

"He won't go away, he says he'll wait. He asked me to give you this—to tell you it's the transcript of an interview he obtained with General Sherman."

Schurz nodded. "Tell him that it is foolish for him to wait. There is nothing that I have to say."

"I'll tell him that."

The transcript lay in front of the secretary, and for a while he sat and stared at it idly. Then he wiped his glasses and fixed them on his nose. He began to read. The dateline was Washington, Jan. 16.

"General Sherman said tonight that the war department had no other information concerning the recent outbreak among the Cheyennes than had already appeared in the *Herald*. The General had just finished his dinner and was going to get ready for the Henry Memorial Exercises at the Capitol.

" 'You have read the details of the story of the massacre of the Cheyennes then, General?' asked your correspondent.

" 'Massacre, massacre!' repeated General Sherman. 'Why do you call it a massacre? A number of insubordinate, cunning, treacherous Indians, who had no more regard for the lives of our officers and soldiers than if they had been dogs, attempted to escape from the custody of our troops and used violence to carry on their rebellious act. They were treated just as they deserved to be, and it's folly to attempt to extenuate such a crime by soft-sounding words.'

" 'But, General, may there not have been aggravating surroundings which led to the attempt of the Cheyennes to free themselves?'

" 'That question is easily answered. The orders were to remove the Cheyennes from Fort Robinson to the Indian Territory. They resisted, revolted, and fled. It was a duty imposed upon General Crook to see that the order was executed. Insubordination in the army is always fatal to military discipline. Shall a lot of Indians be permitted to do what we would not tolerate for an instant among our own race? No, no. The rascals were determined to resist, cost what it might, and as this government is not yet prepared to yield to the dictation of any number of Indians, the measures enforced were just precisely what the exigencies of the occasion demanded.'

" 'You do not suspect, then, that there was anything like jobbery on the part of the Indian Agent that provoked them to act as they did?'

" 'Nothing of the kind. The Cheyennes were ordered to Indian Territory from Fort Robinson; they were in charge of the military to be transferred. They were not inclined to go, and the usual precaution was taken, as was supposed, to make them harmless. That precaution was not thoroughly taken, and the result was a conflict between the Indians and our troops in the enforcement of a military order.' "

It ended abruptly, and Schurz could see Sherman pulling on his coat and preparing to leave the house, his mind washed clean of all conflict and doubt. Envy turned slowly to wonder and then to fear; he sat and stared and stared at the written words of the interview.

Then he rang for the clerk. "That reporter, Mr. Jackson, is he outside?" Schurz asked.

"He wouldn't go away."

"Then send him in," Schurz said.

Jackson came in slowly, inquiringly, his long, ugly face impassive, his loose clothes rumpled. Scenting for the wind, he waited until the secretary asked him to sit down.

"Have a smoke," Schurz said, taking out a box of cigars.

Jackson accepted, bit off the end, and leaned forward to the match Schurz held out. He puffed deeply and said: "That's good—on the government?"

"On me," Schurz smiled.

"Thanks." He still waited.

"You have been away," Schurz said. "You like to travel?"

"I hate it."

"Yes? Well, some should stay at home and some should travel. A good cigar is worth a thousand miles on a railroad, no?"

"I think so," Jackson agreed.

"You were to the Territory?" Schurz said.

"Yes—"

Schurz sighed. "It will do no good, making a big noise about nothing. When a thing is over, it is over, and then it should be forgotten, no?"

"Maybe," Jackson agreed.

Schurz said: "This interview—"

"They told me the Secretary of the Interior had nothing to say."

"But you must not print this," Schurz said.

"I think we'll print it, Mr. Secretary."

"But you must not," Schurz insisted.

"Whatever I think of William Sherman," Jackson slowly said, "I know that the man is honest. Whether he is right or wrong in what he believes, he's honest."

Schurz stared at him, the little eyes narrow, the mouth masked under the impassive cover of beard.

"What happened at Fort Robinson will be forgotten," Jackson said. "Maybe in six months, maybe in six weeks.

295

But will people forget that Carl Schurz said, nothing can be wrong in principle and right in practice?"

"What do you want?" Schurz whispered.

"For such insinuations, you should throw me out of your office, Mr. Secretary." Jackson's tone was light, almost insulting.

"What do you want?"

"I wanted a statement from the Secretary of the Interior. It might mean a raise for me."

"I have nothing to say," Schurz answered stolidly.

Jackson rose to go. At the door he paused and stared quizzically at the secretary. "Mr. Schurz," he said quietly, "it's not the dead Indians—we've had all that before. But those guns at Fort Robinson, they weren't only pointed at the Indians; they were pointed at you and at me." And then he went out.

Perhaps an hour had gone past before Carl Schurz took paper and a pen and began to write. One hundred and fifty of the Cheyennes, the half of the village still alive and uncaptured, were somewhere in the north. In a fashion what Schurz wrote to General Crook was defeat. It left him feeling tired and old; it humbled him. Yet he knew that this, least to be remembered, an obscure order to a more or less obscure military leader, was not the least of his services not only to America but to the man, Schurz. He gave it to the clerk and said:

"Send it off tonight. I'm going home now."

He walked out slowly into the night. He knew that the headlines were done with, that in six weeks or six months no one would remember that there had been a massacre at Fort Robinson in Nebraska. Nor would it

296

mean much that one hundred and fifty primitive savages called Cheyennes would sleep easily in a land that had long been their own.

For Murray, there was no trail's end, even in January when he heard the news from Fort Robinson, even in February when a lieutenant transferred from the Third Cavalry to Fort Keogh in Montana, gave a vivid, first-hand description of the last fight at the buffalo wallow. It was at the officers' mess, and everyone listened intently, admiring the way Wessells had taken advantage of the soft ground. When the lieutenant had finished, he turned to Murray and said:

"You had a few scraps with them, Captain. Tough customers, aren't they?"

"Yes—"

Murray's impassive face revealed only complete lack of interest. He left the table, and the lieutenant shrugged and went on with his story.

Murray had been at Fort Keogh almost nine weeks. The long, fruitless search for Little Wolf's band had led him into the Black Hills, and there the trail had petered out. Somewhere in the vastness of green mountains, numberless valleys, and deep forests were the Indians. To find them in the short space of time before winter snows set in would have been next to impossible. Then, from Colonel Mizner, in Indian Territory, came orders for the return of the two companies of the Fourth Cavalry to the south. At Deadwood, Murray telegraphed for a transfer to General Miles' command, and when it came through, he left his men and went on alone to Fort Keogh in Montana.

His parting with Wint was curious. He said little, seemed almost frantically anxious to be away from them. Wint, uneasy, embarrassed, said the conventional words.

"It's all right," Murray smiled. "Maybe up there I'll find what I'm looking for."

Then he spent nine long, dull weeks in snow-bound Fort Keogh. He had little to do with the garrison officers. He showed plainly that he desired to be alone; his only interest was in news of the Cheyennes, in the vague rumors that filtered through the mountains, a trapper who had heard this, a scout who had heard that, a hunter who had found an old, abandoned camp site. And when news finally came through that the Cheyennes, when discovered, would be allowed to remain in the north, even that interest slackened away.

It was in April that the first real news of the Cheyennes came through to the fort. Lieutenant W. P. Clark, who was out with a scouting detail of two troops in the direction of Powder River, had made some sort of contact with them. Word brought back to Fort Keogh indicated that two of Clark's Sioux scouts had come across the Cheyennes up on the Powder River, that they had spoken with them, and that Little Wolf had agreed to meet Clark.

General Miles, recalling Murray's chase, said to him: "It's curious, Captain, that they should come in peaceably this way. Almost an anticlimax after that chase they led you."

"I don't know," Murray said. "They wanted to go home. I think that was all they wanted."

"Of course," the general added, "the primitive idea of freedom and liberty is not like ours."

"Perhaps," Murray agreed.

"Have you made any plans for the future, Captain?"

Murray said: "No—no, not exactly. I'm thinking of resigning my commission, leaving the army for good."

"You're an old army man. If you don't mind my saying so, Captain, you'll be like a duck out of water."

"Possibly," Murray agreed.

"If there's anything I can do, Captain, anything in the way of a recommendation for a promotion—"

"No, sir. Thank you, but my mind's more or less made up."

Back in October, the Cheyennes, the one hundred and fifty of men and women and children led by old Little Wolf, had lost themselves to Captain Murray, to General Crook, to the world and to Carl Schurz who had written words that meant their freedom. They fled north and north, losing their trail in shallow rivers, meeting the snow and welcoming it, covering their backwash with a white blanket, and seeing finally like a wall in front of them, the green, humped shoulders of the hills.

They went into the Black Hills like a fox to earth. Deeper and deeper, they sought the place they wanted, found it finally, a long, wooded valley, high-walled, close at either end and cut off from the rest of the world. There was shelter and protection, pasturage for their tired ponies, fat bear, deer seeking the same protection that was theirs, wild duck winging down from the icy barrens of Canada, rabbits, squirrels, all the rich, fruitful world they had longed for.

They made life for themselves. As days turned to weeks and weeks to months, as the snow fell and piled in great banks around their tepees, the memory of the long, running battle became less and less urgent. A wall of snow and mountains of snow sheltered them; children were born and nursed at mothers' breasts, and other children, playing in the snow and sifting it to powder, forgot red dust that was also like powder, starvation and malaria and the ominous, stiff-shirted beings who represented civilization.

Yet others couldn't have forgotten, for in the original village the three hundred were almost, through marriage and inter-marriage, a single family; and now, in Little Wolf's band, brothers waited for sisters, parents for their children, children for mothers and fathers.

They waited, and old Little Wolf, carefully hoarding his store of tobacco, sucked his corncob pipe and stared anxiously at the protecting banks of snow. Spring would open the mountains to the world, and then the great net would begin to close about them once more. And with the first breath of spring in the air, he gave orders to the tribe to take down their tepees and prepare to move. Where, he didn't know, but he had the feeling that somewhere in the north was refuge and security, perhaps in the half-mythical place called Canada, where Sitting Bull and his Sioux had gone.

They passed out of the mountains and traveled north

and west to the Powder River. And it was there, near the Powder River, that they met Lieutenant Clark's Sioux scout, Red War Bonnet. And it was there, through a Sioux speaking unfamiliar, halting Cheyenne, that Carl Schurz's decision came to Little Wolf.

AN AFTERWORD

THE STORY told here is, as far as I can ascertain, absolutely true. If incredible, its incredibility can only be explained by the fact that it happened. All of the principal characters in the story, with the exception of Captain Murray, are persons who lived and played their parts much as I have detailed here.

I first came on the track of this story through reading Struthers Burt's "Powder River." A paragraph there gave some hint of what was possibly the greatest struggle against odds in all human history—and also an epic in man's desire for personal freedom. Deciding that the story should be told in full, I set out to gather the facts.

I ran into the usual maze of falsification and inconsistency that rewards any attempt to dig out an untold story already more than sixty years old. The fact that the drama of the situation made for good newspaper copy at the time only added to the confusion. A typical example is the following from the *New York Herald,* of September 20, 1878:

AN AFTERWORD

TOPEKA, KANSAS—Sept. 18

Rumors that the Indians are doing damage such as burning houses near Fort Dodge on the western borders of Kansas. . . . Two or three houses three miles west of Dodge City were on fire this PM, and it is not unlikely that some of the Cheyennes who escaped from their territory a few days ago and who are known to have been turned back and broken up into squads have set fires either to the prairies or the homes . . .

And in the same paper a few days later, datelined:

TOPEKA, KANSAS—Sept. 20

The Indian scare in Kansas subsiding; not a hostile in the state. People reported killed are laughing it off. Great scare is subsiding. Beyond stealing a few head of stock near the line of Indian Territory or perhaps south of it, there appears to be no authentic case of Indian depredations.

Starting on the trail itself, on the Cheyenne Reservation in Oklahoma, I ran into the same difficulty that presented itself to so many of the characters in the story, the barrier of language. The old, old Indians who remembered the flight to the north had never learned to express themselves adequately in English. They still spoke their wonderfully musical and complex tongue, but almost no one I came in contact with could help me to lucid translation. For instance, when I spoke to them of Dull Knife, the old chief who had led the village in its flight, I was speaking of him in English by the name the Sioux had given him. In Cheyenne, he had other names. I began to believe that any literal translation from Cheyenne to English was impossible. So complex is the tongue that young Cheyennes, educated in English schools, are unable to speak to their fathers in their native language.

304

For all that, the old men of the tribe were more than willing to be helpful, and from their great store of memories I got much that was useful. Also, I am deeply indebted to all the people of the University of Oklahoma at Norman, who spared no effort to aid me; and to the young Cheyennes who re-created the life of their ancestors in their own slow, Western drawl.

I have also drawn heavily upon George Bird Grinnell's anthropological studies of the Cheyenne Indians.

Bit by bit, the story took form. It is a tribute to the little Indian village that battles fought hundred of miles apart should have been generally regarded as isolated incidents. At the time, few persons realized that the band which surrendered to General Miles on the Yellowstone River was the same that had left Oklahoma so many months before. Neither the War Department nor the Bureau of Indian Affairs were eager to publicize the facts.

Particularly interesting is this: that among the few persons who went to bat for the Cheyennes were certain fearless, hard-hitting frontier editors. In spite of the fact that they wrote for a western audience, they had enough regard for the truth to print what they believed. The following editorial from the Omaha, Nebraska, *Daily Herald* is a very good example. It was printed in rebuttal to a *New York Herald* story which claimed that since the Cheyennes had enough clothes to start north from Indian Territory, it was foolish to say that they were half naked at Fort Robinson; that their outbreak at Fort Robinson had been prompted by fear of prosecution for their crimes; and that this prosecution was at the suggestion of General

Sheridan with the concurrence of General Sherman and the Commissioner of Indian Affairs.

The Omaha editorial, dated January 17, 1879, is as follows:

The above [referring to the *New York Herald* story] is a tissue of lies. Without knowing anything of the truth or falsity of so much of it as relates to the recommendations alleged to have been made by Sheridan or Sherman, we feel prepared from our knowledge of the entire falsity of the rest of it, to say that that statement is also a lie. The above report was written in the Indian bureau, evidently. Perhaps Mr. Hayt himself was the composer. We shall be obliged if Commissioner Hayt or anybody else in Washington will disprove the following assertations:—

These Cheyennes were surrounded in the sand hills of North West Nebraska in a severe snowstorm on the 20 October last by three companies of the 3rd Cav. under Capt. Johnson. Their number was then officially given as 149. Then they said they would remain peaceably at Camp Robinson or live with Red Cloud's people (on the Sioux reservation in the north) but would die before they would return to their reservation in the Indian Territory, where they had been starved. The commissioner did nothing in the case until Dec. 19, when he ordered their removal to Kansas. Temperature at Camp Robinson indicated 30° below that day. The commissioner must have known this. It was one of the items of news, current in all the journals of the country. The squaws and children hadn't a blanket that wasn't in rags. They did leave their reservation in the same clothing they now wear, but they left in August, and it is now January; besides, clothing often wears out in Nebraska as well as in Washington. The man who opened that telegram was a fool or a cold-blooded scoun-drel. Dec. 20, 1878, the commissioner was informed by wire that before these Indians could be moved, they must have clothing. He never answered that telegram until January 11, the very day of the outbreak.

This whole Cheyenne business is in keeping with the rest of the Indian Bureau management. It is a disgrace to the U. S. A. From Mr. Hayt we are prepared to hear anything. He displayed his incompetency so fully in his dealing with the Sioux as a "diplomatist" that we beg leave to suggest to him that as a private citizen he might be more of a success than as the head of a bureau.

This Cheyenne business must be investigated. We think General Crook should be ordered to Washington to explain what he knows about it. We think that the more Crook's part in it may be scrutinized, the more thoroughly he will be respected by the American people. Somebody must suffer for this infamous piece of incompetency. If we commence with Crook, the bottom facts can be made to appear sooner than by any other method. We want to know all about this and also about the trouble with Red Cloud and Spotted Tail, Sioux, which came near us last fall and which yet threatens our people. We give our word as journalists that every statement in the last paragraph of the N. Y. "Herald" telegram, above quoted, is a lie. Order General Crook to Washington; make him show all the papers, telegrams, and indorsements of his office that bear upon this subject. If he be guilty, then punish him, but if not, and we are willing to wager heavily that he is not, then let the one who is delinquent be sacrificed.

It is interesting to contrast this editorial with the interview General Sherman gave representatives of the *New York Herald,* and it is also curious that Hayt is blamed for something that was to a large extent in the hands of Carl Schurz.

Yet for all his indignation, this editor could not keep the scandal alive. In a few months, it was forgotten; and only today does a parallel begin to appear as all over the earth people begin the long trek to freedom.